SPIDERS OF THE MARKET

ETHNOMUSICOLOGY MULTIMEDIA

Ethnomusicology Multimedia (EM) is a collaborative publishing program, developed with funding from the Andrew W. Mellon Foundation, to identify and publish first books in ethnomusicology, accompanied by supplemental audiovisual materials online at www.ethnomultimedia.org.

A collaboration of the presses at Indiana and Temple universities, EM is an innovative, entrepreneurial, and cooperative effort to expand publishing opportunities for emerging scholars in ethnomusicology and to increase audience reach by using common resources available to the presses through support from the Andrew W. Mellon Foundation. Each press acquires and develops EM books according to its own profile and editorial criteria.

EM's most innovative features are its web-based components, which include a password-protected Annotation Management System (AMS) where authors can upload peer-reviewed audio, video, and static image content for editing and annotation and key the selections to corresponding references in their texts; a public site for viewing the web content, www .ethnomultimedia.org, with links to publishers' websites for information about the accompanying books; and the Avalon Media System, which hosts video and audio content for the website. The AMS and website were designed and built by the Institute for Digital Arts and Humanities at Indiana University. Avalon was designed and built by the libraries at Indiana University and Northwestern University, with support from the Institute of Museum and Library Services. The Indiana University Libraries hosts the website, and the Indiana University Archives of Traditional Music (ATM) provides archiving and preservation services for the EM online content.

SPIDERS

of the

MARKET

GHANAIAN TRICKSTER PERFORMANCE

in a

WEB OF NEOLIBERALISM

DAVID AFRIYIE DONKOR

INDIANA UNIVERSITY PRESS

Bloomington and Indianapolis

This book is a publication of

Indiana University Press
Office of Scholarly Publishing
Herman B Wells Library 350
1320 East 10th Street
Bloomington, Indiana 47405 USA

iupress.indiana.edu

∞ The paper used in this publication
meets the minimum requirements of the
American National Standard for Information Sciences—Permanence of Paper
for Printed Library Materials,
ANSI Z39.48-1992.

Manufactured in the United States of
America

Cataloging information is available from
the Library of Congress.

ISBN 978-0-253-02134-2 (cloth)
ISBN 978-0-253-02145-8 (paperback)
ISBN 978-0-253-02154-0 (ebook)

1 2 3 4 5 21 20 19 18 17 16

To my mother, Juliana
"Sisi Awo" Donkor (1933–2014)

And that, my people, is how Kwaku Ananse, the spider . . .
came into possession of this story. There are those
of you who may say he came to it by trickery.
I prefer to call it, the fine art of negotiation.

Sandra Jackson Opoku, *The River Where Blood Is Born*

CONTENTS

GUIDE TO ONLINE MEDIA EXAMPLES

Each of the audio, video, or still image media examples listed below is associated with specific passages in this book, and each example has been assigned a unique Persistent Uniform Resource Locator, or PURL. The PURL identifies a specific audio, video, or still image media example on the Ethnomusicology Multimedia website, www.ethnomultimedia .org. Within the text of the book, a PURL number in parentheses functions like a citation and immediately follows the text to which it refers— for example, (PURL 3.1). The numbers refer to the chapter in which the media example is found and the number of PURLs contained in that chapter. For example, PURL 3.1 refers to the first media example found in chapter 3, PURL 3.2 refers to the second media example found in chapter 3, and so on.

To access all media associated with this book, readers must first create a free account by going to the Ethnomusicology Multimedia Project website at www.ethnomultimedia.org and clicking on the "Sign In" link. Readers will be required to read and electronically sign an End Users License Agreement (EULA) the first time they access a media example on the website. After logging into the site, there are two ways to access and play back audio, video, or still image media examples. In the "Search" field, enter the name of the author to be taken to a web page with information about the book and the author, as well as a playlist of all media examples associated with the book. To access a specific media example, go to "Search," and enter the six-digit PURL identifier of the example (the six digits located at the end of the full PURL address below). The reader will be taken to the web page containing that media example, as well as a playlist of all the other media examples related to the book. Readers of the electronic edition of this book will simply click on the PURL address for each media example; once they have logged into www.ethnomultimedia .org, this live link will take them directly to the media example on the Ethnomusicology Multimedia website.

Chapter 3

PURL 3.1 | Okalla in full comedic mode at the more recent 2012 NDC rally, dressed in both national and party colors.
http://purl.dlib.indiana.edu/iudl/em/Donkor/910426

PURL 3.2 | Okalla performing at the Kumasi Cultural Center. YouTube video.
http://purl.dlib.indiana.edu/iudl/em/Donkor/910420

PURL 3.3 | Okalla opening for the Omintimum Concert Party Troupe at the Ghana National Theatre. YouTube video.
http://purl.dlib.indiana.edu/iudl/em/Donkor/910421

PURL 3.4 | Okalla singing parodies at a live outdoor show. YouTube video.
http://purl.dlib.indiana.edu/iudl/em/Donkor/910422

PURL 3.5 | Okalla telling jokes and singing parodies at a live outdoor show. YouTube video.
http://purl.dlib.indiana.edu/iudl/em/Donkor/910423

Chapter 4

PURL 4.1 | *Afutuo,* from the opening song to the death of Asantewa. King Karo rehearsing at the Accra Arts Center. Videorecording by Daniel Peltz (2001).
http://purl.dlib.indiana.edu/iudl/em/Donkor/910405

PURL 4.2 | *Afutuo,* from Ma Red's illness to the closing song. King Karo rehearsing at the Accra Arts Center. Videorecording by Daniel Peltz (2001).
http://purl.dlib.indiana.edu/iudl/em/Donkor/910406

Chapter 5

PURL 5.1 | Opening chorus—storytelling session. Ekumfi-Atwia players performing at the Kodzidan. Videorecording by David Donkor (1999).
http://purl.dlib.indiana.edu/iudl/em/Donkor/910412

PURL 5.2 | "Co-wife rivalry" story—from the storyteller's opening disclaimer to the "lizard-catcher's" interlude. Ekumfi-Atwia players performing at the Kodzidan. Videorecording by David Donkor (1999).
http://purl.dlib.indiana.edu/iudl/em/Donkor/910409

PURL 5.3 | "Co-wife rivalry" story—from end of the "lizard-catcher's" interlude to the "Mansa" song. Ekumfi-Atwia players performing at the Kodzidan. Videorecording by David Donkor (1999).
http://purl.dlib.indiana.edu/iudl/em/Donkor/910410

PURL 5.4 | "Co-wife rivalry" story—from the end of the "Mansa" song to the "itch affliction" interlude. Ekumfi-Atwia players performing at the Kodzidan. Videorecording by David Donkor (1999).
http://purl.dlib.indiana.edu/iudl/em/Donkor/910414

PURL 5.5 | "Co-wife rivalry" story—from the end of the "itch affliction" interlude to the riddle-poem/dance. Ekumfi-Atwia players performing at the Kodzidan. Videorecording by David Donkor (1999).
http://purl.dlib.indiana.edu/iudl/em/Donkor/910415

PURL 5.6 | "Co-wife rivalry" story—from the end of the riddle-poem/dance to the storyteller's closing declamation. Ekumfi-Atwia players performing at the Kodzidan. Videorecording by David Donkor (1999).
http://purl.dlib.indiana.edu/iudl/em/Donkor/910416

PURL 5.7 | "Dissatisfied elder" skit-storytelling intermission. Ekumfi-Atwia players performing at the Kodzidan. Videorecording by David Donkor (1999).
http://purl.dlib.indiana.edu/iudl/em/Donkor/910417

PURL 5.8 | "Tree Bear" story—from the storyteller's opening disclaimer to the "poverty has ravished me" interlude. Ekumfi-Atwia players performing at the Kodzidan. Videorecording by David Donkor (1999).
http://purl.dlib.indiana.edu/iudl/em/Donkor/910418

PURL 5.9 | "Tree Bear" story—from the end of the "poverty has ravished me" interlude to the "Kwarteng" concluding skit. Ekumfi-Atwia players performing at the Kodzidan. Videorecording by David Donkor (1999).
http://purl.dlib.indiana.edu/iudl/em/Donkor/910419

ACKNOWLEDGMENTS

I AM VERY GRATEFUL to the many people and institutions from which I received various support, assistance, and encouragement over the course of this project. The research presented in this book has been funded by grants from the Race and Ethnic Studies Institute and the Glascock Center for Humanities Research, both at Texas A&M University. I am grateful to Catherine Cole of the University of California, Berkeley who first encouraged me to think more seriously about the contemporary significance of the trickster, and whose own work continues to be a big inspiration to me. I am thankful for the excellent training and mentorship I got from the theater and performance studies faculty at Northwestern University, where the seeds of this project were sown. I am especially thankful to Professors Margaret Drewal, Sandra Richards, Tracy Davies and the late Dwight Conquergood for their guidance during those nascent stages of the project.

I thank Professor Esi Sutherland Addy of the University of Ghana, who has long supported my scholarship and who, in 1999, invited me to see the performance in the Kodzidan at Ekumfi-Atwia. Samuel Dawson was the best assistant one could ask for when he accompanied me to the village, for which I am very grateful. I thank the people of Ekumfi-Atwia for their invaluable gift of a rare storytelling experience. I must mention the staff and management of the Ghana National Theatre for being generous with access and conversations between 1999 and 2001. I thank Ako Tetteh, Patrick Omane Asiedu, Auntie Ama Buabeng, and Gyifa Glipkoe for their help. William Addo, Anastasia Agbyenegah, and David Dontoh went out of their way to share their experiences after parting ways with the Theatre. I thank the several archivists and librarians at the Ghana National Archives, the Institute of African Studies and the School of Performing Arts at the University of Ghana, the Herskovits Africana Library at Northwestern University, and Graphic Corporation of Ghana for their assistance. To the King Karo troupe—Linda "Ma Red" Amoako, Kwame "Katawere" Gyan, Ivan "Fine Boy" Odartey Lamptey (may they rest in peace), Joe Boy, Miriam "Akyere" Donkor, Asonaba Konadu, Yaw "Tapo" Forster, Asantewa Botchwey, Charlotte Gyanfua, Agnes "Yaa Bayere" Yankson, Maame Yaa, Kwedjo "Abiba" Frimpong, Frank "One Way" Adjei, "Idikoko," and "Okotope"—I offer a heartfelt *Meda mo ase!*

The people whose comments helped shape this book over the several stages of its draft are numerous, so I will mention just a few. I thank my professional editor Jesse L. Rester, whose meticulous eye and encouraging suggestions helped me "sift the wheat from the chaff" to produce clear and compelling prose. I am thankful for the candid critiques and insights I received from my manuscript reviewers, D. Soyini Madison of Northwestern University and Jesse Shipley of Haverford College. Their own solid scholarship in Ghana studies and performance studies continue to inspire and inform my work.

I also thank current and former colleagues in the Performance Studies and Africana Studies Departments for their support and feedback. These include Judith Hamera, Harris Berger, Donnalee Dox, Kirsten Pullen, Jason Beaster Jones, Kim Katarri, Larry Yarak, Violet Johnson, Kimberly Brown, Rebecca Hankins, Michael Collins, Joseph Jewel, Wendy Moore, Tommy Curry, Verna Keith, and Shona Jackson. I share a special comradeship with fellow (including former) joint appointees Phia Salter, Adrienne Carter-Sowell, Sarah Busdiecker, Aisha Durham, Mikko Tuhkanen, and Carmela Garritano. Alain Lawo-Sukaam and Fadeke Castor have been constantly by my side with life-line cheers and friendship in our fellowship of struggle and celebration. Outside Texas A&M, many longtime friends and fellow scholars have been great sounding boards at various stages of the process and include Awo Asiedu, Akua Ayidoho, Godwin Murunga, Ato Ahoma, Kirk Mills, and Mshai Mwangola. Praise Zenenga has always been available for that 3:00 am phone call to offer advice and felicitations in times of both crisis and confidence. I also thank my extensive network of friends in and outside academia, whose cheers and help have fueled this intellectual pursuit.

I cannot express enough thanks to my editor at Indiana University Press, Dee Mortensen, for being supportive of this project long before its completion and for her commitment to seeing it through to publication. My immense gratitude also goes to assistant sponsoring editor Sarah Jacobi and to Mollie Ables for helping to prepare this project as part of Indiana University Press's Ethnomusicology Multimedia Series that has linked this book with video examples online. All three have worked very hard and been very patient in guiding the faltering steps of my first book authorship. I give thanks to Asha Fuller and Clarissa Lega for the book cover image and special thanks to Mary Blizzard for the beautiful and arresting book cover design.

Finally, and most important, I say the biggest thanks to my family. I thank my parents for all their sacrifices: my mother and source of creative/intellectual curiosity, Juliana Donkor, who told me my first Ananse story and who passed away in the final stages of the manuscript, and my father, Samuel Donkor, who instilled in me the joy of reading and the discipline of writing at an early age. I thank all my brothers (Fifi, Daniel, Samuel Appah, Bethel, Samuel Asare, Michael, and Henry) and their families. I love them with all my heart and am grateful to them for their wholehearted support and for helping me to achieve my dreams.

SPIDERS OF THE MARKET

Introduction

> He . . . creates for himself a space in which he can find ways of using the
> constraining order of the place or of the language. Without leaving the
> place where he has no choice but to live, and which lays down its law for
> him, he establishes within it a degree of plurality and creativity. By an art
> of being in between, he draws unexpected results from his situation.
>
>   Michel de Certeau, *The Practice of Everyday Life*

IN 1983, PRESIDENT JERRY JOHN RAWLINGS of Ghana was facing a conun-
drum. Two years after seizing power in a coup d'état, the popular leader
had attempted to reverse Ghana's severe economic decline by launching
the most tough-minded policy reforms in the nation's history. These initiatives drew on the involvement of credit-bearing international finance
institutions (IFIS), including the World Bank and the International Monetary Fund, which mandated spending cuts, currency devaluation, the
privatization of state-owned enterprises, and other economic liberalization measures. The implementation of these changes in Ghana led to job
losses, wage depression, higher costs for goods and services, and angry
public protests.[1] Rawlings's military regime then began to rely more and
more on the use of violent repression to enforce the austerity measures
and maintain control over popular discontent. By the start of the 1990s,
the clamor to end the violence of the military regime had reached such a
pitch that Rawlings decided to resign from the army and institute a return
to elected constitutional government. Taking credit for the move toward
democracy helped Rawlings to revitalize his basis of popular support and
emerge victorious from heavily contested multiparty elections in 1992.
Despite this victory, however, the dilemma of the president's position
only worsened. The pressures toward economic reforms mandated by IFIS

had not decreased, nor had popular dissatisfaction with the implementation of those reforms. Meanwhile, the nation's new constitution placed significant limits on the use of executive power and rendered Rawlings's previous repressive measures unlawful. The regime had to come up with a new way to square the circle of implementing unpopular economic policies in a democratic country.

This book examines how the Rawlings government turned to cultural performances as a means of influencing public opinion and establishing political legitimacy. By recruiting performers and appropriating popular forms of expression and entertainment, the regime sought to intervene in the social values and outlooks that underwrote resistance against its economic policies.[2] As part of its strategy of political legitimation, the government co-opted—or rather, *attempted* to co-opt—three Ghanaian performance genres: *gyimi, concert party,* and *kodzi.* Each is rooted in the stylistic tradition of *Anansesεm,* a time-honored storytelling sensibility associated with the Ghanaian folkloric spider-trickster Ananse.[3] Just as a spider in its web is seen as having a crafty, creative, and sometimes unnerving disposition toward evading predators and capturing prey, Ananse in Ghanaian folklore is likewise a crafty and deceptive figure, full of comic delight and social significance. In Ghana, the term *Anansesεm* denotes both stories about Ananse and the act of storytelling itself. Since storytelling is considered to be crafty, imaginative talk, the line between the storyteller's own personality and that of the spider-trickster is often blurred.

Performance traditions that are centered around a crafty trickster ethos are perhaps not the smartest choice for political co-option. Although Rawlings's legitimation project sought to constrain the range of cultural/artistic expression available to performers, trickster traditions allowed the performers to creatively negotiate and subvert these limitations. This book shows how both trickster behavior and the process of political legitimation can be understood as social performance. The Ghanaian trickster ethos is a wily, counterhegemonic tradition in which resistance against social domination is firmly entrenched and out of which such resistance tends to emerge in an unexpected and novel fashion. Contemporary debates about the economic and political futures of Africa involve attempts to manipulate views of the common good and thus remain centered around moral (rather than technocratic) premises.

THE MILLENNIAL CONFLUENCE OF ECONOMIC
LIBERALISM AND POLITICAL LIBERALISM

The backdrop for the stories in this book is the confluence of two social ideologies in millennial Africa: economic neoliberalism and political
democratization. Neoliberal economic ideology is a view in which the
market is privileged as the ultimate mechanism for organizing all aspects
of life and where private ownership is celebrated as a means of devolving
decision making into the hands of individual agents. Those who embrace
the tenets of neoliberalism argue that the market and the actions of private
owners should be given a sphere of autonomy unregulated by any social
institution.[4] Proponents argue that in contrast to the actions of government, an unfettered market results in a prompt and efficient coordination
of decentralized agents by better accommodating uncertainty, change,
and the distributed knowledge of economic needs and resources. The
neoliberal view of the state is that it should regulate conflict among autonomous individuals and, by forcefully securing law and order, preserve
legal-constitutional procedures that protect the market and private ownership.[5] Neoliberalism's aspiration is toward a mobile, unregulated, global
market and the creation of new markets where none exist. The social world
it envisions is a borderless landscape of opportunity for private actors, one
in which capital, corporations, and solutions flow where needed as individuals make market-driven, self-maximizing decisions and innovations.

In the 1980s, British prime minister Margaret Thatcher and U.S. president Ronald Reagan, backed by pro-market think thanks, used their political positions to expedite the spread of neoliberal policies and practices.
In the United States and the United Kingdom, Reagan and Thatcher attempted to reform what they called the "welfare state" by cutting government expenditures on social welfare, health, and education. They also
tried to expand this ideology to other parts of the world in order to create
investment opportunities for Western-based corporations. Reagan, in particular, used the United States' dominance in the contributions-based vot-
ing structure of IFIs to move these organizations toward backing market-
centered reforms. This demand for neoliberal reforms overwrote IFIs'
previous emphasis on international loans for "development planning"
and "basic needs" with the new requirement that borrowers must pursue

market-based policies. From the 1980s to the turn of the millennium, IFIs routinely imposed neoliberal policy requirements as conditions of lending for crisis-riddled borrowing countries. The philosophies and practices of neoliberalism migrated to Africa largely under these conditions.[6]

Proponents of neoliberalism in Africa confronted widespread and long-established opposition. From the 1950s onward, as African nations achieved independence from colonial governments, a social compact arose in which citizens looked to their new African states to play a commanding role as the primary locus of socioeconomic welfare and development. This outlook was derived, in part, from the arguments of structuralist development economists and dependency theorists, who focused on the inequality between "underdeveloped" countries (which primarily exported raw commodities) and industrially "developed" countries (where most manufacturing took place). These economists argued that the centrality of manufacturing sectors in industrialized countries led to a reduction in prices for primary goods, and therefore "underdeveloped" countries increasingly exported more and more goods for the same value of manufactured imports, making them relatively poorer and poorer with deteriorating terms-of-trade.[7] In order to transform "underdeveloped" countries, it was proposed that these countries should establish state-protected domestic industries concentrated on locally manufactured products. Such state-centered solutions reflected a belief that the market can signal information suitable for immediate production needs but that decisions about long-term investment for the purpose of structural development are better accomplished through centralized planning. An additional aspect of Africans' preference for protectionist, interventionist states was a commitment to policies on behalf of working classes and, for some, to ward off what they believed were the neo-imperialist proclivities of industrialized nations.

In the early years after independence, Ghana and other new African countries enjoyed respectable rates of economic growth. Their state-centered investments in industry, social welfare, and development sustained public confidence in state capacity, and this was the ground from which many political leaders derived their legitimacy. Public desires for more state-provided roads, schools, health stations, jobs, contracts, agricultural products, and so forth consolidated the social compact in a deeply entrenched pattern and reinforced popular expectations of the state as a source of welfare and development.[8] However, these programs were crippled during the global economic crises of the 1970s. African export earnings declined drastically, and balance-of-payment deficits multiplied before the results of long-term structural investments were able to come to fruition. Much of the economic and social progress that had been realized after independence was lost to rising debt, while important economic and social infrastructure depreciated and suffering among African populations increased. Consequently, the ability of the state to meet the expectations of the postcolonial social compact gravely deteriorated.[9]

In the 1980s, the crisis of state capacity opened the door to outside intervention in Africa on a massive scale. A significant aspect of this intervention was the enforcement of policy conditions for IFI loans. In contrast to the idea that the state should have a primary role in economic activities and decision making, IFIs contended that African states were the source of the crisis: They were oversized and overbureaucratized, facilitated clientelism, discouraged private initiative, and made excessive and counterproductive interventions in the operation of market forces. For example, the World Bank's "Berg Report" (officially titled *Accelerated Development in Sub-Saharan Africa: An Agenda for Action*) blamed the crisis in Africa mainly on the inadequacies of protectionist state policies and their restrictions on trade and foreign exchange. IFIs suggested requiring African borrower countries to undertake "structural adjustment programs" (SAPs), which involved revisions in national economic policy that were "nothing short of a Copernican change."[10] Some of these changes were to allow free entry/exit to foreign businesses, more firmly define and protect property rights, cut public spending, and eliminate protections for domestic industry. One of the explicit motivations of these reforms was to make the state less responsive to entrenched popular demands for spending on welfare and development.[11]

The imposition of SAPs raised delicate issues of sovereignty, security, and subjectivity. Many Africans perceived them as unprecedented and humiliating foreign influences on domestic policy. By complying with IFI-mandated reforms, government leaders abandoned the postcolonial social compact, and the policy changes only intensified the decline in infrastructure that had begun in the 1970s. The prices of goods and services rose, food security diminished, real wages decreased, and the quality of health care and education continued to decline. Both rural and urban populations were affected by the reduced ability of the state to deliver what was expected of it.[12] At the same time, critics announced the emergence of a new "neoliberal subjectivity," in which citizens were reenvisioned as consumers, conditions of suffering were attributed to a lack of individual prudence, and employees were increasingly regarded as human resources with an obligation, rather than a right, to work. Some have argued that the ideology of neoliberalism involves a restructuring of the very nature of selfhood and social belonging, profoundly altering "the phenomenology of being in the world." With the abandonment of the state-focused social compact of the post-independence era, Africans had to confront changing understandings of social inclusion, freedom, continuity with the past, and political voice.[13]

In the 1990s, growing public unrest across Africa led to the implementation of a second social ideology: political democratization. A wave of democratic activism resulted in significant changes in governmental structures during this decade as regimes limited executive powers and made concessions to the call for public accountability. However, many of these political transitions did not entail actual changes in leadership, as incumbent regimes were able to reinvent themselves and take credit for reforms in the political process. Often, as was the case with J. J. Rawlings in Ghana, those elected into newly democratic offices were the same individuals who had previously held power without electoral mandate. Despite the concessions to democratic sentiment, many of the habits of authoritarianism were still entrenched in this executive cadre. Furthermore, these changes did not remove the issue of debt or the insistence of IFIS that unpopular neoliberal policies remain in place. Democracy in Africa at the turn of the millennium thus became an incomplete and conflicted foil to the implementation of unpopular neoliberal policies. The primary effect of the transition toward democracy was to force long-standing regimes to look for more sophisticated ways of managing discontent, as they developed strategies of political legitimation and sought to bridge the gap between the exigencies of economic reform and the imperatives of public accountability. The cases presented in this book show how the Ghanaian regime attempted to use cultural performances to actively reinvent the moral concepts of citizenship and the public good. They also demonstrate how performers contended with these manipulative efforts to co-opt their traditions.

GYIMI, CONCERT PARTY, AND KODZI PERFORMANCE TRADITIONS

As mentioned before, the three trickster-rooted performance traditions examined in this book are gyimi, concert party, and kodzi. *Gyimi* is a form of stand-up comedy comprised of jokes, pratfalls, and parodic songs. It probably began in the 1930s when the Ghanaian performer Ishmael Johnson combined Ananse's trickster persona with the vaudevillian antics of blackface minstrelsy to create a comic stage character named "Bob." At first, comedic "Bob acts" were presented as a part of the older genre of touring troupes known as concert party theater. Bob acts were performed either as openings to concert party plays or as comic episodes integrated directly into the play.[14] However, in the 1980s, the late John Grahl, alias "Waterproof," went independent with his comedy and thus initiated a separation of genres that was complete by the 1990s. The comedians who opened for concert party shows were no longer members of the theater troupes; they had no permanent ties to concert party and were often featured in their own independent productions. These stand-up acts developed a large following as a distinct performance genre, which came to be known as gyimi or "comic foolery."[15]

The case of gyimi's use in political legitimation that I address in this book occurred in 1996. Ghana's President Rawlings was facing a loss of public support as a result of his unpopular effort to comply with IFI-mandated tax reforms—in particular, his implementation of a new value-added tax, a format that increased the tax burden on the poor. Violence erupted against groups who were protesting the tax, and opposition parties contended that the bloodshed had been orchestrated by the regime, further undermining the already-tenuous public confidence in Rawlings's commitment to liberal democracy. To shore up his political legitimacy for the upcoming presidential election, Rawlings's political party contracted gyimi icon Bishop-Bob Okalla to endorse the president's campaign.

Okalla is a beloved comic performer who rose from modest means to gyimi fame by way of a platform at Ghana's National Theatre. He enjoys a widespread appeal among gyimi's rural, working-class, and underclass fans. By hiring Okalla to endorse President Rawlings at a campaign rally, the party was attempting to reestablish its legitimacy with this large and important public constituency, making the case that, neoliberal reforms aside, the state was still in touch with the interests of the common citizen.

In normal circumstances, Okalla's duplicitous and ambivalent stage persona—the source of his artistic credibility—would have automatically led his fans to interpret his political endorsement as a farce. It would have been perceived as a backhanded compliment or satire focused on Rawlings's campaign, a characteristically humorous gyimi stand-up performance. In the highly polarized political environment of the time, however, the endorsement seemed to be something outside of Okalla's customary stage persona and the associated trickster performance conventions. The imperatives of the political stage seemed to constrain the meaning of his gesture, forcing the gyimi performer to "play it straight." (Chapter 3 discusses how the conflict between the trickster ethos and the imperatives of political clarity was ultimately resolved in Ananse's favor.) In subsequent engagements, Okalla retroactively constructed a gyimi frame around his presidential endorsement, creating the suspicion among his followers that a very sophisticated trick had been enacted. Without ever actually retracting his endorsement, Okalla executed the trickster's "double maneuver" by bringing the meaning of that endorsement into question and making the sincerity of his support less determinable. By evading the fixed political meaning that the Rawlings campaign attempted to project onto the event, the comedian Okalla left it up to audiences to figure out exactly what kind of performance had occurred.

Concert party theater is an older performance tradition that developed during the colonial era. Concert party troupes were traditionally itinerant performers whose popular routines involved comedy, music, and moralistic melodrama. Their techniques of presentation and reception grew out of the folkloric conventions of Anansesɛm and were based around long-standing tropes of Ghanaian storytelling.[16] Concert party activity experienced a golden era in the post-independence climate, but it declined from the 1970s onward due to the weakening of transportation infrastructure, limited access to musical instruments, rampant military curfews, and competition from video films. In 1994, Ghana's National Theatre and the Ghana Concert Party Union presided over a planned revival of the concert party genre. However, this investment in Ghana's cultural legacy was almost immediately undermined by IFI demands to cut subsidies from public enterprises such as the National Theatre. Cash-strapped and compelled to take a new institutional direction, the Theatre looked to Unilever Ghana, a local subsidiary of a multi-national manufacturing company, to make up for the declining governmental support. Unilever imposed a variety of content restrictions and required the concert party performers to include marketing plugs for the corporation's soap products in their productions. Amid public concerns that desubsidization would undermine the National Theatre's ability to preserve and promote national culture, promoters tried to show that the Keysoap Concert Party Show struck a "reasonable balance" between commercial interests and an authentic, national-progressive cultural product.[17] The billing of the show framed Unilever as a responsible corporate partner devoted to promoting culture and development (not just to selling soap) and presented the Concert Party Show as a culturally authentic program.

In pursuit of this mission to legitimate neoliberal institutions, the National Theatre released instructions intended to codify the culturally progressive nature of Keysoap-sponsored performances. Keysoap concert party troupes were instructed to reject any performers with cosmetically lightened skin, to include plots that resolved conflicts with realistic and noble human efforts instead of through fantastic means such as the actions of ghosts or spiritual beings, and generally to promote the prescribed social themes that the organizers considered "progressive." A concert party production titled *Afutuo Nsakra Onipa Gye Sɛ Nsɔ-Hwɛ* (*Advice Does Not Make a Person Change, Only Trial and Ordeal Do*) was one of the products of this institutionally crafted revival. This moralistic play tells the story of a defiant businesswoman, Ma Red, who contracts cholera and nearly pays with her life after refusing to participate in community sanitation efforts. With its message of environmental health and public responsibility, the production seemed on the surface to be a legitimate ideological investment in structural development on behalf of neoliberalism's proponents. As discussed in chapter 4, however, socially marginalized performers and audiences detected in the play a paternalistic attitude that threatened their agency and range of expression. To these Africans, the character of Ma Red began to expand beyond her intended role of social miscreant and to take on the characteristics of the trickster. For performers who felt manacled to an imposed notion of progress and cultural authenticity that overwrote their immediate material needs and conflicts—particularly the poor terms of their economic relationship with the National Theatre—Ma Red offered a vicarious imagination of power and mobility. By celebrating and lovingly focusing on the character and antics of Ma Red, performers subtly muddied the intended message of the production and brought into question the moral framework propagated by its sponsors.

The third performance tradition, *kodzi,* is simply the word for traditional Anansesɛm storytelling in the language of the Fante ethnic group.[18] However, in the Fante village of Ekumfi-Atwia, seventy-five miles west of Ghana's capital, the word *kodzi* resonates with a special meaning. In the 1960s, local performers in Ekumfi-Atwia undertook a theater project in collaboration with the late Ghanaian dramatist Efua Sutherland. The kodzi produced from this collaboration was a modernist-experimental reworking of traditional Anansesɛm practice. In the traditional community art of Anansesɛm, free-flowing improvisation and audience participation are the norm. Sutherland described traditional Anansesɛm as "all the people present are performers in one way or the other."[19] While specialist storytellers initiate and guide the event, the invocation of the trickster is understood to require transformative involvement on the part of the entire audience. Ekumfi-Atwia's kodzi theater project, in contrast, is a *staged* representation of Anansesɛm, an experimental modification that aims to theatrically invoke the element of community participation. Housed in a specially designed arena called the *Kodzidan* (the house of stories), the experimental kodzi project involves more limited participation and features prerehearsed performers whose skills generate the *illusion* of free flow and participation.[20]

By the 1990s, the kodzi project in Ekumfi-Atwia had long been in decline as a result of socioeconomic marginalization and the depletion of the village's population. It was at this time that Ghana's heritage tourism industry seized upon the kodzi theater as an ideal site for foreigners to experience "authentic" folkloric performances. Heritage tourism drew

Ekumfi-Atwia into the neoliberal legitimation project, offering the village a new socioeconomic lease on life in exchange for collaboration with foreign investment. The Rawlings government, against popular skepticism, began in the 1990s to heavily court such investment from international tourism companies. In an attempt to put a less threatening face on this influx of outside funding, the regime focused on courting African diaspora tourists, who would visit Ghana in order to connect with their black heritage. To sell what these heritage tourists were thought to be seeking—a reconnection with an original identity and world—Ghana offered access to "long-standing" or "traditional" African sites that claimed authenticity by (often unspecified and therefore politically malleable) standards of historical continuity and verisimilitude.[21]

Chapter 5 describes a performance given in Ekumfi-Atwia in July 1999 for a group of visiting African American storytellers. The framing of the event—as a well-preserved and authentic expression of African heritage—obliged the performers to maintain a masquerade and support the visitors' presumed experience of free flow and improvisational audience participation. In reality, however, the kodzi theater tradition of Ekumfi-Atwia is a staged, modern re-presentation of Anansesɛm, but under the aegis of the neoliberal tourism industry these modernist-experimental aspects of the performance had to be hidden rather than celebrated. In this context of historical duplicity, a *truly* unplanned interaction—a young child's brief but meaningful walk onto the stage in the middle of the performance—humorously incited anxiety from the village participants in this supposedly casual and spontaneous event. In this child's entrance, the trickster ethos—the devious and unexpected interruption of ideological norms—reemerged from the obscurity of its appropriated tradition to wreak havoc on the preplanned meanings of the performance.

PERFORMANCE AND POLITICAL LEGITIMACY

An important argument in this book is that the process of legitimating a political ideology or regime can be interpreted as a performance and that in contemporary Ghana these performances of political legitimation are centered around moral premises. Political legitimacy is a measure of how strongly people believe in a leader's right to govern or in the validity of governing institutions. Legitimation is the bridge between brute power and the lawful spirit of a political community, and it is associated with the function of political representation wherein subjects want to feel that their leaders embody their wishes and act in their best interests. The legitimacy of power can be understood in both a narrow, legal-procedural sense (the belief that rulers exercise power in accordance with appropriate laws and customs) and in a larger social-moral sense (the belief that rulers conform with widely held principles and values).[22]

The link between legitimation and cultural performance can be found in the manipulation of public symbols. Political scientists and anthropologists have long recognized that symbols are frequently associated with political power. Leaders manipulate these symbols, appropriating and refashioning them or creating completely new ones, as a means of urging the members of the political community to act in desired ways. Sophisticated symbolic systems are a part of most political establishments, and they often serve to represent regimes as natural parts of the social and/or cosmic order. However, nonelites can also marshal symbols, sometimes the very ones that leaders have used, for alternative purposes, including resistance against political elites.[23] This work of constructing, employing, and/or revising political symbols is a creative endeavor and a form of expressive behavior. Some political scientists and anthropologists have described this phenomenon as the "dramaturgy of politics," and have suggested that the study of politics can benefit from insights into performance and aesthetic theory.[24]

According to Dwight Conquergood, performance is "a powerful locus for research in the human sciences" and continues to generate "a remarkable constellation of thinking" around the concept.[25] In bringing insights of performance theory to bear on the practices of political legitimation in millennial Ghana, it is useful to start with some of the basic concepts of the field. We can start with the idea that human beings are *homo performans,* or naturally performing species—that we recognize, substantiate, and recreate ourselves and others through creative, playful, provisional, imaginative, and articulate expressions that we call performance.[26] The large range of behaviors that can be labeled *performance* include cultural performances such as storytelling, theater, dance, and festivals, which, as Milton Singer points out, have "limited time span, beginning and end, an organized program of activity, a set of performance, and audience, and a place and occasion."[27] They also include ordinary "culturally scripted" human interactions, or *social performance*. For example, the act of shaking hands is a social performance in the sense that it is an exhibition of behavior with a significance that is based on long-standing social meanings in a particular culture. One elaboration of social performance by Erving Goffman is that human beings assume roles in everyday life that have scripted characteristic (e.g., gestures, costume, demeanor) and are tailored toward influencing particular observers or audiences.

Richard Schechner's succinct definition of performance as "showing doing" focuses on the expressive, reflexive, and re-presentational dimension of human behavior. Performance, from his perspective, means giving actions an expressive or symbolic quality with an awareness of how they will be perceived by other people. Our actions become performatively meaningful when they entail exhibition, presentation, representation, or demonstration to others. The significance associated with these actions commonly involves "restored behavior": the iteration, citation, and revision of established practices and their social meanings.[28] Working with a similar paradigm, but focused on modes of language rather than action, Jacques Derrida's starting point is the idea that more than simply true or false statements, uttered words bring something of material, physical, or situational consequence into being. He highlights history and culture as the forces behind this performativity: Speech is performative precisely because it is repeated and cited expression. Judith Butler takes the ideas of reiteration and citation further by recognizing that they are how diverse human agents actively shape social reality. They condition bodies (and behavior) socially by establishing value and cultural convention around such bodies.

Judith Hamera's more recent idea of "technique" offers a specific way to connect sociality with the repetition and citation that performativity entails. Technique, at one level, is simply a repeatable, memorable, represent-able, embodied practice related to aesthetic and other ideals about performance efficacy. At another level it describes a complex web of relationships that links performers to particular communities. Seen at both levels, it constructs readable (legible and intelligible) and reproducible bodies even as it organizes the very social relations that make the reproductions and readings possible. Hamera calls technique a "corporeal chronotope" because it intersects a world with the grammars and protocols that produce that world (hence "chronotope") and because material bodies, not just texts, enact the grammars/protocols (hence "corporeal"). Hamera recognizes that technique disciplines performing bodies in line with dominant ideals, but it may involve reappropriations/diversions for purposes the ideal visions would not condone.[29] In this, she resonates with other scholars—Jill Dolan, Elin Diamond, Dwight Conquergood, Homi Bhabha—who maintain that repetition and citation of inherited hegemonic acts are only one dimension of performativity and that performativity may also involve the repetition and citation of subversive acts that disrupt and disavow what hegemonic performativity enacts.[30]

To view performativity as a potential double gesture of construction and deconstruction or disruption is to recognize that "performance itself is a contested space where meanings and desires are generated, occluded, and . . . multiply interpreted."[31] Attempts to legitimate Rawlings's presidential campaign and/or neoliberal ideologies in Ghana can be understood as a performance in the sense that they involved the exhibition and active manipulation of social symbols and meanings. As Dwight Conquergood says about the politics of performance, "Images and symbolic representations drive public policy."[32] The fact that the political legitimation campaign employed cultural performances—gyimi, concert party, and kodzi—simply makes this more interesting, in that the manipulation of social symbols and meanings involves an overlap and interaction between different *kinds* of performance (the explicitly political vs. the explicitly theatrical). As trickster-defined cultural performances, the specific instances of gyimi, concert party, and kodzi performance presented in this book demonstrate that the possibilities of iteration, citation, and revision that are inherent in performance—and the potential of technique to engender collective bases of reading and evaluating performance out of such iteration, citation, and revision—can cut both ways. On the one hand, it can discipline individuals and communities to reproduce dominant and/or idealized social meanings, and on the other hand, it can also empower them to subvert or alter these meanings.

INTERPRETING TRICKSTER PERFORMANCE

Insights from performance studies can also be very useful in analyzing the significance of the trickster figure, allowing for a more nuanced interpretation than was often present in folklore-studies approaches from previous decades. In extremely traditional terms, the Trickster (capital "T" to represent a broadly theorized construct) is an archetypical figure that is manifested around the world in folklore, literature, and popular culture. Folklorists have identified the Trickster in the Native American Coyote, the Chinese Monkey King, Legba of the Fon of Benin, the Nordic Loki, the Celtic Puck, the Yoruba Eshu, the African American John Conquerer, the French Renard-the-Fox, and many others. The spider-trickster Ananse is of Ghana, but this figure is also a transatlantic transplant to many different parts of the New World, where he is known as Ananci, Anancy, and Aunt Nancy, among others. As the name suggests, Trickster behavior is characterized by deception—ruses, hoaxes, pranks, and the like—and tends to run against the grain of socially accepted conduct. It often violates cultural beliefs, defies authority, and produces improprieties. Yet, invariably, the Trickster's behavior has an aesthetic, skillful, and amusing quality that makes it as appealing as it is aberrant. While it is clear that Trickster entails a kind of counterhegemonic ethos, theorists have often struggled to explain what exactly the figure's contradictory conduct amounts to and to understand what the cultural producers of the figure express with it or mean by it.[33]

To answer these questions, it is helpful to remember that the abstracted ideal of the Trickster is not, in Robert Pelton's words, a universal mold "into which all reality must be poured."[34] However broadly we construe the Trickster figure, we always encounter such expressions in a specific historical, cultural, political, and economic context—as *a* trickster (lowercase "t" to emphasize the contextualization). When we focus on trickster expressions as specific, concrete *performances,* it is easier to see how individual performers use the possibilities of cultural iteration, citation, and revision to engage in many forms of delightful and subversive deception. Through these creative acts of folkloric, literary, and theatrical imagination, performers express their ideas about the world, transmitting established meanings, while simultaneously forging new ones. This approach to trickster performance allows us to recognize a spectrum that ranges from shared meanings to individual ones, thus steering between, as Pelton says, "the devil of idealism and the deep blue sea of nominalism"— that is, between an overexpansive generic construction of the Trickster and an overly specific focus on individual performances.[35]

Another way to approach trickster performance is through the distinction between *subjunctive* and *indicative* modes of performance. In the subjunctive mode, the performer describes a behavior or acts it out but not in such a way that others would interpret the behavior as the performer's true personality. The performer is not a trickster but is merely behaving like one. This is the kind of performance that we most often associate with "acting." The indicative mode of performance is where the expressive meaning of the performance coincides with the performer's own personality and intentions. In this case, the performer does not merely represent a trickster but embodies, or personally takes on, the substance and quality of the trickster ideal. We will see that tricksters often confuse the distinction between these two modes of performance. In reality, the line between the subjunctive and indicative modes, between representing a social meaning and personally embodying that meaning, can often be blurred. The "true self" is seldom completely free of artificiality, and, conversely, performers often find ways to lend their own individual mark to even the most stereotyped roles.

Schechner described the spectrum between the subjunctive and indicative modes of performance as one in which "multiple selves coexist in an unresolved dialectical tension." In other words, the distinction between the kind of people we really are and the way we behave onstage is seldom clear-cut.[36] Often, this takes a meta-expressive form, such as when performers describe their trickster behaviors in ways that are, themselves, tricky and subversively deceptive. This blurring of subjunctive and indicative expression is particularly effective in resisting hegemony and domination, because it undermines honest discussion about subjects that is necessary to achieve political clarity. This essential ambivalence is, indeed, the modus operandi of political engagement in Ghanaian trickster performance, not just the mode of performance.

Other commentators have noted that the ethos of crafty deviance associated with trickster figures is grounded in a spirit of constructive undoing and renewal. While trickster performances often negate dominant community values, they do so in a way that does not posit individualism as a viable alternative (thus negating their negation of community values). Robert Pelton describes Ananse as a contradictor who contradicts everything, even contradiction itself, in a never-ending dialectic of negation and re-negation, and William Hynes describes tricksters as "agents of creativity who transcend the constrictions of monoculturality."[37] By reminding us that there is more to life than established meanings, and reaffirming community life as an endlessly open-ended process, tricksters open the door to creative possibilities. In one traditional story, Ananse plays a trick on a character named "Mr. Hates-Contradiction" because he kills any animal that contradicts him. Ananse dupes Mr. Hates-Contradiction into self-contradiction by making claims that are so incredible that Mr. Hates-Contradiction cannot help but challenge them. After turning the tables on Mr. Hates-Contradiction, Ananse chops him up and scatters his remains as a corporeal testimony that contradiction is unavoidable.[38]

It could also be argued that Ananse *is* contradiction. Both animal and human, both sinister and comically delightful, the trickster embodies irony, ambivalence, double-entendre, indirection, and indeterminacy. Such is Ananse's tie to inconsistency that his own trickery—while irrepressible—is not indomitable. The trickster often succeeds in outsmarting himself, failing to achieve his objective just when it seems most certain. In one story, when Ananse attempts to collect all of the world's wisdom, his bratty toddler son provokes him into smashing the pot containing the wisdom and scattering the contents to the ends of the earth.[39]

When discussing the significance of the trickster, we must always return to contexts. It is interesting that in trickster scholarship, continental African tricksters tend to be discussed in strikingly ahistorical terms, while their counterparts in the African diaspora are understood to be in a constant state of dynamic evolution. For example, John Roberts identifies a recursive process of cultural production in which, by "endlessly devising solutions to both old and new problems of how to live under ever-changing social, political, and economic conditions," African Americans from slavery through post-emancipation invented a variety of black folk heroes that maintained continuity with African roots. The historical development of these New World figures, from trickster through "conjurer" to "badman," is granted an experimental and developmental aspect that is absent from the discussion of continental African reference points.[40] Similarly, Richard Burton's discussion of "Anancy" emphasizes the trickster's evolution as an icon of cultural resistance in Jamaican plantation life between 1800 and 1834, while the primordial, continental Ananse that he references seems devoid of historical context.[41] Other scholars who have directly addressed the Ghanaian Ananse tend to recognize that there is something socially dynamic about the trickster figure, yet they rarely address the changing historical contexts and material conditions that give rise to this dynamism.[42] This book emphasizes the ongoing reinvention of Ananse within a specific location and at a particular time in continental Africa. The Ghanaian figure of Ananse is an ethos that lives in and through history, not outside or above it.

NEOLIBERALISM AND ITS DISCONTENTS

We will see in later chapters that both the implementation of neoliberal policies and the contestation of those policies can take unanticipated forms. While neoliberalism is generally oriented around appeals to individualism and competitive success, the implementation of these ideas involves contending with local histories and coming to terms with recalcitrant outlooks. In the context of postcolonial Africa, as noted above, advocates of neoliberalism were forced to confront a strongly established ethos of cultural authenticity and social solidarity. This led to local developments in which neoliberalism was paradoxically justified through an appeal to the community-based moral foundations of Ghana's social compact. Such varied implementations of neoliberal outlooks are increasingly leading scholars to speak of "local but interconnected neoliberalisms," emphasizing the multifaceted reality of economic policy shifts.[43] The other side of this coin is that the global spread of neoliberalism has led to a wide variety of different local objections. To understand the texture of performance in the web of neoliberal policy disputes, it is necessary to focus on local histories.

Perhaps the most immediate situational factor relevant to disputes over neoliberalism in Africa is the context of postcolonialism. Political relationships and processes of cultural/economic production in Africa are greatly informed by the experience of imperial and colonial incursions and the associated proxy regimes and resistances in African communities—leading to the contemporary state of affairs that is often described as "postcoloniality."[44] In accounting for and responding to the ongoing legacy of imperialism, postcolonial subjects tend to be skeptical about discourses of progress, economic rationality, civilization, modernization, and development, especially when such rhetoric emerges from distant centers of global financial power and is imposed on local communities. Recognizing a geographical overlap between the directional imposition of neoliberal policies and the historical operation of colonial power, postcolonial commentators rightly tend to associate neoliberal ideology with the politics of domination. The classically liberal economic ideals that originated in eighteenth-century Europe—the celebration of individual success in the marketplace and the possession of commodity abundance—were in their own era often cited as aspects of the racial superiority of industrialized nations and as a justification for the "civilizing mission" of empire. It is therefore not surprising that when confronted by the external imposition of neoliberal economic policies, postcolonial subjects often intuit a return to paternalistic attitudes in which agents from financially powerful nations mask profiteering agendas (via political interference, inequitable terms-of-trade, inequitable labor markets, etc.) under the guise of "development."[45]

Postcolonial subjects also tend to have an acute sensitivity to hegemony, the combination of coercion and manipulation through which a social ideology comes to be seen as common sense, even to those who are disparaged or exploited under the ideology. Some theories of hegemony and "false consciousness" have been criticized as mistaking outward signs of compliance with social ideology for the internal acceptance of those ideas.[46] However, recent interpretations of hegemony are more sophisticated in positing a continuum in which imposed ideas are never completely accepted *or* completely rejected. The concert party performers, for example, described conflicted feelings about wanting to be a part of the goals of the Keysoap Concert Party Show, while simultaneously feeling displaced from and uncertain about those goals. In this view, power relations entail an ongoing dialectic of naturalization and denaturalization, as people simultaneously endeavor to position themselves within and yet actively reconstruct their social world.[47] In the same way that the "real self" of indicative performance tends to waver back and forth into the "false/assumed self" of subjunctive performance, our views of accepted common sense versus imposed ideology tend to exist within an ongoing process of negotiation and transformation.

The upshot of all this is that in ordinary life we should not generally expect to see a clear-cut opposition between different social outlooks but rather a more complex interaction, one in which the meaning of ideas and values is negotiated and reinterpreted on a continual basis. It is unsurprising that beyond the more explicit, visible, deliberate, and formal challenges to neoliberalism, we can find a much broader field of subtle and improvised acts of resistance.[48] This complex reality calls for a broader understanding of ideological contestation, one in which we recognize that social performances can most frequently be seen as both propagating *and* reshaping power relationships, often in elaborate and indirect ways. The performances discussed in this book are by no means free from the channels of power, but neither are they absolutely defined by the regime. They respond to the complex ideologies of neoliberalism from within, by turning ideological imperatives to ends other than that for which they were intended.[49]

Of all the varied forms of cultural performance in which we can identify subtle resistances and contestations of power, trickster performances are crafty, ambivalent, counterhegemonic engagements *par excellence*. We will see how gyimi, concert party, and kodzi performances were part of an arena of ideological resistance and contestation that scholarship on neoliberalism seldom addresses. While hegemonic legitimation efforts in Ghana sought to close off the contestability of neoliberalism's social logic, the contradictory trickster ethos was an empowering touchstone that performers could use to resist and contest these ideological presumptions. We can understand the outsourcing of political legitimation work to local performers as a form of cultural co-option and invasion, in which externally imposed policies were naturalized into local moral imaginaries. However, this invasion was not a simple process of domination and ideological closure but rather one in which postcolonial subjects pursued their own agendas. These agents disrupted—or at least unsettled—the work of political legitimation by rearranging imposed ideas for their own, counterhegemonic purposes.

THE AUTHOR'S EXPERIENCES

During a visit to Ekumfi-Atwia, I, along with a visiting African American storytelling group who were in the country as part of the First International Storytelling Conference, had the rare opportunity to see the village's experimental, theatricalized version of Anansesɛm.[50] It was interesting to observe how heritage tourism framed the group's cultural expectations of kodzi. Although these cultural expectations offered certain opportunities to the residents of Ekumfi-Atwia, they also constrained the villagers' cultural expression in the Kodzidan.

The Keysoap Concert Party performances at Ghana's National Theatre were my first points of contact with key individuals during my research into this performance tradition. Among these were leaders and members of the Ghana Concert Party Union (a labor welfare society for practitioners) and the splinter group known as the Concert Party Association. I also met some of the officials in charge of managing the revival of the National Theatre, as well as a few more highly placed executives. Some of them helped me to gain access to official Theatre documents, including internal communications about the concert party revival, an overview of the Theatre's operational years, and the Theatre's recent corporate plan. I attended several of the Theatre's auditions and technical dress rehearsals. I also accepted an invitation from Theatre officials to judge an annual competition for the best groups and comedians of the revival. These experiences helped me to better understand the prohibitions and prescriptions that the Theatre, in pursuing its government-mandated institutional restructuring, had established to regulate performers' stage choices. Eventually I met the lead director of the King Karo Concert Party Troupe and was invited to the group's rehearsals for the play discussed in chapter 4. Seven months of informal conversations, formal interviews, and participation in rehearsals with members of the troupe helped me to more fully appreciate the complicated nature of their relationships to the Theatre's prohibitions and prescriptions and how they navigated and subverted the constraints that were placed on their lives both on and off the stage.

I became more interested in gyimi when I repeatedly heard about stand-up comedy icon Bishop-Bob Okalla. I was struck by Okalla's distinctive comedic signature of risqué jokes, grotesque visual self-representation, physical humor, and parodic songs. I soon learned from conversations with friends, family, Theatre officials, and fellow comedians that Okalla had a reputation for both great comedy and great public controversy. The several times that I saw him on stage at the National Theatre left little doubt in my mind about his comedic genius and his controversial artistic choices. Two examples of his delightful artistic signature and of his propensity for creating a media ruckus, both of which occurred in 1996, came up repeatedly. One was his provocative parody of Christian clergy and liturgy, and the other was his embroilment in the furor over partisan politics after his public endorsement of J. J. Rawlings's presidential campaign. My discussion of Rawlings's appropriation of gyimi for the purposes of political legitimation and Okalla's trickster-defined subversion of these performances is derived from observing the latter's comedic activities (both live and on videotape), as well as from conversations with acquaintances and articles I read in newspapers and other archives.

Current ethnographic praxis in performance studies, specifically of the school of critical performance ethnography, affirms the epistemological validity of personal engagement with the cultural "repertoire" (acts that range from quotidian behavior to specialized embodied forms of expressive culture).[51] The praxis, which the late Dwight Conquergood strongly influenced, recognizes the physical body as the site of, often subjugated, knowledge production. It also emphasizes the temporality, contingency, and investment of the embodied researcher. Central to it is the idea that people, including researchers and "subjects," are agents who interact and create meaning dialogically through performance in a complex flux of power-laden relationships. In its outlook, an ethnographer is more a "co-performer" than a "participant-observer" and so has an opportunity to intimately feel and know what subjects feel and know by being "coeval," or with them at the time.[52] Whether singing along with the choruses at Ekumfi-Atwia, bantering with judges at the National Theatre, cheering

Okalla with a delightfully raucous assembly of his fans, or scrambling with King Karo troupe members to catch a bus after rehearsals, shared and embodied experiences made it possible for me to appreciate "subjects as they work for and against competing discourses in the quest for security and honor in their locations."[53] The results, for this book, are the many insights I could hardly access otherwise.

As a co-performative witness, I feel I have a responsibility to describe my background and the outlook I brought to this project. To start with, I was born in and lived my formative years in Ghana. I speak two of its main languages, Ga and Twi, fluently. In Ghana, I performed on the stage and then later on the TV screen, and I still have a small socially diverse fan base. However, I currently reside in the United States, although I return to Ghana frequently. I began my fieldwork well aware of my unstable position as cultural insider or outsider and had few assumptions about what I know on the basis of a glib, fixed, native versus nonnative binary. What I did not anticipate was how often I would have to underscore the multiple identities I brought into my fieldwork and that often not I, but others, would dictate what was, or was not, important. I discovered that identities are not fixed and autonomous but constructed, relational, and contingent. Indeed, assuming different identities like a shape-shifting trickster, and doing so coevally with research subjects who had to contend with their own structural constraints, helped me to appreciate the limitations of the trickster ethos in power relationships.[54]

Part of what drove me to this project was the opportunity to study performance genres that are primarily improvised in a local Ghanaian language—another good chance to privilege something other than the, more or less, bourgeois, linguistic Anglo-centric "scriptocentrism."[55] This is not to fault writing per se but rather the forces of inscription that attach legitimacy only to what is written down and, in the neo-colonial Ghanaian context, a supremacy that is still given the English language in the social attribution of value. I wanted, in short, to know what people like the performers in this book know—people who are on and from the social and economic margins of society, whose knowledge may be erased or subjugated because it is vernacular and/or embodied. During my research for this book, I discovered that this knowledge is a technique of political engagement based on a trickster ethos that performers used to

navigate the constraints of neoliberal legitimation. Just as those performers navigate their constraints, I use my writing skills to "poach" the space
that these privileged modes of representation occupy, to bring to the fore
the subjugated knowledge that is present in the performers' otherwise
ephemeral, embodied performances.[56]

Performance scholars tend to be skeptical of the belief that nonephem-
eral archival objects (documents, maps, literary texts, letters, videos, films,
CDs, etc.) are more valid systems for storing and transmitting knowledge
than the more immediate "repertoire" of cultural performance.[57] This is
not a dismissal of the utility of the archive but rather an objection to the
myth of immutability and unmediated storage/transmission that is often
attached to archival sources. This outlook accounts for my relative emphasis on participant-observation during the course of this research. Recognizing that both the cultural performance repertoire *and* the archive
are mediated aspects of the generation and transmission of knowledge, I
have approached the latter, as I do the former, as a resource for a cautious,
conditional reconstruction of events and meanings. The archival research
for this book draws from primary and secondary documents, including
letters, photographs, newspapers, and magazines, that I obtained from private individuals or from the University of Ghana's School of Performance
Arts, the Institute of African Studies, and the Balm Library; the Ghana
National Archives; the National Theatre of Ghana; the Ghana National
Commission on Culture; the Graphic Corporation (a newspaper publishing group in Ghana); Unilever Ghana; and the Herskovits Africana
Library at Northwestern University in the United States.

ORGANIZATION OF THE BOOK

Chapter 1 provides a somewhat abbreviated political history of Ghana.
It examines the social ideologies that coalesced during the immediate
post-independence era and the social upheavals that led to and surrounded neoliberal reforms in the 1980s and 1990s. Chapter 2 describes
the Anansesɛm tradition, with details from folklore collections and contemporary storytelling practices. It also includes theories about trickster performance and an interpretation of Ananse's counterhegemonic

ethos. Chapters 1 and 2 provide a foundation for appreciating the different threads of local meaning that were skillfully negotiated by the performers in the case studies in this book.

Chapters 3, 4, and 5 contain case studies in which trickster-rooted cultural performances were appropriated for the purposes of political legitimation. We will see how this appropriation limited the performers' range of cultural-artistic expression and the concomitant, trickster-defined impulse with which performers negotiated and subverted these constraints. Chapter 3 describes the conflicts surrounding the changes in Ghana's tax policies, the populist theatrics of a presidential election campaign, and the artistic signature of gyimi comedian Bishop-Bob Okalla. Chapter 4 discusses the Keysoap Concert Party show in the context of public sector divestiture, multi-national "corporate citizenship," and the ambivalent performances of troupe members both on- and offstage. Chapter 5 focuses on the reemergence of a countermanding trickster ethos in the unexpected antics of a young girl. It also discusses the confluences and collisions of interests among foreign direct investment, African heritage tourism, kodzi theatrical experimentation, and Ekumfi-Atwia's socioeconomic aspirations. In the Conclusion, the case studies are summarized in light of the global expansion of neoliberalism, the appropriation of local imaginaries, and the scope of subversive maneuvers.

1

—— ✐ ——

From State to Market

The History of a Social Compact

THIS CHAPTER EXPLORES the historical and economic situations in Ghana to provide some background that should make it easier to understand contemporary practices derived from Anansesɛm. The events discussed can be broken down into three chronological periods. During the first period, from the 1940s through the 1960s, Ghanaians rallied behind the ideologies of anti-colonial nationalism and pan-African communitarianism. These populist movements led to the rejection of British colonial rule and resulted in the creation of Ghana as an independent nation in 1957. The country's new leaders built a state-oriented economy that, in contrast to colonialism, was morally idealized as nonexploitative. Ghanaians saw themselves as having established a social compact in which legitimacy was granted to a government that defended the interests of the people. The state, more so than the market, was viewed as the primary mechanism of economic development and social well-being.

From the 1970s through the 1980s, however, after a period of escalation of economic crises and multiple regime changes, neoliberal economic policies were introduced in Ghana that broke with this understanding of the state. The government lifted many of its regulatory controls on the economy, auctioned off state-owned enterprises, and eliminated public subsidies. Many considered these new "austerity measures" a breach of the postcolonial social compact. Ghanaians feared a move toward a neocolonial reality, in which the government no longer protected the public interest and instead regressed toward its former role as a conduit for exploitation. These economic policy changes were never fully accepted by the public, leading to a crisis of legitimacy for the state. The military regime that held power in Ghana during the 1980s was able to enact the unpopular changes (at the behest of international finance institutions) by aggressively repressing protest and through the sheer inertia of power. But this inertia did not last.

A third era began in 1992, when the tide of discontent in Ghana forced a transition from military rule to democracy. The political calculus in this new era was decidedly different from that of the 1980s. The tension between the economic policies desired by international financiers on the one hand and Ghanaians' postcolonial expectations of their government on the other hand could no longer be handled with violent repression. The state struggled to find new ways to reconcile these incompatible demands. In the wake of democratization, Ghana's cultural traditions and performances, which politicians have always used in one way or another, acquired a new centrality in efforts to legitimize unpopular policies and manage public opinion.

FROM THE POSTWAR BOYCOTT TO POSTCOLONIAL CONSOLIDATION

After World War II, long-simmering opposition against British colonial rule began to rise to the surface in what was then called the Gold Coast region.[1] A central locus of discontent was the colonial administration's export control regulations, which were tailored to favor large, expatriate-run companies. African merchants felt unfairly displaced by the controls, and the public was increasingly disillusioned by the falling wages and high prices that resulted from these monopolistic practices. In January and February of 1948, opposition leaders organized a boycott of expatriate-run businesses in an attempt to force them to lower their prices. When this economic boycott did not produce the desired changes, people angrily filled the streets to protest the colonial administration's policies. Meanwhile, at the same time as this boycott, African ex-servicemen were

marching to petition the governor about their own grievances. These soldiers had received less remuneration than their British peers during the
war, and they had returned home with expectations for better jobs, a war
bonus, gratuities, and pensions that the colonial administration turned out
to be unwilling or unable to fulfill. Police barred the soldiers' march to the
governor's office, and a British officer opened fire on the group, killing three
of them. As news of the killings spread, the crowds already gathered in the
streets vented their fury by destroying cars, looting goods, and burning
expatriate shops. These protests are considered by many to be the point at
which the road to Ghana's independence became a political reality.

In the wake of the February 1948 protests, a relatively unknown activist named Kwame Nkrumah rose to take up leadership in the movement against colonial rule. Educated in the Gold Coast, England and the
United States, Nkrumah had worked as a schoolteacher before becoming involved in politics. In 1947, he was recruited to become the organizing secretary of a new party called the United Gold Coast Convention
(UGCC), which combined the talents of the colony's primary opposition
leaders. The UGCC advocated the transfer of governmental authority into
native hands "in the shortest possible time." The colonial administration
quickly blamed the UGCC for orchestrating the February 1948 protests,
and Nkrumah was detained for a month along with the UGCC's other principal leaders. These experiences, combined with the colonial administration's portrayal of the UGCC as a "communist conspiracy" during a time of
rising Cold War tensions, led to an internal break within the party. Under
the original leadership of J. B. Danquah, the UGCC took pains to distance
itself from any radical leftist associations. Kwame Nkrumah, however,
emerged from jail even more convinced of the necessity for leftist pan-
Africanism, so the UGCC leaders distanced themselves from him as well.

In a 1947 essay, *Towards Colonial Freedom,* Nkrumah described colonialism as the result of an imperialist expansion driven by the need to
secure raw materials and cheap labor for European industries (as well
as creating new markets where the generic products of such industries
could be dumped for a profit). He characterized the unequal treatment of
Africans not as an incidental, temporary state of affairs but as one aspect
of a larger structural problem. Racism, in other words, was an excuse for
capitalist exploitation, a political instrument that was used to help en-

sure cheap labor and to justify the repatriation of profits extracted from Africa. The result of this system, Nkrumah argued, was not true progress in Africa but rather the destruction of native crafts and home industries. Due to colonialism, Africa had become a "distorted," nonmanufacturing economy focused only on primary exports, starved of modern know-how, and turned into a dumping ground for overpriced goods. Nkrumah argued that colonialists' claims of trusteeship and tutelage in Africa belied their true objective of economic exploitation; hospitals merely served to keep colonial laborers fit for work, schools were designed to produce only trading clerks rather than thoughtful citizens, and roads and railways were built to ease the extraction and export of resources.

In light of this outlook, Nkrumah's aspirations were toward "complete and absolute independence" for Ghana, along with structural transformations to eliminate inequality and poverty. As the other leaders of the UGCC were distancing themselves from such broad economic arguments, Nkrumah was questioning whether his vision was compatible with the sensibilities of the lawyers and merchants who formed the backbone of the UGCC party. Nkrumah was determined to establish a broad political base among the working classes—especially the growing legion of semiliterate elementary school dropouts who were trooping en masse to the Gold Coast's urban centers in search of government work or private clerical positions. These individuals faced extremely limited employment opportunities. They became part of a swelling urban underclass, taking refuge in slums and on the porches of roadside trading houses, earning the nickname "verandah boys." Without sufficient connections or literary skills to obtain well-paying positions, yet educated enough to aspire to city jobs, this social cluster formed a natural reservoir of frustrated ambition. It was common for verandah boys to seek self-improvement in debating clubs, literary circles, and various youth movements. Nkrumah, along with other anti-colonial organizers, used these outlets to sharpen the frustration of the youths into a broader political view of national independence.[2]

For a time, Nkrumah continued his organizing efforts in parallel with Danquah and the other UGCC leaders. Due to the party's unwillingness to discuss structural economic issues, however, in June 1949, Nkrumah formally split with the UGCC and formed a new organization, the Convention People's Party (CPP). The CPP's platform included a demand for self-governance "now" (in contrast to the UGCC's "shortest possible time"), and the party promised to work for an improved society in which Africans "shall have the right to live and govern as a free people."[3] Lured by the prospect of radical change and by Nkrumah's populist message, commoners flocked to the party. The success of the CPP initiated a rapid shift in the Gold Coast's oppositional politics, with a smaller, older, and mostly male alliance of the African bourgeoisie giving way to a broader, fiercer, and gender-inclusive coalition of traders, artisans, civil servants, teachers, workers, and farmers. Nkrumah encouraged his followers' expectations of rapid change, promising that if self-governance were achieved, then a new African "paradise" could be established within ten years.[4]

Emboldened by its growing popularity, the CPP instituted a "People's Representative Assembly" and called for general elections to create a new government. In January 1950, the party attempted to force the hand of the colonial administration by organizing widespread nonviolent demonstrations, strikes, boycotts, and civil disobedience. The administration once again arrested Nkrumah, along with other CPP leaders, but this only increased the party's legitimacy in the eyes of the masses. Eventually, confronted with internal protests and international pressure, the British were forced to accept constitutional modifications that allowed for native representation in the Gold Coast. In the next general election, the CPP won an overwhelming majority of the legislative seats. Forced to reckon with Nkrumah's popularity, the colonial administration released him from prison in 1951 and created a diarchy of sorts, installing Nkrumah in the newly invented position of prime minister. From this point onward, the colonial authority's involvement in practical affairs of state began to diminish, leading ultimately to the formal recognition of Ghana as an independent nation on March 6, 1957.

In his role as prime minister, Nkrumah was immediately thrust into the precarious position of needing to make good on the extravagant expectations that his anti-colonial campaign had raised. He remarked at the time, "We cannot tell our peoples that material benefits and growth and modern progress are not for them. If we do, they will throw us out and seek other leaders who promise more. And they will abandon us, too, if we do not in reasonable measure respond to their hopes."[5] Nkrumah recognized that improvements in the people's welfare—better health services, quality education, and the availability of water and electricity, among other benefits—were the achievements by which he would be judged. He therefore set out to confirm the new government's legitimacy in the eyes of the public by investing heavily in infrastructure. Adopting the main elements of the "ten-year plan" of infrastructure spending that had already been put in place by colonial authorities, Nkrumah accelerated the time frame on these improvements to five years and nearly doubled the projected spending. He then went on to pursue a "shopping list" that included the construction of a hydroelectric dam; a new harbor; several bridges; a large, modern hospital; an expansion of road and train networks; telephone lines; water supply projects; the development of agricultural enterprises; new housing; and new schools and colleges. His administration provided housing loans, free child education, and overseas scholarships for courses of study that were not available locally. Under Nkrumah and the CPP leadership, the government mandated a 30 percent increase in the wages of unskilled workers. It also greatly expanded the size of the civil service and considerably "Africanized" the higher ranks of governmental administration that had previously been dominated by whites.[6]

During the initial years of Nkrumah's leadership, the Ghanaian economy was in a good position to absorb the costs of rapid development. The world price of cocoa, Ghana's main export, was trending upward at a breakneck pace—from £190 per ton in 1948–1949 to £467 per ton in 1953–1954, and then dropping slightly to £352 per ton in 1957–1958.[7] The prices of other exports were booming as well. Governmental revenues, mainly from export taxes, nearly quadrupled from 1948 to 1952 and continued to rise throughout the 1950s. In addition, the colonial administration had accumulated extensive Sterling reserves during many years of export surpluses. Nkrumah felt that these revenues and surpluses should be reinvested in the common good, and indeed, between 1951 and 1959, he was in a position to do just that. His massive expenditures could be seen as politically expedient in that they bolstered his image as a leader who could quickly provide a greater measure of prosperity for his people. However, Nkrumah's policies also stemmed from his long-standing conviction that Ghana's economy had structural faults that were likely to perpetuate poverty and that were in need of serious redress. He had always viewed political independence as merely a path-clearing event for economic decolonization—an opportunity to remove the economic "distortions" that had kept the benefits of material progress out of the reach of the majority. In his own words, Nkrumah believed that independence by itself "does not change this world. It simply creates the right political atmosphere for a real effort at national regeneration."[8]

As Nkrumah's administration continued to lead Ghana into the 1960s, his policies became more explicitly socialist, shifting toward a broader goal of economic "rebalancing." The centerpiece of this era was a "seven-year plan," released in 1962, which decreed "a period of economic reconstruction and development aimed at creating a socialist society."[9] Industrialization was at the heart of the plan, as Nkrumah continued to believe that establishing local manufacturing capacity was the key to Ghana's future. As long as the country's economy revolved around exporting raw resources, it would remain in a state of financial dependency, susceptible to price fluctuations and extortion. In order to make the drastic transformation from a colonial economy to a balanced modern economy, and to ensure that the benefits of economic growth would be fairly distributed to Ghanaians, Nkrumah believed that the planning authority of the state had to overrule the immediate logic of the international marketplace.

Nkrumah probably understood that his move toward investing in local manufacturing capacity would not have the same quick payoff as his earlier investments in public infrastructure. While new schools, hospitals, and running water had a tangible appeal, the long-term goal of economic self-sufficiency required a leap of the imagination. Nkrumah may have also realized that he was running out of time and resources to enact his vision. After peaking in the late 1950s, the world price of cocoa had collapsed, falling from £352 per ton in 1958 back to a low of £170 per ton by 1962.[10] Burgeoning revenues were no longer available to keep pace with increasing spending, and the real fruits of a shift toward a balanced modern economy would take decades or more to arrive. Embarking on an ambitious plan of long-term industrial development was politically risky among a population whose expectations had been whetted by a quick spate of export-funded welfare projects.

However, Nkrumah believed that he could engage with Ghanaian's postcolonial values. In a sense, he was asking Ghanaians to expand the scope of their social compact, considering not just the value of immediate material improvements but also the long-term, sustainable future of the continent. Nkrumah made a moral argument for a socialist future by invoking concepts of fairness, authenticity, and autonomy. He suggested that the refusal to invest in a sustainable future would leave Ghana mired in the backwaters of an alien and exploitative economic order. A failure to regulate capitalist profiteering would undermine the egalitarian promise of the anti-colonial movement. Such a fate would be a betrayal of "the personality and conscience of Africa," which in Nkrumah's view was a traditional ethos rooted in communitarianism—the "duty to support one another and make the happiness of others a condition for the happiness of oneself." It would not be proper for a conscientious African to tolerate conditions of rampant inequality or to allow private profiteers to pillage the community's resources.[11]

Nkrumah was concerned that without a robustly socialist government committed to economic development and distributive justice, Ghana would turn into a *neocolonial* state. It might retain the outward trappings of sovereignty, but its policies and economic conditions would remain at the mercy of foreign interests (in particular, the profit-seeking interests of multinational corporations and financiers). Neocolonialism, Nkrumah warned, is the "last stage" and the "worst form" of imperial exploitation. Under such a system, those who extract profit from Africa would continue to dictate local policy and prices, but they would no longer have to deal with the practical issues of governance or face any kind of accountability for the results of their actions.[12] A strongly protectionist, socialist state was the only moral bulwark that could challenge such an economic system. Nkrumah's vision was that he could help to create a pan-African coalition that would be committed enough to sever the continent's economic ties to colonial powers and pursue an independent, morally superior way of life. He wrote:

> We feel that there is much the world can learn from those of use who belong to what we might term the pre-technological societies. There are values which we must not sacrifice unheedingly in pursuit of material progress.... While we seek the material, cultural, and economic advancement of our people, while we raise their standards of life, we shall not sacrifice their fundamental happiness.[13]

Nkrumah believed that the rifts and abuses of the colonial era had suppressed the "African Personality," an authentic, nonexploitative, community-oriented outlook that was rooted in traditional African culture. The economic goals of socialism were harmonious with these traditional African principles, in that socialism rejects individual profiteering and gives moral priority to distributive justice. By embracing the communitarian sensibility, Africa could "redeem its past glory . . . renew and reinforce its strength . . . [and] smile in a new era of prosperity and power."[14] The quest for the African Personality was a determination to recast African society in its own traditional forms, wedding what is valuable from the past to modern ideas, while developing a new identity that was wider than ethnic and national affiliations.

A DOWNWARD SPIRAL

Unfortunately, Nkrumah's calls for a morally grounded, pan-African socialist future were curtailed when he was toppled from office in a military coup on February 28, 1966. The coup came at a time when Nkrumah's heavy investment expenditures had combined with falling export revenues to produce a massive budget deficit, a swollen external debt, and an overvalued currency. Amid the related hardships (food shortages, unemployment, and a decline in living standards), many Ghanaians came to doubt the value of Nkrumah's forward-looking socialist ideals. They felt that the government was no longer making advances in looking after their short-term interests, so they began to question whether it was truly the right custodian for their long-term interests. Furthermore, Nkrumah's administration had responded to the loss of public faith by taking an authoritarian turn. Confronted with calls for continuing welfare projects that it could no longer afford, the government banned labor strikes and began to detain its political opponents, a move that only hastened Nkrumah's loss of moral legitimacy. When the government was toppled from power in February 1966, there was little protest, despite allegations of foreign involvement in the coup.[15]

The following fifteen years saw seven regime changes in Ghana—two by ballot box, one by an internal coup, and four by the barrel of the gun— a veritable "musical chairs" routine of political succession. The regimes came from widely differing political outlooks, but they all faced one central

Nkrumah's statues. These were pulled down and broken after the overthrow of Nkrumah. They now stand on display at the National Museum of Ghana. Courtesy of the author, July 2001.

problem: persistent, unresolved economic struggles that left them unable to make good on the public's expectations for postcolonial prosperity. The senior military officers who overthrew Nkrumah in 1966 established a rightward-leaning party called the National Liberation Council (NLC), chaired by Lieutenant-General J. A. Ankrah. Declaring that Ghana was on the verge of national bankruptcy, the NLC announced that privatization and an openness to foreign investment/ownership were the paths to faster development. The party worked to roll back Nkrumah's "seven-year plan," auctioning off central state enterprises to foreign and local investors. Following recommendations from the International Monetary Fund (IMF), they cut costs by firing large numbers of public employees and canceling work on Nkrumah's prodigious construction projects. At the same time, they offered immediate public relief by lowering taxes and import duties. The profits retained by Ghanaian cocoa farmers, in particular, were greatly increased by these changes.

It soon became apparent that general prosperity through privatization was even more illusory than prosperity through state-funded welfare projects. Balance-of-payment problems continued, inflation escalated, and the external debt continued to rise. The International Monetary Fund insisted that the regime devalue the national currency. As Ghana's standard of living plummeted, a paralyzing wave of labor strikes spread across the country. The NLC promised competitive elections, and on making good on this promise in 1969, the party was promptly voted out of office. Ghanaians turned to Kofi Abrefa Busia's Progress Party, another right-leaning regime that promised rapid development and improvements in social welfare. The Progress Party continued the NLC's efforts to divest state enterprises to the private sector and eventually went so far as to abolish public housing and transportation allowances. By this time, unemployment in Ghana had reached more than 50 percent. Prices continued to rise, dissatisfaction continued to spread, and labor strikes continued to immobilize the country. In 1971, Busia accepted a hugely unpopular IMF recommendation to devalue Ghana's currency a second time, by 44 percent to the dollar. In the midst of widespread protest, the military stepped in and once again overthrew the government. Busia described the action as "an officers' amenities coup arising from my efforts to save money."[16]

This time, the military leaders that toppled the government adopted leftward-leaning policies. They formed a party called the National Redemption Council (NRC), chaired by Colonel I. K. Acheampong. Seeking an immediate change in social conditions, they partially revalued Ghana's currency, made a public break with the IMF by repudiating foreign debts, and seized for the state the majority shareholdings of foreign-owned timber and gold-mining companies. The NRC mandated an increase in workers' wages and subsidized the prices of essential commodities. The result was that Ghana enjoyed a brief period of prosperity, which was further buoyed by rising world cocoa prices. The boost lasted for less than two years. By 1974, the country was again in economic shambles, made worse by an international oil crisis and worldwide inflation. Facing a tide of unrest, the NRC changed its name to the Supreme Military Council (SMC) and consolidated power by largely replacing the higher levels of government with a military command structure. This did little to resolve Ghana's economic problems, and the country continued to be afflicted by pervasive unemployment, food shortages, decaying infrastructure, and widespread demoralization.

In 1978, the regime underwent an internal convulsion that resulted in Lieutenant-General Fred Akuffo replacing Colonel Acheampong as the party's leader. Then, in May 1979, the SMC quashed another internal military mutiny and detained its leader, flight lieutenant Jerry John Rawlings. Finally, in the following month, junior army officers deposed the regime, executed its leaders, released Rawlings from jail, and asked him to lead a new governing party that they named the Armed Forces Revolutionary Council (AFRC). More the outcome of seething frustration than a well-thought-out political revolution, the AFRC declared itself to be a "house-cleaning exercise." It did not initiate any new governing policies but simply made arrangements for open elections, which took place four months later. Hilla Limann of the People's National Party (PNP) was elected. The PNP contained several of the "old guards" from the Nkrumah years and saw itself as the ideological descendent of what was quickly coming to be regarded as a "golden era." However, the party was internally divided and had no clear consensus regarding the proper course of economic recovery. In a gesture toward the public welfare, the PNP tripled the minimum wage, but it simultaneously reduced the duties levied on cocoa farmers. As a result, government deficits began to soar, and another collapse of the international cocoa market intensified the dour state of economic affairs. On December 31, 1981, barely two years into Limann's first term, the PNP government was overthrown in yet another military coup—this one staged by none other than the soldier who had preceded Limann in office: flight lieutenant J. J. Rawlings.

THE "BEAUTIFUL ONE" AT LAST?

Through all of the tumultuous regime changes from 1966 to 1981, Ghanaians continued to view their government as a primary mechanism of economic development and material well-being. Their acceptance or (more often) rejection of government policy was tied to the assumption that those policies should result in improved social welfare. The leftist-leaning regimes endorsed and traded on this understanding, but even Ghana's right-leaning leaders were forced to contend with the expectation that their privatization schemes should bring about a rapid improvement in the overall quality of life. K. A. Busia of the Progress Party, who is generally understood to be a standard-bearer of Ghana's ideological right, expressed this reality by saying that any government in Ghana must be prepared to respond to the public's longing for "social improvements and higher standards of living."[17] Busia's statement was proven accurate, as the public's tolerance for his economic "liberalization" quickly evaporated when it did not yield an immediate improvement in Ghanaians' welfare. "Austerity measures" and privatization remained limited in scope due to the continuing expectation that the government had a moral responsibility to respond to the needs of the people.[18] Thus, regardless of their stated ideology, the ruling regimes recognized that their legitimacy in the eyes of Ghanaians rested on their ability to provide for the common good. Since Ghana emerged from the colonial era with an abundance of immediate material needs, tensions between short-term welfare projects and long-term economic solutions (of whatever ideological stripe) were almost inevitably resolved in favor of the quick fix.

In asking why their government was unable to consistently provide prosperity, Ghanaians also tended to settle on a short-term explanation: corruption. Assuredly, there was much to complain about in this regard. Nkrumah, in the final years of his tenure, was accused of retaining the lion's share of shrinking government revenues for distribution among the party faithful. His insistence that the few should not benefit from the labors of the many began to reek of *Animal Farm*–like disingenuity, as living standards declined and party officials continued to enjoy expensive cars, luxurious houses, and other trappings of opulence. The military commanders of the NLC invoked charges of corruption to help justify their coup against Nkrumah, but then these same leaders set a new standard of unscrupulousness when chairman Ankrah admitted that he and other party officials had taken bribes from foreign businesses.[19] Busia's Progress Party continued the trend; an investigative commission into the activities of the party found "extensive evidence of malfeasance at all levels of the administration."[20] The leftist NRC/SMC regime that overthrew Busia reached perhaps the highest apogee of kleptocracy, establishing a thoroughgoing culture of fraud and malfeasance in which all levels of the government were pervaded by corruption. Ghanaians called this state of affairs *kalabule:* the habitual embezzlement, diversion, and illegal privatization of state resources. Those who profited the most from corruption were people connected to the regimes, but the ever-widening gyre of venality drew all classes into it, with participation as the price of survival.

As this culture of corruption continued to evolve from the mid-1960s through the late 1970s, Ghanaians' understanding of their social compact and communal welfare began to coalesce into a one-pointed desire: a regime that does not directly steal from the public coffers. Honesty, accountability, and fairness came to the forefront as prerequisites for political legitimacy, more so than any broader political or economic philosophy. It was in this context of pervasive venality that J. J. Rawlings led his insurrection in May 1979. Although initially unsuccessful, it laid the foundation for his image. During his court-martial, Rawlings declared that corruption and social injustices under the SMC regime were the reason for his actions. He also announced, in the face of capital punishment, that he alone was responsible for the insurrection and asked the prosecutors to "leave my men alone."[21] Ghanaians who had come to associate soldiers more with misrule and embezzlement than with courage and integrity found in Rawlings's bold stance a source of inspiration. Posters and graffiti with the phrases "leave Rawlings alone," "Rawlings is our man," "we have suffered too long," "stop the trial or else," and "revolution or death" appeared on the walls of Ghana's military barracks. The lower ranks of the army, who were aware of the public mood and were just as frustrated with the corruption and bad economy as their civilian counterparts, turned on their commanders and freed Rawlings before he was sentenced. Their message was clear: Stop those in power from cheating.[22]

Popular support for Rawlings was grounded in Ghanaians' postcolonial sensibility that leaders should promote distributive fairness and look after the interests of the people. But it reduced this moral outlook to a cult of personality. Rawlings, at the onset of his popularity, offered no economic or political viewpoint at all. He simply convinced the public that he, personally, could be trusted. This appealed to a populace weary of politicians who spoke of equality but enacted corruption. Ghanaians imagined Rawlings as a fearless and messianic champion of justice. They reinterpreted his initials "J. J." as "Junior Jesus," to indicate a courageous, concerned, valorous, simple, and selfless man of the people. Correspondingly, they appropriated popular Christian choruses for the battle cry of the moral revolution, singing:

> J. J., rise up, devil wants to ruin our land,
> J. J., rise up, the devil wants to ruin our land.
> On the day J. J. arrives what would the evildoers do?
> On that day, that day, what would the evildoers do?[23]

Gaunt, shabby, and unshaven, with a cigarette tucked behind his ear, although still young, handsome, and magnetic, Rawlings was the archetype of a populist leader. He was a man who used discarded army airplane seats for home furniture and bought cheap food on credit—an ordinary man familiar with hardship. He made fiery speeches from atop cars and under trees, building rapport with the masses by conveying moral sincerity and sharing in their frustrations.

Rawlings in one of his fiery speeches to Ghanaians, atop an armored military vehicle. From Shillington, *Ghana and the Rawlings Factor,* n.p. Courtesy of Getty Images.

Ghanaians celebrated Rawlings's first coup and transitional government in 1979 as a moral revolution against corruption, and they looked forward with a tentative optimism to the prospect of economic recovery. The winner of the new general elections, however, failed to make good on these expectations. For the next two years, under Limann's PNP administration, the country continued to experience declining incomes, rising inflation, widespread unemployment, food shortages, decaying infrastructure, and the entire litany of familiar socioeconomic ills. Things came to a head when PNP bosses were revealed to have engaged in shady business deals involving the misappropriation of public funds.[24] Given this state of affairs, the "second coming" of Rawlings in December 1981 was hardly a surprise. Rawlings declared his second coup to be a resurrection of the moral revolution, a "holy war" against corrupt politicians. Building on his image of personal integrity, he suggested that he might well be the moral leader that Ghanaian novelist Ayi Kwei Armah had mythologized in his 1968 classic *The Beautyful Ones Are Not Yet Born*—a voice of conscience who could resist temptation. Under the banner of a new regime, the Provisional National Defense Council (PNDC), Rawlings set out to expunge corruption from the state apparatus. He inaugurated "Citizens' Vetting Committees" and a "National Investigations Committee," both comprised of nonprofessionals and both tasked with the job of rooting out governmental embezzlement and fraud. Responding to complaints that the regular judicial system was unwieldy, inflexible, and intimidating to ordinary people, he set up a parallel tribunal system in which commoners could bring complaints.[25] Nonetheless, Ghanaians' reactions to Rawlings's second coup were lukewarm—ranging from cautious approval, to near indifference, to eerie quiescence, to mild consternation. The era was marked by a broad pessimism as Ghanaians waited to see what shape the new administration would take.

"PEOPLE'S POWER" AND GRASSROOTS DEMOCRACY: RAWLINGS VERSUS THE LEFT

Under the PNDC label, Rawlings's initial policy signal was to the Left. Between the time of his original rebellion and his "second coming," he had been taken into the fold of the June Fourth Movement (JFM), a school of thought that drew from Marxist outlooks and claimed the mantle of

Nkrumah's socialist-structuralist vision. Like Nkrumah, JFM leaders attributed Ghana's continuing woes to neocolonial exploitation and economic dependency. By celebrating the leadership of J. J. Rawlings (the movement took its name from the date of his original "housecleaning" of the government), the JFM leaders sought to integrate Rawlings's populist anticorruption campaign with a broader socialist vision. Some elements of this movement were skeptical about the value of liberal democracy. While insisting on the importance of "people's power" at the grassroots level, they recognized that electoral politics was susceptible to ideological and financial manipulation. These elements of the movement therefore embraced and encouraged Rawlings's preemptive populism (i.e., his willingness to seize power by force). They argued that:

> Whether there will be food in the kitchen or not . . . will be determined primarily by who effectively wields state power—the rich men or the poor workers; soldiers, policemen, or farmers—the power to determine who should get what share of the national wealth. . . . Any discussion of the problem of how the people are to free themselves from the present dilemma, which does not take this as a point of departure, is meaningless.[26]

Rawlings did indeed take this outlook as the point of departure for his second coup in 1981. This time, it was not a military dictatorship but rather an elected government that he deposed, and his new party had no intention of being a transitional administration. Dissatisfied with the ability of electoral politics to produce robust solutions, Rawlings castigated the system as a "sham democracy." He argued that under the electoral system, all successful parties had to rely on funds from oligarchs to finance their campaigns and that once in power they would inevitably abandon those who elected them in order to provide their financiers with "dividends" on the "invested" money. Such a system deprives the electorate of any real participation in the affairs of state, leaving the average person as a passive, helpless spectator to politicians' destruction of the socioeconomic fabric. Rawlings claimed that the PNP party he deposed, while nominally leftist, had been reduced to a "pack of criminals" acting as corrupt puppets of vested interests—a claim that appeared to be verified by revelations of the party's financial misdeeds.[27]

The broader public, and even some elements of the JFM, followed this anti-election logic with a degree of apprehension. However, Rawlings moved forward, determined to provide substance and legitimacy to his populist claims. He declared that his government would do "nothing . . . without the consent and authority of the people." He envisioned a greater degree of direct civic participation, saying that ordinary people should "take their destiny into their own hands and feel that they are part of the government."[28] In addition to his public anticorruption committees, Rawlings introduced local People's Defense Committees (PDCs) and Workers' Defense Committees (WDCs), which were tasked with overseeing the fairness and orderly functioning of everyday society. Rawlings attributed the idea of these organizations to his greater awakening since 1979:

> I was slightly naive, in the sense that it never struck me that some kind of supportive system, maybe new institutions, would have to be organized to ensure that the people of this country hold onto their newly won freedom, to ensure that they dictate the terms of their own survival. . . . Now I know better.[29]

The P/WDCs were intended to be mechanisms of direct, popular democracy through which ordinary Ghanaians could participate in important decision-making processes. To the extent that any consensus ever existed about their specific roles, they were supposed to keep an eye out for financial misdealings, provide a forum for airing popular grievances, and undertake voluntary social work projects. In urban areas they were tasked with protecting laborers and tenants from abuse, while also confronting workers who slacked in productivity. In rural areas they were encouraged to organize cooperatives and to help farmers gain access to broader markets and services.

Within months of Rawlings's return to power, however, "excesses" associated with the P/WDCs—acts of harassment, intimidation, and extortion—began to give them an ill repute. It seemed that many of the participants viewed these organizations as a means of carrying out the very activities that they were chartered to prevent. Part of the problem was that the ordinary people—or at least *some* of the ordinary people— interpreted the Left's call for social justice as an invitation to role reversal. Local P/WDC members found in the organizations a first-time opportunity for self-assertion. With no central control over their actions and no standardized procedures of operation and accountability, they exercised "people's power" in an ad hoc fashion. Even "the people" did not escape these excesses. P/WDCs bred overzealous vigilantes who felt free to mete out corporal punishment, forcefully reinstate dismissed workers, and raze stores if their prices were too high. Some invoked claims of hoarding and overpricing in order to seize goods, which they then sold to the public at reduced prices and pocketed the profits. Others set up kangaroo courts and levied fines for real and concocted offences, while harassing locals who fell out of their favor and diverting government aid to their own friends and families.[30]

The rapid onset of these abuses created a crisis for Rawlings. They threatened to undermine his public image as a moral crusader, the central pillar of his political legitimacy. They also contributed to a growing rift between Rawlings and the JFM's leftist caucus. Everyone agreed that the "excesses" were a breach of the social compact, but the leaders quibbled over who was responsible and what should be done about the situation. The JFM blamed Rawlings for establishing the public committees without adequate centralized oversight to provide for accountability. From the JFM's leftist perspective, oppressed individuals "beginning to liberate themselves from years of domination and exploitation" were at risk of prioritizing selfish, parochial gains over abstract goals, if they were not properly guided. The JFM leaders noted that they had asked for a proper supervising body over the P/WDCs to mitigate this risk, but the Rawlings administration had insisted on grassroots populism and minimal oversight and thereby allowed "discredited elements" to hijack the committees.[31] Rawlings, for his part, increasingly attributed the problems in the P/WDCs to leftist ideology run amok. He began to insinuate that the Left's rhetoric was responsible for the grassroots committees' abuses because it stirred up undue antagonism. In February 1982, Rawlings shocked the JFM caucus by embarking on a public tirade against—in his words—"socialist nonsense."[32] During the months that followed, the JFM caucus would come to the conclusion that Rawlings had betrayed their progressive cause.

This sense of betrayal intensified in April 1982 when rumors emerged that Rawlings had secretly decided to pursue financial assistance from the World Bank and International Monetary Fund—both of which would demand currency devaluation and other policy changes as a condition for loans. Ghanaians dreaded such "austerity measures." For many, currency devaluation brought back memories of the escalation in the cost of goods and services that had occurred when the Busia and SMC regimes had tried such policies, and the resulting chaos and disaffection that led to the overthrow of those regimes. The Left, of course, viewed any such concessions as acquiescence to foreign profiteering and neocolonial rule. A JFM delegation called upon Rawlings to explain the truth of these rumors, asking why the administration's economic policies appeared to be shrouded from national debate despite the talk of participatory democracy. Rawlings assured the delegation that "all decisions related to the economy would be subjected to a democratic discussion."[33]

As it turned out, such discussion never took place. The political situation began to deteriorate in June 1982, after three prominent judges and a retired senior army officer were kidnapped and murdered at a military firing range. Despite Rawlings's denouncement of the murders, rumors implicated his regime. All three of the judges were known to have ruled in court cases in which they overturned sentences imposed by the military administration. Anti-Rawlings protests began to spread across the country. Ghana's Catholic bishops released a statement decrying "the indiscipline and arbitrary actions" of those who set themselves up as "demigods."[34] Then, in August, Rawlings announced that despite his previous assurances, his administration's Economic Review Commission had indeed gone forward with preparing a policy agenda centered around currency devaluation. When this was revealed, Rawlings's own cabinet (which had largely been in the dark about the proposal) rejected it. The cabinet established an Alternative Economic Committee to forge a development plan that did not involve "dependence on imperialism."[35] Evidently convinced that this alternative proposal would not be implemented without pressure, the JFM and other leftist groups organized demonstrations in which they criticized Rawlings for forging secret deals with international financiers. Rawlings summoned the Left's leaders and demanded that they cease their campaign, but they would not back down.

Fearing reprisals, and convinced that Rawlings had become their enemy, leftist leaders from within the ruling PNDC party conducted a series of abortive coup attempts during the closing months of 1982. Ultimately these failures merely gave Rawlings the opportunity to imprison and otherwise purge the oppositional elements from within the PNDC party. This paved the way for his administration to consolidate power and move forward with its economic plans, despite widespread protest. In April 1983, the regime unveiled its new "economic recovery program," which included currency devaluation, the elimination of public subsidies, substantial personnel cuts in the public sector, and the reduction of state controls on pricing, distribution, and foreign ownership. All told, Rawlings's economic plan was a fundamental alteration of Ghana's economy on a scale that had not been seen since the country's independence. It became the broadest of the internationally mandated "structural adjustment programs" in Africa and was hailed by Western investors as nothing short of "revolutionary." As a result, Ghana became a "showcase," a "paradigmatic case," and a "prime laboratory" of neoliberal reform.[36]

Rawlings's economic plan struck at the heart of the country's postcolonial social compact. In effect, it was a formal renunciation of the idea that the government should be directly responsible for the well-being of its subjects—a view that was still held by the majority of Ghana's people. Rawlings recognized this and made efforts to preempt the expected outcry. Following the lead of earlier regimes, he sought to rally support through a spate of short-term development projects. At the same time that he was systematically dismantling protectionist and welfare-oriented state policies, he embraced new international loans to bankroll the construction of roads, electric lines, water systems, health clinics, and schools, mostly in rural areas. However, while these projects may have helped Rawlings retain the loyalty of their immediate beneficiaries, they could not forestall the larger effects of "austerity." As the new economic policies went into effect, the average prices of basic goods and services soared. The cost of water and electric utilities and hospital services immediately rose by 150 percent, 1,000 percent, and 1,500 percent, respectively.[37] As a result, even as international funding fueled a spate of new development, the fruits of the economy were increasingly unavailable to the poor. By some formal measures, Ghana's economy "grew" twice as rapidly as the rest of Africa between 1983 and 1991, but at the same time, the living standards of most Ghanaians drastically declined.

The negative effects of austerity were felt most strongly by urban workers and young people. In addition to their declining quality of life and a lack of advancement prospects, the urban poor were confronted by the spectacle of relative inequality as capitalist development projects proceeded. The emergence of enclaves of elite prosperity merely highlighted the hardships confronted by the majority. In the cities, the term "Rawlings chain," referring to a protruding collarbone on an emaciated body, became a metaphor for the economic burden that austerity placed on the poor. The influential Trades Union Congress (TUC), which was overtaken by Rawlings loyalists during the early years of his regime, threw out its leadership and voted in a new, anti-Rawlings coalition. Its member-group, the General Transport and Chemical Workers, described the regime's new economic program as being "anti-people, a killer, callous and inhuman."[38] They began to call for massive wage increases to mitigate the rise in consumer prices and then, as conditions continued to worsen, for a wholesale rejection of Rawlings's economic plan. In 1985, TUC leader A. K. Yankey warned that workers might be forced "to rise up against the government, since it cannot ensure them their survival."[39]

Rawlings's administration was ultimately able to push the unpopular economic policy changes through because it was a military regime that did not hesitate to employ the standard tools of autocracy. Rawlings had a reputation for being tough on those who crossed him. Even in 1979, during his original rebellion against the corrupt NRC/SMC party, Rawlings's transitional government had alarmed some Ghanaians by executing the previous regime's leaders and applying corporal punishment against lawbreakers. Half a decade later, as his new economic policies incited a storm of protest, Rawlings was accused of employing "thugs" to shore up his authority and encouraging loyalists to enact violence against dissidents. Rawlings also did not hesitate to go beyond this "decentralized" coercion and use the full force of the state's security apparatus directly and openly against his political opponents. Strikes and protests were met with armored vehicles and mass arrests. Labor leaders were put under surveillance, and many were forced to curtail their activism for fear of attracting such drastic reprisals as to imperil the very existence of the opposition. State repression was not new in Ghana; starting in the final years of the Nkrumah regime, it had been used by parties of all political persuasions as a means of muting dissent.[40] However, after Rawlings enacted his economic program, this political repression reached such scope and intensity that the country was said to be living under a "culture of silence." The regime announced that opposition to its plan was an act of economic sabotage, and would-be dissidents rapidly disappeared into the maw of the system. Wielding power to arrest and detain whomever it considered a threat to national security, the PNDC's rule was awash with detention, torture, molestation, and murder.[41]

THE SHAPE-SHIFTER: *RAWLINGSISMO* AND
THE RETURN TO MULTIPARTY POLITICS

J. J. Rawlings founded his regime on populist rhetoric and an appeal to direct, grassroots political engagement. As already mentioned, he early on rejected the idea of electoral politics as a solution to Ghana's problems, adopting the argument that the process of formal/liberal democracy was too easily manipulated by corrupt oligarchs. Many Ghanaians accepted this argument at the time. They had witnessed firsthand the corruption of the elected PNP regime. Furthermore, their understanding of the post-colonial social compact was that the legitimacy of government was tied to the perceived character of the regime and how well it responded to the interests of the people, more so than the particular mechanism by which it came into power. This view began to change in the 1980s, however, as Rawlings himself enacted a political about-face and exercised his pre-rogative to foist a massively unpopular economic plan onto the reluctant populace. Ghanaians from a wide variety of backgrounds suddenly began to agree that Rawlings's "alternative democracy" was no democracy at all.

By 1984, Rawlings no longer even saw a proto-democratic role for the local P/WDCs. At the start of his regime, he had described these organiza-tions as the locus of "people's power" and pledged to make them the basis for establishing "elected representatives of the people . . . [at the] district level, then regional, and ultimately at the national level."[42] He had contin-ued to insist on the autonomy and democratic value of these committees even as revelations of abuses and corruption undermined their legitimacy. However, Rawlings quickly brought the local organizations to heel once they started to voice resistance against his economic plan. Concerned that the P/WDCs might become a forum for airing popular dissent against the regime, he took steps to place them under the direct control of the central PNDC party and severely curtailed their power.[43] At this time, Rawlings had begun to seem all but invincible. He had purged the contentious Left from his party's fold, survived attempted countercoups, neutralized the power of the P/WDCs, and repressively cultivated a culture of silence. This status quo was about to encounter a new challenge, however, as "people's power" began to flow in an unexpected direction.

Starting in 1986, workers risked state repression and took to the streets en masse to protest the declining value of wages. The PNDC reacted in typical fashion, blocking public gatherings with armored cars and conducting mass arrests. This time, however, as the opposition began to build, its message was focused on a call for formal/liberal democracy, perhaps even more so than on the conventional leftist grievance of unjust social conditions. Leftist leaders had not entirely abandoned their qualms about the tendency of electoral politics to be manipulated by moneyed interests. However, their experience of betrayal under the "alternative democracy" of Rawlings reinforced those voices on the left who believed that the prospects of formal democracy were better than the alternative. This shift in strategy helped the opposition to establish a larger coalition of support. It made dissidence more palatable to the country's professional classes, including traditionally rightward-leaning organizations such as the Ghana Bar Association (GBA) and the Association of Recognized Professional Bodies (ARPB). The confluence of interests was strengthened in February 1988, when distinguished historian and economic conservative Albert Adu Boahen dared to speak out against the Rawlings regime, calling it "illegitimate." The government responded by threatening the scholar with, in its official words, "conflagration and inferno."[44] In March, Ghana's Trades Union Congress formally declared its support for democratic process, thus helping to establish consensus where once there had been disjuncture. By 1990, Boahen had joined forces with radical socialist Johnny Hansen to form the Movement for Freedom and Justice (MFJ). This new organization cut across traditionally opposing ideological lines to endorse a shared call for formal democracy and multiparty elections.

Rawlings responded to the increasingly unified opposition and its calls for open elections by establishing the "National Commission on Democracy." The regime steadfastly refused to relax its ban on alternative political parties (i.e., any party other than the ruling PNDC). As a counterproposal, however, it put forth an idea for new legislative assemblies that would consist of a mixture of elected and appointed officials. This idea infuriated Rawlings's critics. They saw it as an evasive attempt to dance around the public's demands for reform and prolong the power of the regime. Even as Rawlings went ahead to form the hybrid assemblies, opponents labeled them as an insult to democratic process and encouraged the public to boycott the elections. The MFJ's leaders alleged that Rawlings's gestures toward democracy were enmeshed within a system of intimidation, intolerance, and exclusion. They maintained that the regime held a stranglehold over the electoral process by insisting that all candidates run on the ruling party's own platform and that the hybrid assemblies were packed with loyalists who terrorized and silenced opposing viewpoints.

Opposition leaders were very successful during the closing years of the 1980s in marshaling local and international sentiment against the Rawlings regime. They were aided in these efforts by the fact that nearly all Ghanaians believed the government had breached the social compact and was no longer acting in their best interests. The regime began to lose allies and became increasingly isolated. Nonetheless, most Ghanaians were astonished in May 1991 when the PNDC announced that it would cede to this pressure, lift its ban on alternative political parties, and hold open elections. In a nationwide referendum, Ghanaians overwhelmingly approved the regime's proposal for a new constitutional democracy in which an elected president would share power with a democratic legislature. If this move came as a surprise to the MFJ coalition, the opposition leaders were perhaps even more discombobulated when Rawlings declared his plans to quit the army and the PNDC in order to organize a new party and run for office. They were then even more shocked in December 1992, when, after a year of vigorous campaigning, the previously autocratic Rawlings *won* the open presidential elections.

The almost incomprehensible reinvention of Rawlings as a candidate for democratic office left opposition leaders wondering, "How did he do it?" Many decried what they believed must have been continuing fraud in the electoral process—the intimidation of opponents, the lack of an independent electoral commission, problems with voter ID verification, perhaps even stuffed ballot boxes. Some called for boycotts of the upcoming parliamentary elections—with the result that Rawlings's new National Democratic Congress party (NDC) won nearly all of the legislative seats.

In respect for the ensuing clamor, it is fair to say that Rawlings enjoyed distinct institutional privileges. With the state's coercive instruments at his command, he continued to operate throughout the electoral process as both player and referee. He chose the time and the scheduling of the transition to democracy, stage-managed the debates on Ghana's future, hassled opposition leaders, and disrupted MFJ meetings. One common complaint was that Rawlings had misled the opposition about election timetables, thereby thwarting their campaign planning and getting a head start in the race for president. Despite all of these complaints, however, it does seem clear that between the low point of his popularity in the late 1980s and the onset of democratic elections in 1992, Rawlings did manage to reinvent himself and garner significant public support. The opposition's charges of electoral fraud exceeded the evidence, and monitors from both the Organization of African Unity and the Carter Center in the United States declared the elections to be free and fair. How, then, did Rawlings manage to restore his political legitimacy and emerge as a democratic favorite?

One reason for Rawlings's electoral success was the predictable fragmentation of the MFJ coalition after its members achieved their goal of open elections. The rightward-leaning and upper-class members of the opposition moved to create the National Patriotic Party (NPP) under the leadership of A. A. Boahen, while the socialist-structuralist faction split into no less than four different parties, each claiming the legacy of Nkrumah. With the previously unified opposition splintering into diverse bickering groups, Rawlings loyalists had an easier time currying favor and managing the electoral process. Perhaps even more important than the fragmenting opposition, however, was Rawlings's uncanny ability to use his charisma and institutional power to manipulate public opinion. It was this "soft power," more so than any direct intimidation and fraud, that swayed the elections in his favor. In a sense, Rawlings made good on his earlier contention that electoral politics can be manipulated by those with the social power and resources to do so. Rawlings's electoral campaign managed to sufficiently muddy the waters so that even the two most conspicuous elements of his previous rule under the PNDC—its autocratic nature and its introduction of drastic economic policy changes—became lost or distorted in the popular imagination.

The first aspect of Rawlings's phenomenal shape-shifting ability after 1990 is that he managed to convince significant numbers of voters that liberal democracy had been his goal all along. What better way to negate criticism of his military rule than to transform into an advocate for democratic process? Pointing to the regime's 1991 constitutional initiative, Rawlings suggested that he personally had been the one to bring democracy to Ghana. He invoked his reputation as a grassroots populist, arguing that the country's new elections were the result of "a democratic process set in motion . . . on December 31, 1981."[45] In this claim, he conveniently ignored that what had actually happened on that date was that Rawlings had led a military coup to overthrow a democratically elected (albeit corrupt) government. Rawlings's claim to a liberal-democratic pedigree flew in the face of his ardent and explicit criticisms of electoral process during the early years of his rule, arguments that he had used to justify seizing power by force. His new political persona also seemed to be conspicuously undercut by his record of threatening and imprisoning pro-democracy activists and by his regime's long-standing ban on alternative political parties. Critics pointed out that Rawlings had resisted a return to formal democracy for more than a decade and that he had only conceded in the face of an overwhelmingly unified opposition. Nonetheless, while the opposition decried Rawlings's "sleight of hand," significant numbers of voters came to accept his claims.[46] Rawlings's improbable transformation into an advocate for liberal democracy sowed enough confusion to undermine the position of the National Patriotic Party, whose rightward-leaning lawyers and professionals had historically been the standard-bearers for formal democratic process in Ghana.

In a similarly improbable fashion, Rawlings was able to negate the moral position of the Left by laying claim to the mantle of Nkrumah's socialism. Despite the fact that his regime had sanctioned the most far-reaching economic liberalization effort in Ghana's history, Rawlings was able to convince many voters that he was the heir of Nkrumah's vision. He did this by enacting a *stylistic appropriation* of Nkrumah's socialist and pan-African rhetoric. Starting in the 1990s, Rawlings embarked on an organized effort to resurrect the conveniently deceased Nkrumah as a national symbol. He spoke of Ghana's first leader in glowing terms and inaugurated a Nkrumah mausoleum on the site where the venerable statesman had de-

clared Ghana's independence. He also threw the weight of his regime behind cultural projects that were first envisioned by Nkrumah, such as the
construction of a new National Theatre. This "cultural revival program"
allowed Rawlings to present himself as an authentically African-centric
leader who was bringing Nkrumah's ambitions to fulfillment.[47] As was
the case with his appropriation of liberal democracy, however, Rawlings's
claim to Nkrumah's legacy was largely disingenuous. During the decade
of his military rule, Rawlings had reached out to international financiers
and, at their behest, systematically displaced the state-oriented economic
paradigm that Nkrumah preferred. The Rawlings of the 1980s had made a
firm break with the Left, excised Nkrumahists from his ruling party, and
overtly criticized Nkrumah's legacy as being the cause of Ghana's economic woes. Zaaya Yeebo, a member of the June Fourth Movement who
was, for a time, a part of the Rawlings administration, recalled that from
the very start of his rule, Rawlings was seldom able to "resist the temptation of taking a swipe at Nkrumah and socialism."[48] Rawlings declared,
not long after his 1981 coup, that what Ghanaians got "when Nkrumah
preached socialism . . . [was] detention and hunger."[49]

Nonetheless, Rawlings was able to shore up his populist image by celebrating Nkrumah's cultural legacy. He adopted the mantle of the African
Personality and positioned himself as a patron of cultural performances.
Rawlings attempted to undercut the viability of the socialist caucus in
Ghana by appropriating the Left's moral and populist legacy and grafting
it onto his own, decidedly non-Nkrumahist policies. Nkrumah had linked
the moral outlook of socialism with traditional African sensibilities. Rawlings, in contrast, described socialism as an "empty" theory imposed by
those who held "faith in dogmatic ideologies evolved in societies other
than our own."[50] Thus casting Nkrumahists as head-in-the clouds ideo-
logues, he rejected their substantive economic arguments, while adopting
their populist and African-centric style. For example, Rawlings justified
his regime's embrace of international loans and the required governmental restructuring through the down-home metaphor of a bus ride:

> We are not parlor theoreticians. All our actions have been based on real-
> ism and the hard facts of our economic situation. . . . We are on a long
> journey. We could refuse any help, and thereby compel our people to
> crawl slowly and more painfully along the road to recovery. If we want to

speed up the process and ride part of the way in a bus, then we must pay the fare.[51]

Rawlings sought to characterize his economic program as the most pragmatic way of improving Ghanaians' material conditions, thereby laying claim to the moral terms of the postcolonial social compact. By "getting on the bus" of international finance, Ghanaians would be accepting the friendly hand of communal helpfulness, and they would at last be able to relax and enjoy the ride. Of course, this rhetoric merely displaced substantial questions about who was driving, where the bus was taking the country, and whether a ride on the international marketplace would truly be smoother for most Ghanaians. But what Rawlings's populist rhetoric did accomplish was to create a kind of ideological dissonance—a confounding stylistic counterpoint to the Left's argument that unregulated capitalism is "anti-people." By signaling left while turning right, Rawlings blurred and undercut the moral identity of the Left and succeeded in stealing the political thunder of the opposition.

During the late 1980s and early 1990s, a popular consensus emerged in Ghana. The long-standing social compact was interpreted as a combined desire for political honesty and transparency, formal democratic process, and substantive social justice. Rawlings held onto power primarily by convincing the electorate that he was an advocate for all of the above—even though in reality the policies and actions of his regime had advanced none of the above. The "alternative democracy" through which Rawlings came into power and maintained his position cannot be confused with formal democratic process. Nor can his adoption of populist imagery and style be confused with substantive, organized efforts to improve social equality. Due to Rawlings's masterful political shape-shifting, however, neither the structuralist-socialist Left nor the formal-liberal Right was able to mount an effective campaign against his regime. Rawlings's political longevity was a product to his enduring image—Eboe Hutchful calls it "Rawlingsismo"—of being a selfless, straight-shooting, if unconventional and temperamental, "man of the people."[52] This charismatic leadership helped Rawlings to stay at the country's helm despite, or perhaps even in correlation with, his willingness to bend all the rules of logic and consistency in order to suit his ongoing political relevance. Rawlings had little time for idle pleasantries and no patience with diplomacy, and yet he projected an aura of down-to-earth approachability. Many Ghanaians identified with him on a personal level as an embodiment of their aspirations to individual power, moral certitude, and self-assurance. His campaigns for support were continuous and wide reaching. One day he would arrive in a military utility van to help begin digging the foundation for a new construction project, and another day, he would swoop down in an Air Force helicopter to get dirty with villagers putting out bush fires, carrying sacks of maize, or digging ditches. Rawlings's image insulated him against incurring personal blame for much of the repression and abuse that occurred during his military rule, and it garnered more patience than otherwise would have been possible for his economic policy changes.

TRICKS OF ADJUSTMENT: CULTURAL PERFORMANCE AT THE NEXUS OF POLITICAL AND ECONOMIC REFORMS

Rawlings's presidential inauguration in January 1993 heralded a convergence of economic liberalization and political liberalization in Ghana. Some theorists have argued that the former tends to breed the latter—that is, freer markets tend to loosen the state's controlling grip on society.[53] Ghana's experience, however, brings into focus a more nuanced interpretation: that economic deregulation and the erosion of state services is often foisted onto an unwilling population, whose protests and disaffection then give rise to greater democracy. In other words, it is not "structural adjustment" programs that incite political reform but rather the social distress caused by those programs that leads to a clamor for political change. In Ghana, the transition to formal democracy came about because large numbers of people were dissatisfied with the government's refusal to defend the common welfare and because these people concluded that democratic elections were the best way to pursue their economic interests. It is important to note that the groundswell of democratic opposition that emerged during Rawlings's military rule was violently resisted by the regime precisely because it posed a threat to the ongoing implementation of unpopular economic policies.

International finance organizations were complicit in this repression. The World Bank, for example, explained that authoritarian regimes are "far more likely to be strongly committed to adjustment and thus to be better performers at it than democratic regimes." The institution therefore adopted the practice during the 1980s of lending financial support to authoritarian leaders who would be willing to enact stringent economic changes in the face of opposing "short-term domestic pressures."[54] Bjorn Beckman argued that the World Bank's later language of popular "empowerment," first introduced in a 1989 report, was a disingenuous confidence trick and a "poor substitute for democracy."[55] By dwelling on overdramatized, camera-ready examples of rural development, international financiers whitewashed the broader reality of deteriorating living conditions (especially in urban areas) and the aggressive repression of resistance that was conducted at the behest of these financiers. Beckman described this system as "managerial populism"—a term that might well have been referring to Rawlings's regime. The managed populism of neocolonial control presented a facade or smokescreen centered around images of smiling natives, behind which it acted systematically to subvert democracy and undermine the public welfare.

The Rawlings regime and its international financers had a fair amount of success in managing the demand for democracy in Ghana, controlling the transition to electoral politics, and confining the spread of opposition. Nonetheless, the regime found its sphere of activities to be severely curtailed by the new rulebook. After winning his presidential election, Rawlings chafed against the checks on his executive powers. He referred to the new state of affairs as "constitutional anarchy" and complained that:

> We seem to be bogged down by details, and if we become obsessed by procedural details rather than results, national development can end up as a hostage. . . . The complexities of constitutional procedures are slowing down government's ability to respond to the concerns of the people.[56]

Critics on both the right and the left were quick to point out that such statements appeared to be a throwback to Rawlings's earlier views on "alternative democracy." Opposition leaders cried out that "the leopard cannot lose its spots." In their view, Rawlings's conversion to constitutional democrat was a thin veneer, as was his invocation of "the concerns of the people." Rawlings seemed to be increasingly trapped between the pressures of international financiers and the constraints of the democratic process. His ability to use autocratic power to impose policies, repress dissent, and manipulate opinion had been significantly curtailed. Rawlings found it so difficult to adjust to these new constitutional constraints that he even physically assaulted his own vice president when the latter dared to question the regime's economic plans.[57]

Rawlings's political woes were further compounded by the failure of his economic policies to improve the country's standard of living. As the years went by, no amount of rural photo opportunities could supplant the ongoing crisis of inadequate access to goods and services. The country continued to be rocked by economic shocks brought on by local droughts and fluctuations in export prices. Employment rates did not improve, and younger Ghanaians continued to find that they had few opportunities for education and advancement. At the same time, the distribution of income in the industrial and urban sectors had become conspicuously more uneven. Overt signs of new wealth among the elites—large, modern houses; traffic jams; and richly stocked superstores—continued to emerge in juxtaposition with the hard fact that for the majority of the population, daily survival had become precarious.[58] The economic safety net that the state once offered was long gone, leaving Ghanaians to negotiate the effort of survival on an individual basis.

The outcome of this is what some theorists have called "social adjustments"—necessity-driven changes made at an individual or household level in order to contend with macro-level developments over which people feel they have little or no control. Otherwise understood as desperation measures, these strategies emerged out of a partial breakdown of the social compact in which short-term individual survival took precedence over the contemplation of any broader solution to the crisis.[59] The imperatives of economic "austerity" effectively trapped many Ghanaians into such a condition, narrowing their vision to daily perseverance and eroding their capacity to contemplate the bigger picture. Strategies of social adjustment—ranging from informal employment to "dietary innovation" (i.e., finding cheaper substitutes or doing without expensive desirables in one's diet)—became the norm in Ghana during the 1980s and 1990s. As the country's economic divisions deepened, the most vulnerable individuals—the urban underclass and the rural poor—began to rely on these makeshift strategies almost exclusively. Their alienation from the country's power structures and formal economy threatened to unravel Rawlings's populist image. At the same time, however, the short-term personal calculus of survival often fed a deepening pessimism that made the idea of organized, principled opposition seem out of reach.

Cultural performances came to the forefront in this postliberalization climate for two reasons. First, for the Rawlings regime, the decision to embrace constitutional democracy meant that direct repression could no longer be used as freely as a means of managing dissent. Constitutional constraints and the imperative of regular elections reduced the viability of "hard power," with the result that political symbolism and the ideo-logical legitimization of the regime gained an unprecedented importance. Rawlings thus redoubled his efforts to co-opt Nkrumah's political play-book and embrace the dusty mantle of the African Personality. Second, however, cultural performances also continued to provide a voice for the values and aspirations of Ghana's people—including their skepticism to-ward political appropriations. In an era of declining expectations, and after a long period of frustration with corruption and abuse emerging from both sides of the political spectrum, Ghanaians looked to cultural performances as a means of ad hoc resistance. Within the convoluted ideological environment of economic liberalization and electoral politics, these performances became a means of reaching toward the remains of the social compact.

In discussing the creativity, or forging, that is at the heart of cultural performance, *forging* does not refer to "counterfeiting" or "sham" but to the act of skillfully making something out of something else—or even out of nothing. Rawlings's strategies of political legitimation are described here as "shape-shifting," "sleight of hand," and "confidence tricks." This is language that draws from the well of crafty creativity, used to describe political manipulations that might be considered playful had they not had such a serious purpose. Also, this concept of creative forging applies even more compellingly to the survival strategies of those who seek to "make do" in the face of social breakdown and despair. Theirs are what Michel de Certeau identifies as the "bricolent" practices—the "artisan-like in-ventiveness" by which people constrained within oppressive conditions tinker with the status quo, using what little they have to pursue an escape from what they cannot leave.[60] Cultural performances are not merely "heightened occasions involving display." They have been understood as a locus of possibility and rewriting, where witty action and reinvention can potentially turn a stacked deck into "a potent set of wild cards . . . for refiguring possible worlds."[61] Amid these restless creative energies, no one can retain a smug confidence in the stability of his or her own ideological constructs. Mobilizing cultural performance for the purpose of political legitimation is therefore flirting with a transgressive force, one that is just as likely to interrupt ideological closure as to enact it. In the following chapters, we will see that this was especially true for Rawlings's attempts to channel Ananse, the Ghanaian trickster spirit.

2

Once upon a Spider

Ananse and the Counterhegemonic Trickster Ethos

> Poor painted Queen, vain flourish of my fortune,
> Why strew'st thou sugar on that bottled spider
> Whose deadly web ensnareth thee about?
>   Queen Margaret (to Queen Elizabeth) in Shakespeare's *Richard III*

WHEN CONTEMPORARY GHANAIAN performers navigate the web of tensions among public needs, political pressures, and cultural traditions, they have a long-standing reservoir of counterhegemonic maneuvers to fall back upon. This chapter discusses the time-honored trickster ethos of Ghanaian folklore, which is centered around tales of the crafty spider-spirit Ananse. The folkloric stories reveal Ananse's propensity for misdirection and "double maneuvers"—antics that can simultaneously confirm *and* undermine the sanctity of established beliefs, values, rules, and authorities. In an Ananse story, we are never quite sure if the trickster is endorsing the status quo or critiquing it. We will also see that Anansesεm (the practice of telling Ananse stories) is a tradition in which the trickster's deceptive ethos is seen as a defining quality of performance itself. Ananse is not merely the topic of these stories; he becomes an integral part of the storyteller's persona, and the trickster's unreliable craftiness becomes a part of storyteller-audience interactions. In the spirit of Ananse, storytellers are seen as ambivalent and deceptive figures who appear to be undermining social mores, while endorsing them at the same time (and vice versa). Anansesεm practitioners thus often use their performances to challenge distinctions between what is true and false, what is real and imagined, and what is authoritative and questionable. This form of storytelling has long served as a counterhegemonic influence in West Africa and beyond, allowing performers to surreptitiously call into question the legitimacy of socially dominant groups and their ideologies. This chapter describes how Anansesɛm practitioners maintain their agency in politicized performance spaces by obscuring the relationships among their stories, themselves, and their audiences—by cannily confusing the distinction between trickster representations and trickster embodiments.

MISTAKEN IDENTITY: THE SPIDER-TRICKSTER VERSUS THE "GREAT SPIDER"

In the foreword to Efua Sutherland's famous play *The Marriage of Anansewa,* the grande dame of Ghanaian theater poses a question: "Who is Ananse?"[1] Indeed, the identity of the trickster-spider has often been veiled in mystery, and for many years, Ananse left only faint and confusing traces in the historical records. In 1705, the Dutch merchant Willem Bosman was perhaps the first outsider to report that the natives of Africa's Gold Coast region spoke of a "Great Spider" who went by the name of Ananse and was said to have created the human race. Two British narrators, George MacDonald and Alfred Ellis, made the same observation during the nineteenth century.[2] In 1909, a British couple, Decima and Frederick Guggisberg, provided a more detailed description of the spider-spirit and explained that Ananse is "a frequent figure in the folklore," while also characterizing him as a deity and again repeating the European perception that West Africans believe mankind originally came from Ananse.[3] However, all of these Europeans confused the identities of two different spiders: the "Great" one and the deceptive one. A traditional Akan story succinctly explains the difference:

> *Ananse Kokuroko* [the Great Spider] had a plantation that was so big you couldn't see from one end of it to the other. When his crops were ripe, however, *the trickster Ananse* stole a good portion of the harvest. Upset that the trickster was stealing his crops, the sky god hired a medicine man to catch the thief. The medicine man took a drum, did rituals on it, and

then hid it on the farm. The trickster Ananse came to the farm again and looted as much of the harvest as he could carry. As he headed back home, however, the drum attached itself to the spider and beat with each step that he took. Ananse dropped the loot and ran, but he could not escape from the drum. So he crawled very quietly home to bed. At dawn the drum left him to go eat. When the drum returned, Ananse grabbed hold of it, snuck into his mother-in-law's room nearby, and fixed the drum on her!

At dawn Ananse said to his mother-in-law, "That is Nyame's thief-trap on you! Just be quiet about it until I can figure out how to remove it." But then Ananse the trickster headed straight to the sky god and told him, "I know where the thief is hiding! Send your servants tomorrow so that we can root her out." That night, however, Ananse's mother-in-law escaped from the drum when it went out to eat, and the trickster awoke to find the drum attached back on him! Just then, Nyame's servants arrived, calling out, "Ananse, come and show us the thief!" Unable to get out of bed without revealing his deception, Ananse replied, "I am unwell!" The king's servants brought him a carriage, but still Ananse pretended he was too weak to get up. So they tried to help him, at which point they saw the drum on his back and realized that he was the thief! So they seized the trickster Ananse and brought him before Ananse Kokuroko, who handed down the sentence: "Take Ananse to the executioner!"[4]

In 1916, Captain Robert S. Rattray, another British commentator, confirmed that the "Great Spider" (*Ananse Kokuroko* in Akan) was often used as a sobriquet for Nyame, the supreme sky god. European observers, he explained, had been confusing this "Great Spider" Nyame with the very different personage of Ananse the trickster-spider. This understanding was further confirmed in 1966, when Ghanaian native Charles van Dyck emphasized that in Akan the term "Great Spider" is reserved for Nyame alone and is "never given to the spider of the folk stories."[5]

Still, the mistake is understandable, because Ananse (the trickster-spider) maintains a particularly close and convoluted relationship with Nyame, the "Great Spider" or sky god. In Akan folklore, Ananse appears to be particularly favored among Nyame's many servants and attendants. Nyame entrusts Ananse with important errands. For example, in one popular story, the sky god asks Ananse to steal Death's golden sandals, snuffbox, and whip. Nyame also frequently challenges Ananse to complete difficult tasks or puzzles, such as weeding Nyame's nettle-infested farm, determining which one of Nyame's sons would be the better heir, capturing various wild and magical creatures, or even attempting to conceive a child with Aso, the wife of Akwasi-the-Jealous-One.[6] Ananse seems to have unlimited access to Nyame; the trickster can appear before the sky god whenever he wants, even if it is just to wish him good morning, a familiarity that is not granted to any other figure in Akan folklore. Despite their often antagonistic relationship, the two are described as "great friends."[7] Ananse sometimes even goes so far as to bring his own challenges and audacious bets to the sky god (for example, when Ananse seeks to trade a "beautiful maiden" for the sky god's sacred sheep, or when he claims that he can cure one of Nyame's relatives for half of the usual medicine man's fee).[8]

Nyame has honor and irreproachable status. He is addressed using the royal honorifics *ohene* and *nana*. He has servants, attendants, farmhands, executioners, and medicine men in his employ. His farm is so huge that you cannot see where it ends. Ananse's fortunes, in contrast, are eternally mercurial, so much so that the phrase "Ananse's wealth" is often used as an ironic reference to doubtful and temporary achievements. Ananse does well enough on one occasion to obtain a farm so big that "a sound at one end of it could not be heard at the other"—an apparently diminutive and derivative version of the sky god's farm—but Ananse is never able to retain these fortunes for long. Nyame sometimes refers to Ananse as a *kwahwiaban*—a vagrant with no reputable livelihood.[9] Most of the time, Ananse is idle and lives in squalor. He steals from and defrauds others to get by and is well known to authorities. As the Ghanaian scholar Kwesi Yankah suggested, Nyame and Ananse are almost always engaged with each other, and they are almost always at cross-purposes.[10] Ananse seems eternally dedicated to contradicting and antagonizing the sky god, and yet in doing so he shares a unique intimacy with Nyame:

> Nyame and Ananse, two great friends, argued over what is more painful, incrimination or bodily injury. Ananse said that incrimination is more painful, but Nyame insisted that injury holds the greater pain. Nyame cut Ananse with a sharp knife in order to make his point. Ananse hurt badly! But when his wound healed, Ananse decided to take his revenge. He dug a tunnel underneath the kitchen of Nyame's mother-in-law, hired a band of musicians, hid them in the tunnel, and instructed them that when they heard the mother-in-law cry out, they should sing a song that he taught them. Ananse then crept into Nyame's house and defecated in

the mother-in-law's hearth stove. "Who did this?!" cried the mother-in-law upon discovering the deed. Hearing their cue, the hidden musicians sung the song that Ananse had taught them: "Nyame has defecated! He has defecated!" Nyame's mother-in-law, thinking that she heard the disembodied voices of spirits naming the perpetrator, confronted Nyame and gave him an earful. Nyame was so ashamed that he almost committed suicide. "So," Ananse told him, "you must admit that I was right!"[11]

Sometimes Ananse the trickster seems to be almost the degenerate double of the sky god, or at least a close relative. He is portrayed in some stories as being married to Nyame's sister or daughter. Ananse also occasionally identifies himself as Nyame's half-brother, and at times Nyame acknowledges him with the title "washer of the sky god's soul."[12] In other words, the relationship between the "Great Spider" (Ananse Kokuroko) and the trickster-spider Ananse is one of tremendous familiarity and interdependence.

NOT GOD AND NOT NOT GOD: ANANSE AND THE "COINCIDENCE OF OPPOSITES"

How, then, are we to regard Ananse? Is this trickster who interacts so freely with the supreme sky god a deity in his own right, a subordinate spirit, a twisted reflection of Nyame, or merely a folkloric personage? W. H. Barker remarked in 1919 that "no satisfactory solution has yet been found" to the question of Ananse's identity. Native opinion on the matter was varied, Barker explained; one source confirms that Ananse is "related to Nyame" (how so is unspecified), whereas another explains that the two are not related. One source clarifies that Ananse was a historical personage and a principal founder of the Akan people, whereas another source indicates that Ananse possessed the full powers of a god.[13] Barker despaired of ever settling such contradictions, but this has not prevented other commentators from taking a more definitive stance.

Some scholars have argued that Ananse has a finite, anthropomorphic image in the folklore and therefore cannot be seen as a true deity. He is frequently addressed as *Kweku Ananse*, where *Kweku* is the standard "day-name" given by Akans to human males who are born on Wednesday.

Animals (e.g., spiders) are never given such names.[14] Ananse is also depicted in the stories as having a normal human family, including his wife, Aso, and four children (the eldest of whom, Ntikuma, is often suspicious of his father's tricks). Ananse works as a farmer and lives in a normal human village, facing the same daily struggles, needs, and desires as his neighbors. These attributes led Efua Sutherland to propose that Ananse is "a kind of Everyman," who reflects ordinary human passions, ambitions, and follies in a way that is "artistically exaggerated and distorted."[15] However, the same can be said of any of the figures that inhabit West African mythology. Even the supreme sky god Nyame is often described in the stories as a farm owner and a married man. In the preceding story about Nyame and Ananse, Nyame is blamed for defecating in his mother-in-law's kitchen. What image could be more human? Ananse's anthropomorphic characteristics thus do not firmly distinguish him from the gods.

Yet, critics may maintain that Nyame is known for invoking a specifically religious attitude among mortals, while Ananse is not. There are no shrines to Ananse, and there are no ritual worship practices associated with him.[16] In the stories, Ananse often seems to set himself apart from such practices:

> Once, Ananse saw that the priest of a shrine had raised a fat sheep to sacrifice to the shrine's deity. Hungry for a good roast, Ananse decided to play a trick. He went to the priest and said, "I admire your deity so very much, and I want to put myself up as an offering. Give me your sacrificial sheep to eat so, thus fattened, I might be an appropriate offering." When the priest agreed, Ananse gave Rat a tiny piece of the meat and recruited his help. On the day that was appointed for sacrificing Ananse to the god, Rat dug a tunnel under the priest's shrine and hid there with a set of drums. The moment the priest finished his prayers and the acolytes lifted a knife to Ananse's throat, Rat began to beat the drums and sing, "Ananse's blood is offensive to me! Spill it here and you shall taste my wrath! You, your children, and your entire clan!" Shocked by the disembodied voice and thinking it to be that of the shrine deity, the priest ordered his acolytes to release Ananse and set him free![17]

Ananse is not exactly human, but he is not exactly a god either. He is not an object of religious veneration, but he does seem to be capable of duping Death and regularly embarrassing the gods. He is Nyame's servant, subject, errand boy, soul washer, friend, and brother. Thus, as Kwesi Yankah states, "Ananse's religious significance in the Akan world view cannot be asserted with certainty."[18]

Attempting to limit Ananse to the categories of god, spirit, or human minimizes the fundamentally ambiguous and anomalous character of the trickster. Ananse is always negating and transforming himself, and he finds no boundary sacrosanct, including the boundaries between the divine and the ordinary. The novelist Sandra Jackson-Opoku has Ananse declare, "I am more than a spider, much more than just a man. I am the one who spins the rainbows, who rides the winds, who can even negotiate the skies on a line of my own making. . . . I was here at the beginning and will yet be at the end."[19] Unlike Nyame, whom Akan belief places up in the skies, or humans, who are identified with the earth below, Ananse is often found in transit between the realms, moving impulsively back and forth across these borders. As William Hynes explains it, the trickster is a "coincidence of opposites." He is not a deity and is not a nondeity; he is something different and more than either—"not fully delimited by one side or the other of the binary distinction, nor by both sides at once, nor by their oppositions."[20] Ananse visits everywhere, including supernatural places that are usually off-limits to mortals; he holds a dual citizenship and wanders with impunity throughout the various metaphysical realms.

CREATIVE-TREACHEROUS/WONDERFUL-LETHAL: THE SPIDER, THE WEB, AND THE FOLKLORIC IMAGINATION

In the nineteenth century, Alfred Ellis reported that West African natives saw Ananse as "sometimes a man and sometimes a spider." Ellis therefore thought it "probable" that Ananse stories were based on the exploits of "some early chief who was known to his fellows as 'spider.'" Of course, this notion that Ananse stories are based on some historical personage is pure conjecture.[21] What is known for certain is that in addition to being a brother to the gods and having the same needs as an ordinary mortal, the folkloric Ananse also has the crafty and sometimes disturbing characteristics of an arachnid. Among the Akan, spiders have the reputation of possessing both an admirable intelligence and an intimidating, treacherous nature. Their webs are both beautiful and deadly. Spiders can jump alarming distances, run sideways with ease, walk across water using surface tension, and even float on the wind by casting their silken threads as a kind of parachute. Sometimes their webs are lacy and symmetrical, but often they weave tangled and irregular architecture in the dark and secluded parts of buildings. Sometimes they create burrows with trap doors, behind which they lurk, waiting to jump out at their prey.[22]

As a spider, Ananse employs his creative intelligence to gratify his ravenous appetite. He uses his cunning awareness of human and animal psychology to concoct ad hoc strategies for preying upon others. Ananse is often described as "wiase nyansafo" (worldly wise), which means that he is endowed with a cleverness that can become its own limitation as well as its own reward:

> Ananse paid a visit to his mother-in-law, arrived after supper, and was offered cornmeal pulp to eat. Disappointed with the bland food, Ananse told his host that he was allergic to cornmeal, hoping that he might be offered something finer. He did not realize that cornmeal pulp was all there was left to eat in the house. "The market is closed," his mother-and-law explained, "so you'll just have to stick with water until the morning." Ananse then regretted declining the offer. He was starving, but asking for the food would expose his lie. "I know what to do," he thought. When he was given water and soap for his bath, he poured the water and lathered the soap on himself in front of everybody, with his clothes still on. "Are you okay?" everyone asked with great concern. "I am fine," Ananse sighed, and then explained, "It is merely my great forgetfulness, the same forgetfulness that made me inadvertently tell you that I am allergic to cornmeal even though I am not!" Hearing this, his mother-in-law served Ananse the very same meal that he had earlier refused. Ananse gulped it all down and licked his hands clean![23]

As intrinsically marvelous as the spider's mobility, camouflage, and web-spinning might be, these acts of cleverness are nonetheless infused with a less-than-wholesome purpose. Colonial observers were not entirely exaggerating when they described Ananse as an "emblem of more or less successful cunning and unscrupulous rapacity."[24] The trickster is known to lie, cheat, and deceive without qualms:

> Ananse and Donkey were friends. Donkey fell in love with a beautiful girl a few towns away and was trying to muster the confidence to approach her. However, Ananse was jealous. He said to Donkey, "Let me take your

message to her. I will make you look chiefly!" Donkey agreed, but when
Ananse spoke with the girl, he extolled his own virtues instead, bragging,
"The next time I visit, I will have my servant carry me here!" Returning to
Donkey, Ananse lied to him, saying, "She requires a proof of your great
strength. I told her that you are fit to carry me all the way to her village."
Pleased at the chance to impress the girl with his strength instead of with
words, Donkey carried Ananse there, only to find that it was all a part of
the spider's scheme. Donkey could not bear it when Ananse married the
girl. Deeply pained, he cried out, "Na-hi! Na-hi!" And so, when you hear a
donkey bray, it is a lament of betrayal.[25]

In his spider-like nature, Ananse is thus an immoral (or at best amoral)
figure. He is admirably creative and transformative, but he is also referred
to as "pɛsɛ m'ko m'nya ni" (selfish one), "difode panyin" (greedy one), and
"man bɔ ni" (breaker of states or homes).[26] He is a parasite and an insatiable, perpetual malcontent who exploits all opportunities to get something for nothing. He can be disloyal, cruel, lecherous, unscrupulous,
vain, and competitive in the vilest manner. He knows no inhibitions and
recognizes no taboos.

Since Ananse takes on an anthropomorphic form in most of the stories,
one might imagine (as Alfred Ellis did) that the trickster's character is
unequivocally human and that his personality is related to the spider only
through a kind of analogy. However, the truth seems to be more complex:

Ananse and Goat made a farm together. Goat, of course, did most of the till-
ing, planting, and weeding, but as harvest time approached, Ananse insisted
that they divide the farm in half. Still, Goat's half turned out to be more
productive. So Ananse put locusts in a jar and said to Goat, "I found these
locusts on the farm! You should burn your part, and I will burn mine." Goat
dutifully followed this suggestion only to discover that he had been tricked:
Ananse did not burn his half of the farm! So Goat decided to make Ananse
pay. One day he offered Ananse a juicy rack of his specially seasoned deer
roast. Ananse licked his lips, "Nice! What is this?" Goat said, "I fell into a
pan of boiling oil and found out that I am quite tasty!" That evening, Ananse
smeared oil around his waistline and lit himself on fire. However, instead of
a great-tasting roast, all he got was hellish pain as the flames burned off his
middle part! And that is why spiders have tiny waists.[27]

In this story, Ananse undergoes an anatomical transformation that is said
to explain the shape of a spider's body, indicating a strong ontological

identity between the folkloric trickster and his animal counterparts. Similar tales abound—including one in which Ananse burns his head while trying to steal hot beans in his hat, rendering the spider bald, and another in which an irate Nyame slaps Ananse to the ground, rendering the spider flat.[28] Another set of traditional Anansesεm stories provide explanations for the behavioral traits of real-life spiders—including a description of how Ananse runs across the water to escape from Crocodile, and a story in which he is compelled out of shame to hide in the dark corners of houses.[29] The Ananse of the folktales can also be found taking shelter in his web in the branches of palm trees, or retreating to the rafters or the ceiling of a house after being discovered in his trickery.[30]

These tales suggest that Ananse is something more than a human with a spider-like personality. Some commentators, in fact, take the opposite view: arguing that Ananse is not human at all but rather an exaggerated spider. Emmanuel Asihene, for example, describes Ananse's spider-ness as his true identity. Asihene explains that the animal spider is creatively personified in the Anansesεm stories but that "in time of calamity, especially when humiliated ... [Ananse] shows his *true colors* as a real spider."[31] In Asihene's interpretation, the typical narrative arc of Ananse stories is a kind of unmasking in which our impressions of the human-seeming trickster gradually yield to reality as his actual spider-nature is revealed. Kwesi Yankah takes a similar view, arguing that Ananse's false human image "tapers off occasionally and *betrays* [his] animal tendencies."[32] Many commentators have taken the liberty of interpreting the human/ spider dynamic in Ananse as representing the interplay between a thin veneer of "civilized" human behavior—understood as a fragile, superficial overlay—versus what they see as the essentially selfish and cruel impulses of primal or animalistic nature.[33]

Others (including the author) believe that Ananse is both *always* fully man and *always* fully spider. In the same way that he blurs and supersedes the boundaries between the human and the divine, he also moves with impunity to erase the conceptual distinctions between what is human and what is animalistic. This is not meant in the same sense as, for example, a werewolf, which changes back and forth, but rather Ananse has both anthropomorphic and arachnoid features at the same time. Thus, he can never be identified as only spider or only human. Even when he is at his

most human, Ananse still bears the name and identity of the spider. And
even when his (mis)adventures result in his taking on arachnoid features
(baldness, a thin waist, hiding in the rafters, etc.), he still does not completely lose his human form. The stories unsettle any distinction between
the man and the spider. When we observe Ananse now as a human and
then as a spider, we are not seeing changes in his form but rather shifts in
the narrative point of view that emphasize one or another of his characteristics. Ananse's dual human/spider nature can thus be understood as
another expression of the trickster's fundamental "doubleness" or ambiguity. He is not an animal, and he is not a nonanimal; he partakes of both
realms and is limited by neither.[34]

PERMITTED ICONOCLAST: ANANSE, THE SOCIAL
ORDER, AND THE PRESERVATIONIST ARGUMENT

Ananse's antics have an unavoidably political dimension. The trickster seems to be the very embodiment of social chaos and instability—
constantly subverting identity and authority, and even challenging the
gods. Many scholars have been left scrambling in their attempts to identify
his "function" within the social order. Why would authorities fail to prose-
cute Ananse and those who convey his stories when the trickster so clearly
defies social norms and established power structures? One explanation, as
developed by the folklorist John Roberts, is that Ananse's antics are considered to be acceptably frivolous outgrowths of a lower-class mentality.
Roberts argues that Ananse's deceptiveness and social creativity provide
a model of "valuable adaptive behavioral traits" for the disenfranchised
members of society. Elites, in contrast, could take the sky god Nyame as
their model; they are viewed as honorable and forthright and are lifted
above the fray by virtue of their positions. While those on the bottom
might need to get by day to day by using their wits, elites survive by using
a much broader, pervasive, and straightforward application of power. Thus,
Roberts suggests, elites are not particularly threatened by Ananse's antics,
as the disorganized chaos of the trickster's short-term greed inherently
prevents him from mounting a sustained challenge to the power of authorities. In this view, Ananse's disreputable scheming poses no real threat to

the social order. In fact, as expected plebian behavior, it is actually a part of the established social order. The forthright patricians survive by their might, and the inglorious plebes survive by their wits; interdependence and hierarchy remain intact, and the social order remains secure.[35]

Roberts's argument may seem to disregard how Ananse's activities are a breach of social decorum and an affront to the status quo. Far from modeling expected plebian behavior, the trickster often ventures into realms of indecency and audacity (stealing, adultery, deceiving a priest, etc.) that would not ordinarily be tolerated. He operates far beyond the usual bounds of custom and law.[36] Still, many scholars continue to insist that the preservation of the social order must somehow be the ultimate goal and paramount logic of Anansesɛm. As these scholars see it, any perceived conflict between the trickster's stories and the social order must be illusory or superficial. The most nuanced of these arguments tend to suggest that Ananse plays a kind of "system maintenance" role either by acting as a cautionary tale and a scapegoat for moral indignation or by providing a fantasy of transgression that allows otherwise powerless individuals to safely (and ineffectively) vent their frustrations. We'll address these arguments in turn now.

Kwawisi Tekpetey is perhaps the most persuasive advocate for the view that Anansesɛm provides didactic lessons about crime and punishment. He maintains that the stories expose Ananse's "unchecked, selfish greed . . . for the dangerous evil that it represents in the society." The ultimate message of Anansesɛm performances, according to Tekpetey, is that the trickster's deceptiveness and greed are crimes to society. Other scholars who make similar arguments include Christopher Vescey and Charles van Dyck.[37] They believe that by thwarting society's most important rules, Ananse acts as an object lesson, revealing the damage that can be suffered by both victims and perpetrators when laws are broken. This view of Anansesɛm, however, is too reductionist. It does not give adequate credence to the delight with which audiences respond to the trickster's exploits. Nor does it adequately account for the many stories in which Ananse escapes punishment and at times even profits from his misdeeds. Charles van Dyck attempts to hedge on this point, admitting that "justice does not always prevail" in the stories but insisting that this feature of Anansesɛm is merely an attempt at social realism. According to van Dyck, the stories in which Ananse *does* pay for his crimes show how the law catches up to evildoers sooner or later.[38] Others, however, feel that the delayed or averted "justice" in many of Ananse's stories is part of a performance ethos that is far more ambiguous. Although sometimes Ananse is punished for his antics and at other times, he gets away with it at the last minute, it is in fact his clever maneuvers or surprising triumphs that are most important to the audience. The march of "justice"—or the evasion thereof—is, if anything, more of a social backdrop for the trickster's topsy-turvy antics than an overriding narrative lesson.

Other Ananse scholars look at the trickster's transgressions as a kind of politically sanctioned "pressure relief valve"—a harmless outlet for frustrations that might otherwise become an insurgent force against the social order. These arguments come from a much broader literature on permitted social deviance. Andrew Stott, for example, explains that established power "absorbs the potential for change, permitting itself to be questioned for the . . . purposes of seeming to appear open, before finally reasserting itself once more."[39] Well-defined performance spaces such as those of storytelling, theater, and ritual have often been described as a natural locus of this kind of temporary, licensed rebellion—scenes where the participants are separated from their everyday worlds and their usual identities and are thus allowed a very brief reprieve from the demands of social structure.[40] Part of the appeal of Ananse's dual human/animal nature, and of the amorphous characteristics of tricksters in general, may well be that these performances offer a fanciful and cathartic escape from the confining obligations of social identity.[41] This begs the question, however, of whether such scenes of permitted transgression are *purely* orchestrated for the maintenance of existing social norms. An alternative interpretation might be that they are expressive occasions in which suppressed desires have burst into view and made their presence known and in which the existing power structures are struggling and failing to entirely circumscribe the influence of these unsanctioned ambitions.

The practice of telling Ananse stories, however, cannot be categorized as either a safe, sanctioned performance or an unconstrained expression of rebellion; it is in fact both. This is why Anansesɛm is always both subversive *and* supportive of the social order. The trickster does not want to be pigeonholed as either an opponent or an ally. Although he may alternately reinforce social norms and undermine them, he never does either in a straightforward or predictable fashion. When we appreciate Ananse's inherent doubleness or ambiguity, we understand that seeing him as unequivocally oppositional or unequivocally reinforcing is doing him a disservice; the trickster will always be available to serve hegemony but will never be fully contained by it. In relation to this, we will now explore how Ananse's politically salient doubleness becomes evident in the performance of his stories.

"OWNER OF THE STORIES": THE ANANSESƐM STORYTELLER AND THE ANANSE-LIKE TEMPERAMENT

A good way to begin our exploration of Anansesɛm performance is by dissecting the term itself. *Anansesɛm* is a compound noun that joins *Ananse* with *asɛm,* which means news, a narrative account, an utterance, a concern, a behavior, a situation, a dispute, or even legal proceedings, depending on the context.[42] In the term *Anansesɛm,* the *asɛm* is the root, and *Ananse* is the modifier that tells what *kind* of news/utterance/behavior/ situation is being conveyed. Thus, one translation of *Anansesɛm* is "Ananse news." Similar compounds can be created for other kinds of "news," including *tetesɛm* (historical stories), *sikasɛm* (financial matters), *anigyesɛm* (joyful situations or news), and many others. In these constructions, the modifying nouns tend to be of two different types. They can indicate the *content matter* of the "news," as is the case in *tetesɛm* (news about the past), or they can indicate its *defining quality,* as is the case in *anigyesɛm* (news that is joyful). Additional examples of these two different kinds of modifiers can be seen in table 2.1.

Our initial impulse might be to interpret *Anansesɛm* as "news about Ananse"—in other words, stories that contain accounts of Ananse's exploits. As befits the trickster's doubleness, however, the modifier can also be read in a different fashion: *Anansesɛm* can be understood as "news that is Ananse-like." In this latter interpretation, it is not the *content* of a story that makes it Anansesɛm but rather the trickster-like *quality* of the storytelling experience. This concept is supported by the fact that the Akan give the name *Anansesɛm* to *all* folktale performances—regardless of whether

TABLE 2.1

The linguistic morphology of the word *Anansesɛm*

Root noun	+ Modifier noun	= Compound noun
asɛm	*Ananse*	*Anansesɛm*

The modifier can indicate the content matter of the news

asɛm (news)	*aware* (marriage)	*awaresɛm* (marital issues)
asɛm (news)	*tete* (past)	*tetesɛm* (history or past occurrences)
asɛm (news)	*sika* (money)	*sikasɛm* (financial matters)

The modifier can also indicate the defining quality of the news

asɛm (news)	*atoro* (untruth)	*atorosɛm* (untrue statements or lies)
asɛm (news)	*anigye* (joy)	*anigyesɛm* (joyful situations or news)
asɛm (news)	*serew* (humor)	*aserewsɛm* (humorous statements or behavior)

or not Ananse appears in the story. The trickster spirit is so closely associated with the act of storytelling, the persona of the storyteller, and the interactions among the performers and with the audience that he has bestowed his name upon the entire genre of folktales. The reason that storytelling is considered "Ananse-like" is probably because Ananse himself is a clever linguist and a spinner of yarns. The trickster is a master of the kind of creative deception that informs art. As Lewis Hyde describes it, he "makes lies seem so real they enter the world and walk among us."[43]

Several of the traditional Anansesɛm tales provide their own account of how the trickster came to be so closely associated with storytelling. All of them explain that Nyame, the sky god, was once the possessor of all stories. One day, however, Ananse went to Nyame and said, "I'd like to buy your stories." A popular version continues as follows:

Nyame replied to Ananse, "Great and powerful towns have tried and failed to purchase the stories. How do you, of so little means, expect to do so? The price is to get me a live python, a hornet's nest, a leopard, and an *Aboatia* (a magical dwarflike creature)." Ananse said, "Okay, I will get them for you." Ananse soon found Python and pretended to be in doubt about his length. "If you have any doubts, then measure me!" Python said. After stretching out the snake, Ananse quickly tied him to the measuring stick, taking him captive. Next, he sprinkled water over the hornet's nest and yelled, "It's raining! Take shelter in my gourd!" The hornets did so, and he covered the gourd, trapping them. Ananse then dug a hole. Leopard came by, fell into it, and then pleaded, "Help me out!" Ananse replied, "I'll have to tie your feet and mouth first, or you'll tear me to pieces when you are out!" Leopard agreed, and of course Ananse kept him tied up after pulling him out. Ananse then placed a gum-covered doll in the forest with a bowl of mashed yams to attract the Aboatia. When the Aboatia arrived, it greeted the doll. Angry that the doll did not reply, the Aboatia struck out at it. Doing so, it became caught in the sticky gum. Ananse was thus able to take all of the snared creatures and deliver them to Nyame. Impressed, the sky god declared, "My stories are now yours. From now on, they will bear your name: They are Anansesɛm!"[44]

It seems that what Nyame wanted from the potential "buyers" of the stories was not wealth—for Nyame lacks little in this regard—but rather the crafty mind that would be able to accomplish seemingly impossible feats. Ananse is of course the ideal candidate, because he is fantastically eager to exploit every opportunity to overcome his personal and material limitations. That Nyame would entrust the stories only to an individual as crafty as the trickster may say something about the value and utility of the tales, in that they rightly belong only to one who can wield them with the appropriate inventiveness.

It is useful to remember that Anansesɛm originates in a context of oral folkloric transmission, in which the stories' only existence outside of the mind is in the practice of storytelling itself. The Akan people have long composed their stories with an eye for the demands of performance. The owner of the stories, then, is one who not only knows the relevant content but also understands what the stories are meant to *do* in the hands of a crafty teller. As the archetypical owner of the stories, Ananse provides the model for this appropriate storytelling behavior. The Anansesɛm storyteller participates in the trickster's creativity and craftiness during the course of performance. He or she becomes, for a time, an innovator who has minute-by-minute control over the course of the narrative. Audiences take particular delight in the storyteller's ability to play upon traditional themes and images, as well as upon more immediate contexts and events, to create original Anansesɛm variations and subvert the participants' expectations.[45] Just as the trickster shifts form and creates false impressions to accomplish his miscreant misdeeds, the storyteller enacts changes of voice and mannerism to ensnare audiences in a narrative web. The tellers do all of this while simultaneously speaking with the authority of an eyewitness—as if they were *right there* when Ananse navigated the skies to Nyame's abode or when he cleverly obtained Death's golden whip and sandals. Engaging in such narrative craftiness and improvisation allows storytellers to prove their artistry and, like Ananse, demonstrate their right to be the owners of the stories.

"NOT TO BE BELIEVED": VERITY, FABRICATION, AND DOUBLENESS IN ANANSESƐM PERFORMANCE

Anansesɛm performances range from simple domestic affairs, in which members of a family share tales among themselves, to more complex dramatized forms, in which an entire community may participate. The larger performances sometimes even include bands of musicians and group dances. However, the differences between informal domestic storytelling and larger public performances of Anansesɛm are for the most part only a matter of scale. No matter how large the audience, Akan storytelling practice revolves around an ethos of innovation and direct participation. There are no detached spectators in Anansesɛm; everyone who is present at the gathering is potentially a part of the performance.[46] In most cases, Anansesɛm begins with a series of rousing songs and free-for-all dancing—a kind of community warm-up. This soon segues into a call-and-response exchange between the storyteller and the participating audience members.

The initial call-and-response in Anansesɛm establishes the trickster-like atmosphere. It is usually a humorous disclaimer indicating that the veracity of the ensuing narrative should be regarded with pleasurable suspicion. For example, at one performance, the storyteller cried out, "Anansesɛm yɛ asisie!" (Anansesɛm is an act of hoaxing!). The audience replied, "Sisi me!" (Hoax me!). In such exchanges, the co-performers (the storyteller and the audience members) acknowledge that such an Ananse-like ruse will be a defining quality of the storytelling event and one that the audience expects. Of course, the call-and-response is not always this direct. In one popular exchange, the co-performers emphatically disavowed any claim to veracity by shouting, "Yɛ' nse sɛ, 'nse sɛ!" (We are not saying this is so, we are not saying so!). The audience replied, "Yε nse sε!" (We are not saying so!).[47]

We can thus see how the elusive truth-status of Anansesεm allows performers to navigate the force fields of surveillance and power. By vocally rejecting the veracity of everything that is to follow, the participants create a space in which unsanctioned outlooks can be spoken and then plausibly denied. At the same time, however, this over-the-top insistence that the upcoming performance is false, wayward, and insincere may itself be a ruse. When the trickster-storyteller goes out of his way to insist that he is *not* telling the truth, the veracity of the denial itself may be called into question.

In some call-and-response exchanges, the navigation of Anansesεm's truth-status takes on even more subtle, obscure, or confusing forms. In one pattern, for example, the storyteller shouts, "Ananse kotoku!" (Ananse's sac-bag!), and the audience replies, "Tenteenten a εsen kurotia!" (So long it traverses the town's boundaries!).[48] This disclaimer begins with the storyteller simply referencing one of the spider's accoutrements—the grotesque and swollen sac where it stores its eggs. Presumably this is a crude/humorous reference to the unsavory and disturbing nature of the Anansesεm performances that are about to unfold. Merely by referencing this aspect of Ananse, the storyteller proclaims that there is nothing here that will be appropriate or meaningful. The audience then responds by indicating that they will accept the sac but only if it "traverses the town's boundaries"—that is, only if it extends to encompass the whole of society. The co-performers thus indicate that the audience has entered into the fantastical world of Anansesεm—a realm of impossibly oversized sacs— and at the same time convey their insistence that in this realm, everyone and everything must be held accountable to the trickster's twisted logic.

Another call-and-response pattern, common among the Fante people, is notable for its apparent contradiction. The storyteller shouts, "Kodzi wɔ ngye ndzi!" (Kodzi is not to be believed!), and the audience replies, "Wɔ gye sie!" (It is for keeping!).[49] The Fante often substitute the word *kodzi*, meaning "go eat," for Anansesεm. In addition to referencing Ananse's insatiable hunger, it carries the metaphoric connotation that the folkloric stories are nourishment that people must consume for survival. The necessity of eating/consuming the life-giving stories (*ko dzi*) is thus directly juxtaposed here against the purported claim that these stories should *not* be accepted/consumed (*n dzi*).[50] The disclaimer can thus be translated as "That which must be believed is not to be believed!" The audience's response then confounds this contradiction even further by asserting that the stories that should not be consumed are rather to be "kept." This somewhat confusing play on words reveals the critical skepticism toward narrative closure that is a fundamental part of Anansesεm. Here, anything that is presented as "to be believed" will soon be unmasked as something that should not be believed. Storytelling is a terrain in which the act of signification is revealed to be (at best) an exercise in contradiction and partial truths. Any legitimate story that wants to be accepted as the unqualified truth must be hiding its own partiality, limitations, or falsehoods—and such a story will not survive long in the realm of Anansesεm. The only vital foundation that must be "kept" during the course of this narrative turmoil between hegemonic and counterhegemonic truths is the critical/skeptical disposition that Anansesεm seeks to inculcate in its participants.

Once Anansesεm performers have established this boundary-disturbing attitude toward narrative truth, they then point out that their tale has its serious points as well and in fact also contains certain truths about the world. Following the call-and-response portion of the performance, the opening phrases with which storytellers typically begin their narration are intended to convey the *genuine actuality* of the events that will be depicted. This opening may take the form of an insistent rhetorical question, such as "Enyε Ananse na n'ɔwɔ hɔ?" (Did Ananse not live/exist once upon a time?). Alternatively, it may state the point directly: "Kurotwiamansa na n'ɔwɔ hɔ" (There once lived/existed He-Who-Holds-the-Nation-in-Fear), or "Kan tete no, na anka Owu nni hɔ" (In the past, Death did not exist). The opening may also establish an etiological framework, such as "Menka nea εyε a Ananse ti pa yε" (Let me tell the story of how the spider got a bald head). In contrast to the antics that herald the start of an Anansesεm performance, the rhetorical framing of the story's opening lines nearly always invokes an attitude of exaggerated seriousness. These openings introduce the story as if it were based on ontological facts—important events that happened and that have shaped the present course of the world. Juxtaposed against the disclaimers of the preceding call-and-response, the serious attitude of the story openings helps to create an even greater sense of confused affect and narrative turmoil. Thus, from the earliest stages of an Anansesɛm performance, the story takes on a kind of ontological doubleness; it is both meaningful and trivial, both actual and imagined, both true and false.

This ambiguous framing makes it possible for both the storytellers and the audiences to explore outlooks and desires that would not ordinarily be sanctioned. While the general context of a designated performance space may give storytellers a certain license, by the time that Anansesɛm performers have fully launched into their narratives, they have additionally wrapped themselves in a many-layered aura of misdirection and artistic ambiguity. From this platform they have a remarkable capacity to express otherwise intolerable and illegal behavior, including indecency, critiques of sacrosanct values, and even insults directed at real-life organizations and political figures.[51] The trickster-like doubleness of Anansesɛm performance thus helps to protect the expression of subordinated and disorderly voices. More than just a harmless "pressure release," Anansesɛm can provide a community-wide, participatory investigation into the limits imposed by the social order and the possibility of alternative, critical outlooks.

MBOGUO: MULTIVOCALITY, DOUBLENESS, AND CRITICAL CONSCIOUSNESS

Anansesɛm performances are structured as serial narrations. At various points the storyteller will pause for a while, encouraging audience members to step in and flesh out the performance with their own contributions. In addition, audience members are permitted to (and often do) interject their own observations and declamations at any time during the story, helping to shape its trajectory. These intrusions frequently involve audience members adopting the persona of one of the story's characters and conveying their unique perspective through expressive or humorous speech, mime, song, or dance.[52] Thus, the performance structure of Anansesɛm is a robustly participatory experience and a truly community-based art form. The ability of diverse participants to enter into the performance space and interact with the storyteller's narrative is a further aspect of Anansesεm's disorderly, critical dialogue and blurred social boundaries. The counterhegemonic outlooks that may be expressed during the performance are not the responsibility of any particular storyteller but rather emerge organically during the course of participatory *interaction.* The unsanctioned displays of alternative outlooks in Anansesεm are thus not merely witnessed by onlookers but have the potential to be actively shaped and embodied by anyone who is present at the performance.

The interludes in which audience members provide their own contributions to Anansesεm are appropriately called *mboguo,* or "knock down," as they displace the storyteller's narration and allow other participants to subvert, complicate, and/or supplant the act. As early as 1930, the British observer R. S. Rattray described the importance of mboguo in Akan performances:

> During some storytelling evenings, between the various tales and often, indeed, in the very middle of a story, actors will sometimes enter the circle and give impersonations of various characters. In this connection I have seen inimitable representations of an old woman dressed in rags and covered with sores; a leper; a priest with an attendant carrying the shrine of his god; an accouchement [birth], with midwives in attendance, who from time to time adjured their patient to confess with whom she had committed adultery, lest she should die; [and] a case of theft, referred ... to the *nkontwuma* [diviner] man. These impersonations are extremely realistic, clever and, like the stories themselves, call forth roars of laughter from all who witness them.[53]

There seems to be some variety in the level of detail and preparation that goes into any particular mboguo intrusion. In some cases, as Jonas Yeboa-Danqua observed, designated "actors" may be on hand during an Anansesεm session to step in and give the principal storyteller a chance to rest (a needed reprieve, because "storytelling among the Akan ... is really dramatic")! In contrast, other mboguo intrusions may arise entirely spontaneously, as audience members become caught up in the mood of the story or are simply overcome by an urge to show off.[54]

The prevalence of mboguo in Anansesεm prevents the storytelling act from becoming the sole property of any single author or authority. It also unsettles any possibility of narrative closure, as the performance tradition encourages differing, sometimes conflicting, voices to constantly revise and subvert the direction of the story. Interjections from the audience typically contribute to the ongoing ambiguity and questionable truth-status of the storyteller's claims. Some of these audience challenges take on more-or-less standardized forms. For example, after hearing the storyteller relate a particularly incredible turn of events, it is common for an audience member to shout out, "Na wo wɔ hɔ bi?" (Were you there?). Storytellers invariably respond by claiming that they were personally involved when the events unfolded: "Na me gyina hɔ bi!" (I stood right there!). In a similar fashion, an audience member may respond to an incredible claim with a call of "Sisi me!" (Keep hoaxing me!), to which the storyteller replies, "Mirisisi wo, mɛsisi wo bio!" (I am hoaxing you, and I will keep hoaxing you!).[55] These exchanges are frequently followed by a more extended mboguo, in which "actors" or other audience members will step in and offer their own performances and subversive interpretations. In another formulaic exchange, the storyteller and audience members explicitly encourage such an interruption:

> INTERJECTOR: Anansesɛm yɛ nsi-si, to no yie! (Storytelling is a hoax, tell it properly!)
>
> STORYTELLER (*to interjector*): Wo na wo nim to! (You are the one who knows how to tell it!)
>
> AUDIENCE (*to interjector*): Sɔre kɔto ɛ! (Get up and go tell it!)[56]

These interjections are both a jovial expression of incredulity and an encouragement of the fine art of fabrication. Regardless of whether or not the interjector ultimately does "get up and go tell it," the customary exchanges gesture toward the multivocality of Anansesɛm and help to ensure that the developing narrative remains wrapped in an aura of mystery and ambiguity.

Anansesɛm performance also has several formulaic codas that may signal an end to a performance segment or may transition into an ongoing or alternative interpretation of the story. In one of the most common, the storyteller says, "M'anansesɛm a metoe, sɛ ɛyɛ dɛ o, sɛ ɛnyɛ dɛ o, me de soa wo" (Whether or not my telling is delightful, I put it on your head), or "M'anansesɛm a metoe, sɛ ɛyɛ dɛ o, sɛ ɛnyɛ dɛ o, momfa bi nkɔhyɛ kɛtɛ ase na ade kye a, mode ato borɔdedwe awe" (Whether or not my telling is delightful, keep it under your sleeping mat so that tomorrow, you may cook it with green plantains to eat).[57] These statements serve to remind the audience members that they are not obligated to be just passive observers but are welcome to express their own judgment of the performance, to reinterpret it after their own fashion, and to take critical possession of the stories (to "keep," "cook," and "eat" them) on their own terms.

In another standard coda, an audience member may speak out to initiate a "judgment" of the performance and take the narrative in a new direction, often inciting another round of storytelling interaction:

INTERJECTOR: W'anansesɛm a wotoe yi, woboa! (You were lying in your telling!)

STORYTELLER: Meboa ne sɛn? (What do you mean?)

INTERJECTOR: Woboa ne sɛ, da bi.... (What I mean is that, once upon a time....)

The interjector will then go on to invoke a different story or an alternative perspective, goading the storyteller into ever more complex revisionary antics.[58] As various audience members humorously joust with the storyteller throughout the Anansesɛm performance, offering up a constant stream of criticism and reinvention, the very nature of authoritative truth and falsehood gives way to multivocal expression and shared creativity. The accusation of "lying" in this context, like the accusation of "not telling it properly," is always understood to evince both skepticism about deterministic truth-claims and an encouragement for further creative fabrication. A large part of the delight that Anansesɛm participants take in the performance is based around the creativity with which counterclaims can be navigated and incorporated into the ongoing ambiguity of the story. An Akan proverb urges, "Wo twa atoro a, twa nea tokro da ho na wo kyere wo a, w'anya baabi a dwane afa" (When you craft a lie, craft one with an opening, so when you are found out, you will have room to escape). In the ethos and aesthetic of Anansesɛm, the "lie" is most convincing when it comes with a built-in rejection of authoritative closure.[59]

Taken altogether, then, Anansesɛm is a tradition that is grounded in collaborative fabrication and a rejection of mono-focal outlooks. The social order is a construct, Ananse tells us—a pragmatic, fragmented, and continually reinvented construct that can turn ominous if it is allowed to coalesce into a domineering ideology. We must always remember to question such stories, to expose their partiality and dismantle their claims to inviolability, even while we affirm the need to continually create new interpretations and new forms of order. Ananse's crafty doubleness allows him to give voice to these new possibilities and to outsmart authoritative outlooks—even to outsmart himself if he appears to be in danger of reaching an unproblematic conclusion. Being at once spider and man, human and god, artistic and avaricious, dexterous and diabolical, wily and wayward, he is always ready to escape from the constraints of his lie and to take up refuge in a new one. Ananse is more of an *ethos* than an individual; he is a recursive transgression whose nature and social logic is the impulse to undermine all forms of hegemony. Anansesɛm performance tells us that this ethos is an embodied one and that we are to receive it "for keeping." It may rest dormant under the sleeping mats of our memories, but when social constriction activates it, we may discover that we, too, possess the nimbleness of the spider.

3

⸿

Selling the President
Stand-Up Comedy and the Politricks of Endorsement

ON MAY 11, 1995, a coalition of political opposition leaders in Ghana known as the Alliance for Change organized a demonstration they called *Kum-me-preko* (Kill me once and for all). The immediate cause of this protest was President Jerry Rawlings's decision to implement a new 17.5 percent value-added tax (VAT) on goods and services. Rawlings enacted the new tax in an attempt to meet the requirements of Ghana's "structural adjustment program"—a series of drastic policy changes mandated by debt-holding international finance institutions (IFIs). The VAT was intended to make up for the loss of revenues caused by the concurrent lowering of the corporate tax rate and the elimination of import and export tariffs. In effect, these tax reforms were designed to shift revenue burdens away from large-scale businesses and toward consumers, thereby creating a more inviting climate for private investment in Ghana.[1] Unsurprisingly, the new tax policy immediately came under fire from labor unions and the general public for increasing the tax burden on the poor and in some cases catapulting the prices of goods and services out of the reach of ordinary citizens. The organizers of the Kum-me-preko protest called the VAT a "gruesome policy measure."[2]

For the regime's opponents, the new tax was a clear and concrete illustration of the effects of neoliberalism. The VAT became a rallying point that allowed a diverse coalition of Ghanaian opposition leaders to set aside their differences and organize a challenge against the president's legitimacy.[3] These opposition leaders decried the VAT on two counts. First, many argued that it was a demonstration of Rawlings's betrayal of the poor and his capitulation to neo-imperialist policies. Second, it was widely argued that the drastic changes in tax policy were an affront to democracy, because the regime had quickly pushed them through the party-controlled parliament without allowing for prior debate in the parliament or in the public media. This combination of factors united opposition leaders from diverse political perspectives and cast a significant shadow over Rawlings's commitment to economic justice and popular rule. The president's position became even more tenuous when, during the course of the Kum-me-preko demonstration, armed supporters of the regime set upon the marchers and killed four people, including a fourteen-year-old boy.[4] The Alliance for Change charged that members of Rawlings's National Democratic Congress (NDC) party, including a minister, a deputy minister, a member of parliament, and the party's general secretary, participated in orchestrating the attacks.[5] A leading opposition newspaper, the *Ghanaian Chronicle,* critiqued the government for flouting the constitutional guarantee of public dissent and called the violence against the demonstrators "Hitlerism in Ghana."[6]

The NDC's suspected hand in the Kum-me-preko violence brought President Rawlings's populist image into question and undermined the credibility of his commitment to the democratic rule of law. Thus, three years into his first term as an elected president, Rawlings faced a major crisis of legitimacy. As the NDC looked forward to the upcoming 1996 presidential elections, it became apparent that drastic measures would be needed to restore the public image of the regime. This chapter focuses on one aspect of this legitimation effort: Rawlings's decision to appropriate popular forms of entertainment in support of his presidency. In particular, the president sought to secure a public endorsement from Ghana's top comedian of stage and television, Bishop-Bob Okalla. A paragon of the stand-up comedy genre known as *gyimi* (comic foolery), Okalla is part of a stage tradition whose history goes back eight decades and that is rooted in the traditional Ghanaian folkloric practice of *Anansesɛm* (trickster performance). Okalla built his career on outlandish stunts and satirical performances that captured the frustrations and aspirations of his rural,

working-class, and urban-underclass fans. In seeking Okalla's endorsement, President Rawlings was attempting to demonstrate an affinity with
these constituencies and their political/economic concerns. However,
given Okalla's artistic signature of public indirection, crafty trickster
maneuvers, and political satire, there was a great potential for ambiguity
in how his endorsement of the president might be interpreted. This chapter
discusses the conflict that emerged between the comic duplicity of the
gyimi tradition and the unequivocal partisan support sought by the NDC.
We will see how Okalla was ultimately able to construct an aura of ambiguity and crafty humor around his political endorsement, drawing on trickster traditions to navigate and subvert the pressures of the political arena.

THE DRAMA OF LEGITIMATION

Electoral campaigns are inevitably focused toward widespread political mobilization. Whether leaders are doing proximal politics—in which
they enact oneness and/or closeness with "the people"—or whether they
are constructing a Manichean divide that pits "us" against a supposedly
dangerous "them," the campaigns usually include dramatic elements
intended to make participants feel they are truly a part of the political
scene. At the same time, electoral campaigns are rituals that legitimize
the liberal-democratic system. The slogans, marches, flags, songs, and
propaganda are part of a national theater in which candidates display their
mass support and competitive appeal, affirming both their own popular
legitimacy and that of the democratic system. These campaigns are often
centered around what Paul Starobin has called "myth-making tools"—
standardized formats of political performance that leaders use to convey
their ostensible qualities.[7] In his campaign for reelection, Rawlings enthu-
siastically grasped such tools to try and repair the dent that the VAT and
the Kum-me-preko violence had made in his populist image.

The NDC party convention, held in the city of Sunyani in September
1996 to inaugurate Rawlings's presidential campaign, was the site of a
grand foray into political myth-making. The drama of legitimation at the
convention involved three gestures—or "acts," if you will. The "opening
act" was Rawlings's declaration of his commitment to socioeconomic

justice. This act began in the days leading up to the convention with the president's formal initiation of public service projects around the Sunyani area. Prominent among these projects was the announced construction of Sunyani Regional Hospital, an ultramodern health facility with a price tag of approximately US$55 million.[8] The opening act continued in the convention program with the unveiling of a new NDC party manifesto. The document expressed a commitment to aiding "disadvantaged areas and deprived sections of the society," and it emphasized that Rawlings's original military rebellion had been in the service of the "struggle for improved welfare for all."[9] The president's speech at the convention again reiterated this theme of commitment to the common good. Rawlings touted his record in providing health care and electricity, while declaring his "irrevocable commitment to uplifting the quality of life for the people." He stated that one of the goals of the regime was "to prevent a few from using their wealth and education as a basis to claim power."[10]

Rawlings's "second act" was his use of the rhetorical tool that can be called "legitimation-by-contrast." The president attacked opposition leaders, characterizing them as insensitive, acrimonious, and unscrupulous. Inverting popular skepticism about the sincerity of his commitment to democracy, Rawlings accused the opposition of "building a campaign of rumors, allegations, and insinuations to manipulate the electoral process." He also dismissed the criticisms of his neoliberal policies as sheer envy:

> The opposition finds it painful to see the roads, the safe water, the schools and clinics, the hundreds of thousands of jobs created. . . . They have even said . . . that providing electricity is cheap vote-catching. . . . In saying these things, they reveal their lack of concern for the people, especially those deprived sectors of the society who were for so long neglected and taken for granted.[11]

While opposition leaders had criticized Rawlings's "electricity politics" as a cynical and clientelistic exchange of services for votes, the president counterattacked by saying the criticism of his policy arrangements revealed a lack of care for people who had been "neglected and taken for granted." The president offered a symbolic opportunity for the audience to identify with this constituency and thus hypothetically benefit from his reelection. Positioning the opposition as pessimistic outsiders who failed to recognize how much people stood to gain by working with the regime, Rawlings embraced his supporters (and potential supporters) as insiders who could expect a place at the table.

The "third act" of the NDC party convention was described by Rawlings as "a show of support and solidarity."[12] Thousands of devotees arrived in the city from all points of the compass, clad in party colors and parading through the streets amid drumming, singing, and dancing. So huge was the crowd that some had to climb into trees or stand on the rooftops to see the proceedings. Speaking before the gathering, Rawlings affirmed that the NDC "belongs to the people" and would not shut its doors to "any citizen of goodwill."[13] Rawlings's use of the phrase "show of support" to describe this event underscores not only its staged aspect but also the applicability of performance-centered interpretations. The distinguishing characteristic of performance (as opposed to other behavior) is frequently defined as "showing doing"—in other words, performances occur when our actions take on an expressive or symbolic quality, when they are primarily oriented toward conveying meaning or providing an example to others.[14] Rawlings's *show* of support was an exhibition of mass involvement in the convention proceedings, conveying a claim of affinity between the regime and the public. It was at this dramatic climax that the NDC displayed the message of Bishop-Bob Okalla (PURL 3.1).

Rawlings had sought Okalla's endorsement because of the performer's modest origins and his wide recognition as an icon of "the people." Born Samuel Buabeng in 1961, Okalla dropped out of school before completing his secondary education, electing instead to pursue a career as a soccer player. When these aspirations were undone by a broken rib at the age of thirteen, he turned to earning his living as a baker. Around the same time, he developed an interest in theater and joined a concert party troupe called Kusum Agoromma. In 1994, the National Theatre of Ghana initiated a revival of the concert-party genre, and Buabeng heeded the audition call under the stage name of Bishop-Bob Okalla. He became one of the first two comedians featured in the revival.[15] From this platform Okalla almost instantly rose to fame. Press reviews praised his comedy as "the best so far" and called him the "almighty" and "indomitable." In December 1995, he was one of three "master comedians" to appear in an event dubbed "the greatest of all concert-party shows." That same year, Okalla won the

Best Comedian Award of the Arts Reviewers Association of Ghana, and in August 1996, he was selected as a "distinguished individual of excellence" at the National Festival of Arts and Culture.

Along with Okalla's rise to fame, his tradition of stand-up comedy began to develop into an autonomous genre. Before the concert-party revival, stand-up acts were mainly performed as comic relief within the context of melodramatic concert-party plays, or sometimes as warm-up acts for the plays. The National Theatre recognized that the comedy acts had their own appeal, and as successful comedians developed their personal fandoms, the Theatre began to give these acts independent billing. The indulgent, delightful buffoonery and slapstick antics in the comedians' routines was soon tagged with the label "gyimi" and became a fully autonomous form of entertainment. Gyimi performances feature comedians in grotesque makeup and incongruous costumes with oddball accoutrements, whose jokes involve ludicrous narratives, song-parodies, and physical humor. So successful was Okalla's gyimi that the press described him as the "crowd puller," "the hottest comedian in town," and the "grandmaster of comedy."[16] At the NDC convention, Okalla stepped onto the rally platform wearing a flowing, light-colored shirt; a red, white, and green (the NDC party's colors) scarf; and a hat embossed with the party's emblem. He acknowledged the crowd with one outstretched arm, and with the other, he waved a placard that read "Vote NDC, Vote Rawlings." He then credited President Rawlings with "building a National Theatre" where "people of humble birth . . . could also appear and display comedy."[17]

SPEAKING TO THE WIND: INDIRECTION, ARTISTIC
SOPHISTICATION, AND SOCIAL RELEVANCE

An Akan proverb says, "As you speak to the wind, you speak to God." This can be applied to the immanence of divinity in the material world or the belief that sincere aspirations will reach the ears of a Supreme Being. Another use of this proverb, however, is less metaphysical and more political. In this sense, "speaking to the wind" is a metaphor for indirection, for the art of making one's intentions so equivocal that they are not easily identified. "God," in this metaphorical usage, means power that can only be successfully addressed through such indirection. In Akan cultures, reverence for elders and the seat of political authority calls for considerable self-restraint in the flow of critical discourse before the face of power. Indirection entails polysemy (the coexistence of multiple domains of meaning), which channels high-stakes discourse into potentially ambivalent or ironic expressions. This serves to develop the craft of negotiation beyond the realm of brute argument—and in the case of encountering repressive and vindictive authorities, it allows contentious meanings to find a certain degree of concealment among innocuous ones.[18] The Akan proverb about speaking to the wind is a meta-communicative illustration of indirection—an indirect expression about indirect expression.

Ghanaian popular artists place a premium on the skills of indirection and wit, which are regarded as a sign of artistic sophistication and a means of making social commentary without being "pinned down." Okalla was well known for indirection because of his penchant for backhanded praise and political parody in his stand-up comedy routines. From this view, the significance and intent of Okalla's political endorsement at the NDC rally were potentially up for grabs. Were they serious gestures or just ambivalent stunts? While Okalla's artistic signature would seem to point toward a glib and typically dubious foolery, the intent of the NDC party and the surrounding context of polarizing partisanship and violence seemed to confine the meaning of his appearance into something more unequivocally partisan. This political delineation of Okalla became even more pronounced in the weeks after the rally, when he accused the Ghanaian press of harassing him for endorsing Rawlings. He complained:

> For two nights, thugs I suspect are members of the New Patriotic Party [the leading opposition party] besieged my house at Kwadaso in Kumasi and tried to force their way into my room for mounting the platform [at the NDC rally]. . . . I had to flee from Kumasi to Accra. I have sent my wife and children to my hometown because we feel our lives are in danger.[19]

Whatever the true intentions of his performance might have been, Okalla's entrance into the political fray made him into a polarizing figure and led to disenchantment among his fan base. Confronting a loss of popular support, Okalla, in his next press release, issued a statement addressed to his "admirers," in which he seemed to apologize for the loss of his ambivalent and comic public persona. Threats received from "unidentified persons," he explained, had "totally disorganized" him. He reassured his admirers that he had "no leaning toward any particular party," that he was "not in politics," and that his services were "always ready for all." Okalla then explained that his presence at the NDC rally was a professional engagement and that he had been "paid the appropriate fee for the performance."[20]

For popular Ghanaian artists such as Okalla, the capacity to embody multiple meanings makes it possible to connect with multiple experiences and aspirations. It also enables performers to cloak critical remarks in innocuous garb, thus demonstrating their sophistication and granting voice to marginalized communities. Such meanings do not even have to be intentional; if the symbolic constructs of a performer are sufficiently ambivalent, they can be reinterpreted, transformed, or extended by audiences to articulate unexpected values. This means that indirection is not just a hallmark of artistic sophistication in Ghana but also a benchmark of social relevance. The difficulties encountered by Okalla after his presidential endorsement stemmed from the progressive loss of this aura of indirection. In an article that appeared in Ghana's *Mirror*, titled "Is Okalla Finished?," arts and entertainment critic Nanabanyin Dadson attempted to make sense of the performer's endorsement and his subsequent partial retraction:

> It seems to me that besides providing entertainment, artistes are looked upon endearingly by society as a special group of people who are expected to be non-partisan, maintain credibility, and be able to "speak for them" when necessary. This expectation . . . has been so high that anytime that any artiste . . . is seen to have turned into a praise-singer for people in power, such members of society are pained and feel let down. . . . So where does that leave our popular artistes? How do they exercise their freedom to associate with a political party and at the same [time] maintain their credibility and popularity? I haven't got the answer, but it appears to me that it is a can't-eat-your-cake-and-have-it situation; either they go it softly on their political leaning and maintain their following or go into politics head-on and "resign" their special status accorded them by society.[21]

The danger that Okalla faced from political violence (if his allegations of harassment were true) was compounded by this even more immediate threat to his artistic career. No longer seen as "speaking to the wind," Okalla had drifted from his place as an entertainer and stumbled contentiously into the role of a public political figure.

To illustrate the reasons for Okalla's plight, it is useful to compare his situation with that of another contemporary Ghanaian performer, the highlife musician Nana Ampadu. The indirect political aspects of Ampadu's music were a significant part of its appeal. For example, Ampadu's breakout record was a hit single titled "Ebi Te Yie" ("Some Are Well Seated"), which tells a folkloric story about a meeting at which different animals shared their social concerns. At the meeting, Leopard sits behind Antelope and puts his feet on Antelope's tail, pinning it to the ground. This prevents Antelope from rising to address the assembly. Exasperated, Antelope ultimately petitions for an adjournment of the meeting because "some are well seated and some are not." While the critical dimensions of this allegory are hard to miss—it describes how the veneer of formal process can mask other political realities—the specific applications of the story are vague enough to allow for potentially different interpretations. This is especially true because Antelope's problem is in finding himself involuntarily "well seated," a situation that inverts the usually powerful connotations of the phrase.[22] The song also includes an indirect affirmation of the value of indirection. Antelope does not explicitly declare the problem to the assembly; instead, he uses a witty and humorous locution to seek a way out of his predicament, while avoiding a potentially deadly confrontation with his predatory tormentor.

Ampadu continued on in his career to release a number of similarly successful, politically resonant songs. In "Asɛm Bɛ Ba Dabi" ("There Will Be Trouble Someday"), a variety of animals excuse themselves from helping to uproot a prickly raffia palm tree that has grown up at the bank of their river and are later punished when the plant is used to create a trap that ensnares them. In "Ɔda Mo Do Yi Ɔda Wo Do" ("A Burden on Me Is a Burden on You"), a draconian law is only narrowly averted when its supporters realize that the law might someday be applied to them as well as to their enemies. The interesting thing about Ampadu's career is that during the course of this popular success, his affiliation with the Rawlings government remained very public. The NDC party used jingles that Ampadu wrote and recorded during Rawlings's first presidential campaign in 1992. Like Okalla, Ampadu explicitly endorsed Rawlings, saying, "I have admired him since the beginning of the revolution. He is a simple man who likes the rural folk."[23] Ampadu's political songs were often interpreted as supporting the regime—for example, with Rawlings identified as the wise Tortoise who encourages the other recalcitrant animals to dig up the prickly tree in "Asɛm Bɛ Ba Dabi." However, many, if not most, of Ampadu's fans took an opposing view and adopted the song for their own purposes, overlooking Ampadu's political statements and identifying Rawlings with the troublesome tree that needed to be uprooted.[24]

Ampadu's career illustrates the importance of indirection in Ghanaian popular culture and its relationship to artistic sophistication and social relevance. As long as Ampadu's artistic persona was ambiguous enough for fans to apply their own interpretations to his work, they were willing to overlook his occasional political statements as a dubious anomaly. Ampadu was thus able to enjoy a delicate distinction between his personal politics and his artistic signature. This brings up a question: What was different in the Okalla affair? Like Ampadu, Bishop-Bob Okalla built an artistic reputation for witty ambiguity and double meanings. In contrast to Ampadu, however, Okalla's reputation suffered drastically as a result of his political entanglement with the Rawlings government. What did Okalla do to alienate so many of his fans and require a declaration of his political neutrality? At least part of the explanation is that Okalla participated in a strongly trickster-based comedic practice in which the line between stage persona (subjunctive performance) and personal traits (indicative performance) was traditionally blurred. This meant that the tinge of partisanship very rapidly eroded Okalla's artistic claims to indirection and ambivalence. We will see in the next sections that Okalla's career was marked by ongoing controversy as he repeatedly struggled to protect his ambivalent artistic signature from the prospect of being "pinned down." The unusual degree of blurring between the artist's personal life and staged performances in the trickster tradition contributed to these dilemmas—but it also provided Okalla with the tools to counter political pressures.

"SELLING," NOT "SELLING OUT": COMEDIC INDIRECTION AND THE ART OF DUBIOUS PRAISE

The origin of Bishop-Bob Okalla's stage persona is in the stock character called "Bob," which was made famous by concert-party troupes in

colonial Ghana. In the 1930s, Ishmael Johnson, the "Original Bob," created the character using the spider-trickster of Ghanaian folklore, Ananse, as his prototype.[25] Like Ananse, the Original Bob had a big, bulging
stomach. He "lived for his appetite and survived by his wit."[26] Johnson
embellished the traditional figure of Ananse with material from a variety
of other sources. He appropriated blackface minstrel makeup from the
films of the American vaudevillian Al Jolson, along with elements taken
from comedy sketches, foxtrots, and ragtime performances by African
American seamen that he met along Ghana's western seaboard during the
1920s. It is from these same seamen that he got the name "Bob."[27] Johnson's
"Original Bob" was a houseboy who spoke pidgin English—a mischie-
vous, joke-cracking domestic servant who made trouble for his employers.
He wore "highly idiosyncratic" makeup: a "painted white line down his
nose, white circles on his cheeks, and a white rim around his lips." He also
wore a tailcoat, a scarf, loose calico pantaloons, shoes of different colors,
and "a long mustache that jutted out from his nose like whiskers on a cat."[28]

Bishop-Bob Okalla's contemporary comedic persona, like that of Bob
Johnson, is *bricolage.* It is comprised of selectively chosen emblems from
his professional comedic lineage, as well as items drawn from his personal autobiography and creative impulses. Signs from his professional
lineage include the name "Bob" and also the use of white circles around
his eyes and mouth—redesigns of the facial makeup that Ishmael Bob
Johnson adapted from minstrelsy. He wears a wooden, hourglass-shaped
pestle around his neck in place of a bowtie; the origin of this accessory is
unclear, but it has been part of the costume ensemble of many a Bob. The
name "Okalla" is autobiographical and derives from his resemblance to a
famous Nigerian goalkeeper of the same name. He earned the nickname
"Bishop," he says, because he likes to pray before any activity.[29] He often
clutches a thick Bible-like book from which he makes outrageous quota-
tions. Other autobiographical elements include his soccer boots, soccer
hoses, and a baker's apron, representing the trades he dabbled in before
achieving his fame in comedy. Some elements of his stage apparel seem
to be the results of utter whimsy. On his arms he wears stockings that
reach to his lower biceps and make his hands look as though they are
enclosed in misshapen mittens. He is usually bare-chested but wears two
flying ties, made stranger by their juxtaposition with his pestle bowtie,

and he wraps a belt over them around his waist. He typically wears a bandana on his head but sometimes replaces it with a baseball cap worn backward or a headpiece that looks partly like a Turkish fez and partly like a Christian bishop's miter. Okalla's trademark accouterment is his "wrist-clock"—a large wall clock that he wears on his wrist like a watch (PURL 3.2, PURL 3.3).

Bishop-Bob Okalla can provoke laughter merely by stepping onto the stage. In such situations he presents a deadpan, exaggeratedly be-mused countenance that seems to ask, "What did I do? Are you laughing at *me?*"—thus often reducing audiences to further eruptions of laughter without uttering a word. By cultivating an attitude of dubious serious-ness that overlays his oddball act, Okalla layers his performance with ironic ambivalence and, in quintessential trickster form, induces a certain amount of discomfort or exasperation in the audience. This ambivalence extends beyond his nonverbal expression and can also be found in his rou-tines of jokes. For example, following his return from North America and Europe on a trip sponsored by the Unilever Corporation's Keysoap brand, he staged a routine in which he flaunts what he calls his "improved" looks:

> I do look good—I have gained weight. Well, thank you, and thanks to Keysoap. You know? That is what traveling abroad is like. When you travel abroad and you do not gain anything at all, rest assured you will gain weight.[30]

Okalla plays on perceptions of Europe and North America as places of extreme affluence and luxury, acknowledging his audience's longing for the "good life" they believe can be found there. Without the means to visit, they can vicariously experience his corporate-funded tour abroad. However, Okalla's ludicrous stage appearance is such a contradiction with his claim of "looking good" that his statement becomes a mockery of such aspirations. After saying that all he gained abroad was weight, Okalla turns to reveal to the audience his padded, oversized backside, eliciting groans of repulsion and delight. By the end of his performance, Okalla has both highlighted and destroyed the audience's fantastic images of life abroad. Similarly, he has both praised Keysoap and undercut that praise: If all he gained on his trip was a huge rear end, then perhaps Keysoap and its producers are not such great benefactors.

Okalla's routines are also interspersed with comic song parodies. The delightful and recognizable melodies of these songs have a tendency to capture the socioeconomic circumstances of soap production, circulation, and consumption. One of Okalla's songs parodies a popular highlife tune as follows:

> When we were courting, we bathed with Keysoap
> When we were newlyweds, we bathed with Keysoap
> How come we now wash with Alata soap?
> You have reduced me to disgrace
> I know we can't afford expensive soap
> But Alata soap is something I cannot bear![31]

The song ostensibly praises Unilever's Keysoap as a symbol of social status and marital fulfillment (thus satisfying Okalla's sponsorship obligations); at the same time, it provides an indirect and humorous commentary on commodity fetishism in the context of unfulfilled economic promise. Like Okalla's "wrist-clock," the highlife associations granted to Keysoap in the parody are so exaggerated as to be comical. Meanwhile, the theme of luxurious courting followed by hardship and disgrace is one that potentially invites a critical view of Keysoap's promises—and by extension, the broader promises made during the course of neoliberal reform and privatization in Ghana.

Okalla's song goes on to describe the plight of any local producers who might seek to compete with his sponsor's product:

> You think you can beat Keysoap?
> Soap people, forget it!
> You arrange your soap at dawn
> It is still displayed at night!

Again, in this refrain, ostensible pride in Keysoap's market dominance is combined with a disconcerting portrait of impoverishment. The refrain's cheerful melody and Okalla's humorous head-bobbing antics are in sharp opposition to the image he presents of struggling soap peddlers in Ghana's informal economy (a familiar occupation to his urban-underclass fans), setting up shop from dawn to dusk without making any sales. This image of local merchants stripped of their prospects by the monolithic marketing resources of a multinational corporation has to be understood in the

context of accusations that large multinationals such as Unilever undermine fair trade practices by exerting political and economic pressures. At
the time Okalla introduced this song, Unilever had recently come under
fire in Ghana for language in its contracts that not only banned distribu-
tors from selling competing products alongside Unilever's but threatened
them with retribution if any of their associates (family members, employees, etc.) used a product or even showed "direct or indirect interest"
in a product manufactured by a competitor of Unilever.[32] These kinds of
monopolistic practices, combined with political interference, corporate-
funded community development projects, and aggressive marketing, produced an ambivalent climate in which audiences could strongly identify
with Okalla's simultaneous messages of enchantment and frustration.

Ghanaian political humorist Kwesi Yankah once said that Okalla's
achievement in relation to his corporate sponsors was that he "sold" their
neoliberal vision. The ambivalent connotations of this phrase astutely capture the indirection in Okalla's performances. While on one level he sold
Keysoap in the sense of promoting it, on another level he "sold" his sponsors by attempting to trick them, integrating potentially critical messages
directly into his laudatory acts.[33] The open juxtaposition of antithetical
elements in Okalla's performances confounds any attempt to give them a
purely subversive *or* supportive interpretation. One might argue that the
name association in Okalla's performances fulfills the marketing goals
of his sponsors despite, and perhaps even partly because of, the more sophisticated and humorous layers of meaning that fans can identify in his
messages. Alternatively, one might argue that Okalla embraces the "arts
of political disguise," in part by seeming to serve his sponsor's interests,
in order to provide a mainstream expression of subtle criticism that can
be recognized by his fans, while remaining "too ambiguous to be action-
able by authorities."[34] Okalla gives the Keysoap brand dubious praise in a
dizzying feat of verbal and nonverbal indirection in which both message
and messenger are full of ironic ambivalence.

Yankah has suggested that when Okalla appeared to endorse the president at the NDC political rally, he was merely extending his penchant for
ambivalent and dubious praise in a new direction: from "selling" the Keysoap brand to "selling" Rawlings as a populist liberal democrat.[35] From
this perspective, Okalla's praise of Rawlings for "building a national

theater" where humble people could "also appear and display comedy" takes on a potentially subversive and humorous meaning. Perhaps it refers not to the National Theatre where Okalla performed but rather to the nation's political stage and the drama of legitimation that played out there. The performer's dedicated fans, who are attuned to the ever-present role of ironic ambivalence in his routines, would have expected such two-sided word play from Okalla. They would have been more likely to read his endorsement as humorously dubious praise rather than as unequivocal support for the president. This situation is in contrast to that of the musician Nana Ampadu, who, as discussed earlier, was able to maintain a delicate distinction between his personal political endorsements and his artistic signature. In Okalla's case, appearing on the stage at the NDC rally, complete with his typically unorthodox dress and accoutrements, was most likely to be seen as an extension of his artistic routine. For this very reason, though, fans were not likely to be offended by Okalla's antics at the rally because they were not very different from his usual performances. This leaves a key question: If Okalla's appearance at the rally was not particularly likely to offend his fans or threaten his career, then why did he lose support, and why was his presidential endorsement partially retracted? To answer this question, it is necessary to look at the events that took place after the electoral rally.

MOUTHS BE GUN: FIGHTING WORDS AND THE PARTISAN MARK

Okalla's endorsement of the incumbent president did not strip him of his artistic aura in the eyes of most of his fans. According to his later press statements, however, it appears that at least a few supporters of the opposition party did not appreciate his humor. Alternatively, it is possible that Okalla's entire construction of being pursued by opposition "thugs" was an elaborate attempt at staging political drama. His accusations of harassment led to sharp rebuttals by opposition leaders, who insisted that they were not involved and would never countenance such behavior on the part of their supporters. In the opposition-aligned newspaper *The Statesman*, critics questioned why Okalla did not make a police report or provide any evidence of the alleged harassment. They described the performer as a buffoonish mouthpiece of the regime and noted that he had appeared on a live radio show in Kumasi on the day after he claimed to have been forced to flee from that city.[36] In their view, Okalla had become nothing more than a propagandist. The allegations of "thuggery" were particularly upsetting to opposition leaders because they involved a word that had taken on intense partisan meaning in the months after the violence against the Kum-me-preko demonstrators. Reports of "thuggery" appeared almost daily in the opposition press, blaming Rawlings's supporters for ongoing political intimidation and questioning the sincerity of the president's newfound commitment to democracy.[37] By appropriating one of the opposition's favorite terms, it is conceivable that Okalla was attempting to ridicule these recurrent accusations. It is also conceivable, as Okalla later said, that he truly was "totally disorganized" by threats from "unidentified persons."

Whatever the truth or intent of Okalla's allegations, his use of the highly charged notion of "thuggery" was unable to elude its partisan and politically combative implications. In making these statements to the press, Okalla lost his ambiguous artistic signature and was captured in a decidedly un-funny aspect of the partisan fray. A political cartoon that appeared directly under the opposition's response to Okalla in *The Statesman* underscored the view that certain words spoken in a polarized political context can be as dangerous as a lethal weapon. In the cartoon, two men stand face to face in front of flags marking polar positions, "FOR" and "AGAINST." Both men are obviously angry, with furrowed brows, large eyes, open mouths, bared teeth, and clenched fists. Canon-looking gun barrels surrounded by droplets of sputum aim out of each one's mouth toward the other. Between these two men, the cartoonist's inscription drives home the point about rhetorical force in the political arena: "MOUTHS BE GUN."[38] The intensity of polarization and violence associated with thuggery in Ghanaian politics made it unlikely that fans would be willing to grant Okalla an artistic "pass" on this particular entry into the partisan arena. Okalla's allegations of thuggery, located not in the festive theatricality of the political rally but in the thick of the rhetorical battle between Rawlings and his political opponents, marked the performer with an unequivocal partisan position. This mark of partisanship was potentially career ending for Okalla; it threatened to collapse the delightful and sophisticated

A cartoon about the potential danger of polarized political speech.
Courtesy of the *Statesman*, September 26, 1996, p. 1.

ambiguity of his presidential endorsement and his Keysoap routines into a nonambivalent and partisan meaning.

Okalla's subsequent attempts to repair this damage indicate the nature of his professional difficulties. In his later press release, the mention of "thugs I suspect are members of the New Patriotic Party" changed to a complaint of harassment from "unidentified persons." Okalla did not retract his accusation of harassment, but he removed its explicit political aspect, relegating it to a personal conflict that had no defining significance for his artistic persona. He then remarked on his presidential endorsement, saying that he has "no leaning toward any particular party," that his appearance at the rally was a paid performance, and that his services "are always ready for all." In these statements Okalla backed away from perceptions that he had taken a public political stance. More than a simple declaration of neutrality, though, his partial retraction was a clever, career-saving tactic to restore humorous ambivalence to his presidential endorsement and to eliminate the corrosive intrusion of a non-trickster-like partisanship into his public image. By saying that his previously established penchant for dubious praise might be applied to anyone, at any time, Okalla gave his fans a reason to interpret his political forays in a skeptical light, and he assured them that he intended to maintain his reputation for indirection and artistic sophistication.

Scrambling to salvage his ambiguity was not a particularly new experience for Okalla. In a previous incident, he had faced public controversy when critics had tried to pin him into a (very different) partisan position. In that case, Okalla's troubles came about when his parodies of Christian church songs began to generate charges of blasphemy, leading to the alienation of a significant portion of his television audience. Okalla's appellation, "Bishop-Bob," is indicative of his penchant for staging dubious adaptations of church music and liturgy. For example, one routine in his repertoire begins with a story about a church scandal:

> There used to be only a select few pastors around. However, these days there is a proliferation of questionable pastors. You know of a few, right? These days, while one pastor fasts in sacred duty, another one sins on the side. Is this any good? Once upon a time a pastor founded a church, which quickly filled up with members. He appointed a young lady as "pastor-woman" for the church.[39]

Okalla propels his hips suggestively each time he says "pastor-woman," suggesting that the position of the young lady was not for the purposes of gender parity. The audience participates in Okalla's double entendre, briefly turning the narrative into a call-and-response:

OKALLA: In the morning she was "pastor-woman." At noon . . .

AUDIENCE: Pastor-woman!

OKALLA: Evening . . .

AUDIENCE: Pastor-woman!

OKALLA: Even at night . . .

AUDIENCE: Pastor-woman!

Continuing the narrative, Okalla explains that the pastor's wife suspected the affair and decided to go to church one Sunday. She sat in the chair reserved for "pastor-woman." When "pastor-woman" sees the pastor's wife in her seat, she angrily walks up to the pulpit, snatches the microphone from the pastor, and begins to sing:

I'll love him, and hold fast to him
I will lay my body and my all
Upon his bed!

Okalla's audience, familiar with the melody and lyrics of this church song, join in with the singing and probably recognize the gist of the parody even before the revised last line reveals that devotion to Christ is no longer the song's topic. This bawdy routine resonates in the atmosphere of religious charlatanism and scandal that blossomed during the late twentieth century as economic conditions in Ghana deteriorated. Audiences were likely reminded of an all-too-familiar clerical infidelity that made newspaper headlines in the months prior to Okalla's performance, when a "street brawl" erupted in Sunyani between supporters of two different women who both claimed to be the lovers of the same evangelist. (A police source later stated that the evangelist in question had "since been missing from the town.")[40]

Beyond his direct digs at clerical hypocrisy, Okalla also tends to borrow religious praise songs for a variety of comic purposes. In a rowdy parody that he calls the "Glass and Bottle Church," Okalla replaces the name of God in a popular Christian song with the names of beverages that are well known to his audience:

OKALLA: Star, you're so good

   Malt, you are kind

   Guinness, you are wonderful

   Akpeteshie, you are . . .

AUDIENCE: Excellent![41]

Culminating in a dubious celebration of *akpeteshie*—a local alcoholic brew with a reputation for being cheap but potent—Okalla's parody takes aim at Christian temperance campaigns and provides an affirmation of the underclass identity associated with this drink. At another level, the exaggerated substitution of beer for "God" and the hesitation before the final affirmation has the potential to incite reflection on the problems of economic stratification and alcohol consumption. Okalla signifies a social difference with his reference to different class-marked drinks: While lager and malt beer in Ghana have long been associated with large commercial enterprises and the comfortable position of the middle class, locally distilled akpeteshie survived a government ban in the colonial era and became associated with urban popular culture, social protest, and poverty-induced alcoholism.[42]

Okalla's borrowing from Christian liturgy and praise songs in such performances led to a flurry of protests in Ghanaian newspapers in the early months of 1996. One letter, for example, stated that:

> This so-called "Bishop" Bob Okalla uses the Holy Bible to ridicule men of God during his concert party show, which is telecast regularly on GTV. This man appears on TV wearing a priest cassock, holding the Bible and sometimes the cross. He ridicules pastors and says profane things as quotations from the Bible. . . . I hope the organizers of the Concert Party Show will . . . stop this comedian from using his show to offend many Christians.[43]

These public objections underscored the new challenges faced by Okalla as his position at the National Theatre caused his fame to grow. Okalla had crafted his comedy to appeal primarily to a live audience of mostly urban-underclass fans. This audience, though largely sympathetic to Christianity, recognized their own experiences and frustrations in Okalla's crafty unsettlement of the boundaries between spiritual and corporeal frames of reference. Intimately familiar with the ideological contradictions referenced by Okalla, they embraced the humor of his ambivalent word play. However, televised performances at the National Theatre brought Okalla's act to a wider audience of Ghanaians, including a powerful constituency of Christians who hailed from a very different social background than did most of Okalla's live-theater fans. For many of these television viewers, Okalla's act resonated more as "sacrilege" than as "socially significant artistry."

The blasphemy controversy, like the later "thuggery" controversy, presented a risk that Okalla's act would be pigeonholed into a distinct partisan position. If this were to happen, Okalla would thereby be dismissed by many potential audiences—including his critics, who objected to his apparent meanings, and his established fans, who delighted in the ambivalence of those meanings. Okalla's response to the controversy reveals an astute recognition of the new social force that he faced and the artistic quandary that his position entailed. In April 1996, Okalla obtained an interview with the Ghanaian newspaper *The Mirror*. He prevailed upon the paper to publish an extensive profile of his life, from humble beginnings to rise to fame, and he took the opportunity to thoroughly confuse anyone who might regard him as impious. After mentioning that he was a member of the Christ Believers Church, Bishop-Bob Okalla thanked his admirers and asked that they "continue to pray" for him. The reporter asked him about how his act "has lately elicited some criticism from his Christian fans" and printed Okalla's response:

> I am greatly disturbed by those who accuse me in recent times of being blasphemous in my shows. Let me say first and foremost that I use names from the Bible only for the show and have no intention of blaspheming. God is my strength in whatever I do, and there is no way I'd turn my back and ridicule my benefactor. What you see me holding on stage is just an ordinary book and not a Bible, as many believe. . . . I just mean to entertain, and it is unfortunate my intentions are misconstrued.[44]

A picture in the article shows Okalla smiling and well groomed, wearing a casual shirt with no makeup or costume, and seated in a leather armchair. Next to this, however, is a larger picture that depicts Okalla on stage with a grotesque countenance and his typically outrageous costume, makeup, and props. Underneath is a caption that describes Okalla's usual stage performance but also explains how "ordinarily, Okalla is a cool guy who says, 'I am God fearing.'"

The juxtaposition of images is ambiguous. Okalla is an ordinary, "God-fearing" guy in a leather chair, but he is also someone who habitually dons absurd apparel and substitutes the names of beers for the name of God. The presentation of a "serious, pious Okalla" tries to convince the public that behind the makeup is a responsible citizen—but for fans who are familiar with the play of contradictory messages in Bishop-Bob Okalla's act, it is not entirely clear that this "serious" message is to be taken seriously or that his comedic message is "just comedy." On the one hand, Okalla posits a "mimetic gap" between his routines and Christian liturgy. The book that he uses only *appears* to be a Bible, but it is really not a Bible at all, and Okalla only *appears* to be criticizing religious hypocrisy, when his real purpose is to "entertain."[45] On the other hand, the social references in his "Bishop" routines, as well as the irreverent imagery, music, and lyrics, undoubtedly *are* drawn from a religious context. Okalla does not deny that he parodies religion, but he does take assertive steps to stifle the critics who call him a "blasphemer" and give him little credit. His treatment of religion, he suggests, is not a straightforward travesty but rather a much more ambivalent parody.[46] By presenting messages of piety and impiety that are blatantly contradictory, Okalla ensured that his public image would remain ambiguous enough so as not to be firmly categorized into any partisan position.

THE LIE WITH AN OPENING

Okalla's response to the blasphemy controversy was a form of indirection. It was a rhetorical feat of doubleness in which he both thwarted his critics and reassured his fans that he was still their artistically sophisticated and socially relevant comedian. By presenting a pious image in the *Mirror* article, Okalla contradicted his irreverent Bishop act without actually retracting it. He allowed his fans to make what they would of the contradiction. Okalla used exactly the same strategy to undercut the taint of partisanship that occurred after his allegations of thuggery. By emphasizing that he "is not in politics" and that his services "are always ready for all," Okalla introduced a questionable mimetic gap between the *appearance* of political partisanship and his actual feelings toward the regime. He did not retract his endorsement of the president or his allegations of thuggery, but he contradicted these statements by pointing out that his words were part of a paid performance. As with his "pious" response to the blasphemy allegations, his "apolitical" stance created a contradiction into which his fans could posit their own interpretations. In effect, Okalla's explanation deftly but precariously moved to maintain his reputation for dubious praise, while gesturing to placate the fans whose political sensibilities his allegations might have offended.

Okalla's strategy of ambivalence brings to mind another Akan proverb about indirection that advises, "When you craft a lie, craft one with an opening, so that when you are caught, you will have a way of escape." The word "lie" in this context, akin to its usage in African American linguistics, can signify creativity, craftiness, and imagination in dealing with social obstacles.[47] The proverb captures what Joyce Jonas refers to as the trickster's singular ability to extricate himself from tight situations, an ability associated with his "talent for spinning yarns."[48] Okalla's tactics reveal him as the embodiment of the Ananse trickster who delightfully but dangerously plays with ambivalence so he can negotiate and undermine different interests—social, religious, artistic, political, and economic. By embracing an artistic persona that is both delightful and grotesque, both subversive and deferential, Okalla imbues his performances with Ananse-like ambivalence and dubious praise. Through this indirection, he was able to find his "opening" and avoid the taint of partisanship by retroactively framing his political statements as a paid performance.

Okalla presents a compelling example of "the agency of a named individual" who negotiates the web of social processes.[49] Despite the appropriation of his ambivalent comedic persona by the ruling party in its quest for legitimation, and even despite his own undermining of ambivalence through his rhetorically forceful allegations, Okalla still emerged intact and with room to be flexible. Okalla's *politricks*—his trickster-like play with the political pressures that he encountered—allowed him the space to precariously navigate among powerful interests. He moves, in the end, to remain "true" to his fans. Okalla challenges, by rendering them ambivalent, the mythologized boundaries of the social order—the lines between sacred worship and comic delight, between piety and blasphemy, between high-class and low-class soap, between liberal democratic ideals and popular cultural values, and between the politics of theater and the theater of politics (PURL 3.4, PURL 3.5).

4

Ma Red's Maneuvers

Popular Theater and "Progressive" Culture

IN 1994, THE GHANA NATIONAL THEATRE embarked upon a project to revive the concert party, then a moribund, near-century-old form of popular theater rooted in *Anansesɛm*. Concert party theater historically drew much of its patronage from the rural peasant classes and the urban underclass. The revival of this form, conducted in collaboration with the Ghana Concert Party Union, was therefore initially conceived as a means of stimulating the country's populist traditions, consistent with the Nkrumahist ideal of African cultural revival and with the National Theatre's public service mission as a state-owned enterprise. However, during the following year, the National Theatre underwent a significant reorganization as part of J. J. Rawlings's neoliberal policy shifts. In a move that was strongly criticized as a vulgar commodification of Ghanaian heritage, the funding of the Theatre was partly divested to private commercial interests. The result was a growing sentiment that the government was abandoning its responsibility to develop and protect Ghana's native culture. This dissatisfaction created a threat against the political legitimacy of the Rawlings-led regime—and specifically, against its co-option of Nkrumah's community-oriented cultural vision.

This chapter discusses the strategy of legitimation adopted by the restructured National Theatre and its new multinational corporate sponsor, Unilever. We will see how the shift from a public theater revival toward a privately sponsored commercial enterprise was presented as a balance between national cultural promotion and private investment. Unilever's "responsible," "enlightened," and "progressive" corporate image was used to justify the involvement of private interests in public endeavors (and, by extension, to justify the neoliberal policies of the Rawlings regime). As a result of this privatization in the National Theatre, the artistic expression of concert party performers was constrained because they were limited to themes and representations that satisfied the sponsors' narrow (and questionable) interpretations of "progress" and "social responsibility." As a way around this, the King Karo Concert Party Troupe used a *trickster maneuver* in one of their plays. This play subtly expressed those stipulated themes and representations, while at the same time presented an alternative message that allowed for the display of unsanctioned ambitions.

LEGACY AND LEGITIMACY: GHANA'S CULTURAL POLICIES AND THE NEW NATIONAL THEATRE

On December 30, 1992, only days after his election as the president of Ghana's reconstituted liberal-democratic government, former flight lieutenant Jerry John Rawlings inaugurated the Ghana National Theatre. As mentioned in chapter 1, at the time, Rawlings was under great pressure to reconstruct his public image as he transitioned from leading a military government to presiding over a liberal-democratic one. He wanted to establish a sense of continuity between the grassroots politics that had defined the early part of his military rule and his subsequent turn to formal democratic norms. Rawlings hoped to reinforce his popular appeal by stylistically appropriating Nkrumah's pan-African rhetoric and resurrecting the deceased premier as a national symbol (even as he simultaneously pursued policies that would have made the esteemed independence-era socialist turn in his grave). The National Theatre was a key element of Rawlings's efforts to accomplish these political goals.

The original desire for a Ghana National Theatre can in fact be traced directly to Nkrumah's pan-African rhetoric of the 1950s and 1960s. Arguing that colonial education had produced a false consciousness in which Africans were forced to defer to European discourses and representations,

Nkrumah believed that a National Theatre Movement (NTM) could help colonial subjects take pride in their native traditions and identify with the authentic, community-oriented "African Personality." Shortly after Ghana's independence, Nkrumah's minister of education, J. B. Erzuah, announced that the creation of a National Theatre would be part of the regime's commitment to cultural revitalization.[1] Notable playwrights such as Efua Sutherland, Joe de Graft, and Michael Dei-Anang embraced this call and produced work that was supported through the NTM program. However, the full funding and construction of a National Theatre building did not come to fruition during Nkrumah's abbreviated presidency.

When soldiers ousted the premier from office in 1966, the new rightward-leaning military regime showed little interest in continuing support for a public theater program that was so closely aligned with Nkrumah's socialist ideology. Nonetheless, the ideals of cultural authenticity and national sovereignty remained strong in Ghana, and each of the short-lived post-Nkrumah regimes was forced to contend with the populist understanding of the social compact that had been forged during the independence movement. In 1975, the NRC/SMC regime once again formally identified the African Personality as a "guiding principle" and emphasized that cultural tradition was too important to be left at the mercy of the markets.[2] In 1979, President Limann's culture minister likewise told the parliament that Ghanaian artists could look forward to a renewal of Nkrumah's policies and that the government was committed to supporting a national culture that would not be "adulterated or de-personalized by vulgar commercialism."[3] However, despite all of these pledges and rhetoric about state-sponsored cultural-artistic production, none of Ghana's various regimes prioritized the National Theatre Movement at the level that it had achieved in Nkrumah's platform—until J. J. Rawlings decided to take up the mantle.[4]

In 1983, around the time that Rawlings's military government first began to embrace neoliberal policy changes, it launched a program that it labeled "Toward a Creative National Culture." The outlines of this program were lifted pretty much intact from Nkrumah's earlier platform. Rawlings emphasized the development of popular artistic traditions and began to plan for the construction of a grand National Theatre building. As was the case with Nkrumah's cultural policy, the program was

intended to demonstrate the regime's commitment to local empowerment. Interestingly, however, Rawlings failed to directly credit Nkrumah
and the anti-colonial movement as the model for these endeavors. He preferred instead to present the program as an outgrowth of his own political revolution, even as he adopted Nkrumahist language and referenced
artistic landmarks that clearly predated his regime. For example, when the
long-awaited National Theatre building was finally opened in December
1992,[5] Rawlings's inauguration speech acknowledged the contributions of
"legendary" figures Efua Sutherland and Joe de Graft for "creating a new
horizon for the performing arts" at the dawn of Ghana's independence.
Rawlings went on to suggest that the Theatre would encourage pride in
native performance traditions and affirm the value of "communal work
and communal living." He also emphasized that the Theatre would have
an inclusive mandate to support not only "lettered" and urban artists but
also Ghana's less literate, rural traditions—"performance groups of excellence from all over the country."[6]

Rawlings's nod to independence-era artists—and his invocation of a rural and communitarian ethos—were part of his *stylistic*

The National Theatre Complex in Ghana's capital city, Accra. Courtesy of the
author, July 2001.

appropriation of Nkrumah's legacy (see chapter 1). While voicing these familiar messages, Rawlings stopped short of any outright acknowledgment that
Nkrumah's regime had been the origin of the National Theatre project.
He thus avoided drawing any undue attention to the contrast between
his own recent policies and those of the independence movement, while
at the same time subtly suggesting (to any who might consider it) that his
new policy direction was in fact leading Ghana toward a fulfillment of the
otherwise aborted Nkrumahist cultural project. Rawlings also made small
but meaningful adjustments to the earlier statesman's rhetoric. For example, the mandate of Rawlings's National Commission on Culture, which
had ministerial oversight of the National Theatre project, was to make the
"values . . . enshrined in the tenets of the 31st December Revolution [i.e.,
Rawlings's 1981 military coup] enduring," while at the same time promoting a "distinct Ghanaian personality to be reflected in African and world
affairs" (Provisional National Defense Council Law 238, article 2, sections
i–iii). The small but critically important shift from Nkrumah's "African
Personality" to a new, individualized "Ghanaian personality" (note lowercase here) signaled a new balance of ideological power. It can be read as a
retreat from the values of pan-African communitarianism in the direction
of a denatured, unthreatening form of national branding—one that would
encompass the *image* of African culture, while being politically inert and
thus more palatable and inviting to Western investors.

POPULAR VERSUS NATIONALIST SENSIBILITIES:
A BRIEF HISTORY OF THE CONCERT PARTY

Shortly after the inauguration of the National Theatre building, the theater program managers identified the concert party tradition as an ideal
candidate for revival, in accordance with their mandate to support popular art forms. Ghana's concert party theater has its roots in the populist
borrowing and hybridization that emerged out of the more elite "concert"
genre of the late nineteenth and early twentieth centuries. These original,
colonial-era concerts were imported forms resembling American vaude-
ville or British music hall variety shows. They were sponsored by private
social clubs, music halls, and schools. Performers in these acts mostly

recited ballads and popular tunes from abroad, such as Al Jolson's "Yes, We Have No Bananas," and songs of loyalty to the Crown, such as "God Save the King" and "God Bless the Prince of Wales." They also included magic/illusionist acts and comedy sketches such as farcical drilling exercises and drunken scenes that mocked the conscription of Gold Coast Africans into the military service.[7]

These original Ghanaian concerts were reflections of colonial social formations. By the early twentieth century, there was a small, established group of Africans (mostly chiefs and wealthy merchants) who maintained their professional standing by sending their sons to be educated in English schools and by adopting upper-class British attire and social forms. There was also a much larger "intermediate" class of Africans who obtained a limited degree of Western-style education in local schools and who aspired to salaried jobs in commercial houses and government service.[8] Those who sponsored and attended "concert" performances came from both of these classes, ranging from the barely literate to the most Western-educated of the African elite. For all of these attendees, the concerts were a way of expressing British enculturation and the associated social aspirations. They were public scenes in which Africans could proclaim their identification with "worthy examples" of Western dress, dancing, music, art, and social interaction—forms that the British colonial state fetishized as measures of status and means of personal advancement.

However, significant tension between the most privileged African elites and the members of the more aspirational "intermediate" class continued. Elites looked down at the "intermediates" with disdain not only for their limited Western education but also because they lacked a fully Westernized sense of decorum. For example, after one concert put on by the Cape Coast Wesleyan School, members of the African elite spoke out in frustration against the active and vocal responses of students in the audience who hailed from the intermediate class. These rowdy, engaged responses were in keeping with traditional African festival and Anansesɛm modes of spectatorship, but the elites considered them disorderly, disgraceful, and uncivilized.[9] Over time, some of the younger members of the intermediate class began to chafe under this treatment. Frustrated by the airs of the elites and a lack of opportunities for upward mobility, they began to create artistic and social innovations that embraced African traditions and thus contributed to the first stirrings of popular anti-colonial sentiment. One of these innovations was the series of moves that transformed "concerts" into the "concert party" genre.

In Sekondi, where the highbrow Optimism Club rented its facilities to Western-style performers, students from the lower-status Methodist School across the street had the chance to closely observe and imitate various concert entertainments. Three students in particular—Bob Johnson, Charles Horton, and J. B. Ansah—studied the techniques of concert performance and adapted them into a new, hybrid form of comic sketch. Johnson, Horton, and Ansah made innovations to the Western-style concerts by adding elements of the Akan language and native traditions alongside to the usual English-language repertoire. They created a three-part performance structure: a signature opening tune, a short duet or comic monologue, and then a "trio" or three-actor sketch. The trio was comprised of stock characters who worked together to mock the affectations and artificiality of life among the Westernized *nouveau riche.* They included Lady, a formally educated African woman whose Westernized "refinement" generated the central conflict of the play; Gentleman or Master, an affluent and formally educated elite; and Houseboy, a "Bob" or comic persona who, like Ananse, lived by his stomach and survived by his wits and whose antics typically undermined his master's cultural pretensions.

Johnson, Horton, and Ansah took their show on the road, wandering through the countryside and making their version of the "concert" available, for the first time, to members of the peasant classes who lived outside of the seaboard cities. Inspired by their success, other performers followed suit, notably the Axim Trio, the Dix Covian Jokers, the Keta Trio, and the Saltpond Trio. To the frustrated members of the intermediate class, the life of the concert party troupe soon became emblematic of a freewheeling escape from regimented clerical labor and scarce prospects within the colonial enterprise. Even though the performers were often regarded, even by their own family members, as disreputable vagabonds who were wasting their education and social prospects, the genre flourished. Left to their own devices and operating largely outside the purview of the colonial administration, concert party performers continued to innovate in response to their expanding audiences.

By the 1950s, concert party troupes had firmly redirected the appeal of a predominantly elite, English-language platform to serve the interests of a much broader and rural-inclusive audience. Beyond the three customary stock characters, the performances grew to depict family members, chiefs, priests, government agents, and various supernatural creatures, swelling the original trios to troupes of between fifteen and twenty-five actors. Abandoning the Western songs and ballads previously used in concerts, they shifted to local, proverb-laden guitar music and integrated these sounds with the dramatic action, emotional tone, and narrative content of the performance scenes. Brief comic sketches grew into complex, extended narratives. Expanding beyond the original themes of upper-class African pretensions, concert party troupes developed a paradoxical, clownish, makeshift, and very nearly chaotic aesthetic—a "highly disjunctive topsy-turvy style . . . a rattletrap ride . . . from sentimental pathos to ridiculous buffoonery."[10] These anarchic artistic developments occurred alongside and in reference to transformations in the colonial order. By 1950, Nkrumah's calls for immediate independence and equality had driven him out of favor with the African elites, and he had begun to establish a political base among the intermediate and rural classes. Concert party performers were at the forefront of this disaffected class sensibility, and they made their presence known. The Burma Jokers changed their name to the Ghana Trio (indicating their support for transforming the Gold Coast colony into the independent nation of Ghana) and ended their shows with pro-Nkrumah messages. The Axim Trio staged performances titled "Nkrumah Is a Mighty Man," "Nkrumah Will Never Die," and "Nkrumah Is Greater than Before." Meanwhile, the Akan Trio released a song titled "Onim Dεε fɔɔ Kukudurufo Kwame Nkrumah" ("Knowledgeable, Courageous, Kwame Nkrumah").[11]

Concert party troupes continued to be cultural standard-bearers throughout Nkrumah's presidency. They were even able to survive Nkrumah's overthrow (probably, in large part, because they had remained financially independent of the National Theatre Movement). The 1960s and early 1970s were perhaps the peak of the concert party tradition, a time when there were at least fifty active troupes in the country. In the capital city of Accra, twenty-four troupes participated in the "National Festival of Concert Parties," organized in 1973 by the Arts Council of

Ghana. A handful of these performers even hit the big screen: The Ghana Film Industry Corporation produced *I Told You So,* an adaptation of the concert party format, and the Ghana Broadcasting Corporation produced *Osofo Dadzie,* a television series that featured concert party artists. From the late 1970s into the 1980s, however, the troupes began to fall on difficult times. Economic depression and drought reduced the disposable income that audiences had available to spend on shows, while a scarcity of imported fuel and the debilitated road infrastructure rendered travel costly and cumbersome. Military curfews and general political instability curtailed the country's nightlife and thus reduced the interest in concert party events. Even musical instruments, which audiences now considered *de rigueur* for shows, had become hard to obtain. By 1988, the number of concert party troupes on record had decreased to thirty, and by the time of the National Theatre's staged revival, nearly all of the remaining troupes were on the verge of disbanding.[12]

A PRECARIOUS PROFESSION: THE COMMERCIALISM AND UNIONIZATION OF THE CONCERT PARTY

We have seen the efforts of J. J. Rawlings and the National Theatre to revitalize the concert party performance tradition, but it is also important to examine the perspectives that led the Concert Party Union to collaborate with this national sponsorship. Doing so was something of a sea change for the concert party tradition, which for many years took pride in operating outside the purview of both colonial and postcolonial state apparatuses. Historically, concert party was defined by an anarchic spirit of grassroots entrepreneurship. The performers thought of themselves as artists but also frankly admitted that their primary goal was to make money—in fact, many of the performers depended on this income to survive.[13] The concert party's ground-up entrepreneurship helped to distinguish this genre from the colonial-era "concerts," as well as from most other "literary" (script-based) theater productions, which were generally funded by government programs, schools, or private social clubs. (The commercial spirit of the concert party, it should be noted, also distinguished it from fully traditional, community-based African performances, in which audiences were comprised of neighbors and kinsfolk, and formal compensation was not expected.)

In the early years of the concert party, troupes were cooperative undertakings in which income from the shows was divided up more or less equally among the performers. Depending on the success of the troupe, these earnings could range from a bare subsistence level to the occasional extravagant windfall.[14] By the 1970s, however, this small-scale entrepreneurship had evolved into a tiered system in which an ever-changing periphery of "bandsmen" performers were paid in wages. A core group of troupe managers or founding members handled the hiring and firing of bandsmen, scheduled the troupe's touring itinerary, and regulated the profits (or losses) of the venture. Performance wages were generally fair at first, allowing "bandsmen" to make decent money, and some of these performers went on to establish their own independent troupes after developing their skills in wage positions. However, theirs was an unregulated profession in an unpredictable, informal sector of the economy. As conditions in Ghana began to decline, the ability of wage performers to sustain a livelihood became increasingly precarious. For instance, when one itinerant troupe ran out of fuel during the world oil crisis of 1973, the performers not only failed to make money, but they also took many days to return to their base of operations because they had to beg for gasoline gallon-by-gallon along the way. In other cases, a troupe might arrive at a performance venue only to discover that a local chief had unilaterally discounted the gate fee by half and would thus be faced with the quandary of having to either accept the imposed price control or just cancel the performance and risk the ire of disappointed audiences.[15]

This situation worsened in the late 1970s as troupes began to increasingly rely on external promoters to organize their shows (especially during the financially slow rainy season). These professional managers would generally negotiate a fixed seasonal payment to a concert party troupe, thereby reducing the burden of financial risk. They would also handle logistical issues, the advertisement of shows, rental arrangements, and so forth, allowing performers to focus more exclusively on their art. However, these benefits came at the cost of entrepreneurial independence. Performers soon chafed under what they saw as exploitative contracts: In some cases a single promoter could earn a larger share of the profits than what the entire concert party troupe received. Many troupes became locked into financial relationships with promoters after having to ask for loans or advanced payments to survive a slow season. Others complained that promoters used their cozy relationships with local authorities to deny permits to noncompliant troupes and thereby sabotage their independence.[16]

The vagaries of road life and the increasing financial precariousness of concert party work reinforced the outlook of those who saw the performers as vagabonds and the profession as irresponsible foolishness. "If you are poor, you have no respect" the leader of the Jaguar Jokers troupe once observed. In response to these anxieties, many troupes came together to provide a limited safety net for their members. For example, if a member of the Jaguar Jokers was sick or in financial difficulty, he might be paid more until his situation improved, or if a troupe member died, the others would help pay for the funeral.[17] Of course, performers were well aware of the limitations of this form of assistance. Facing increasing exploitation as their original freewheeling entrepreneurship became absorbed into the society's larger market structure, the troupes began making efforts to unionize. The first effort, the Ghana National Entertainments Association, was formed during President Nkrumah's tenure. It was comprised of twenty-eight founding troupes and sought to regulate "the management of affairs of artistes," to "operate as a mutual aid organization," and to "eliminate middlemen from this field."[18] As was the case with many of Ghana's trade unions, this effort dissolved after the overthrow of Nkrumah. A second effort, the Ghana Cooperative Indigenous Musicians Society, was founded in 1977 with the support of more than forty troupes, but this union proved to be equally short-lived, collapsing in 1980.

Further unionization efforts remained stalled until the 1990s, when Adelaide Buabeng, a veteran concert party performer, attended the funeral of her friend and fellow artist, the comedian Kojo Stamp. Stamp's modest coffin, with barely ten people around it, was laid on two simple planks and driven to the cemetery on a dump truck instead of a hearse. This pauper's end compelled Buabeng to consider her own future and that of other aging practitioners. She convened a meeting in which many of the genre's central artists came together to contemplate the bleak circumstances that concert party practitioners faced. They resolved to found a new organization, the Ghana Concert Party Union, and to take whatever steps were necessary to provide assistance to impoverished performers. In addition to employing aging performers as mentors and consultants, providing emergency financial aid, and engaging in collective bargaining on its members' behalf, the Union also established a platform for renewing public interest in the concert party genre. Buabeng, who in 1993 obtained a position as a wardrobe mistress at the National Theatre, became instrumental in lobbying for a government-funded revival. Noting that English-language performances dominated the National Theatre's programs despite Rawlings's mandate to include native traditions, Buabeng petitioned, and eventually got the attention of, the Theatre's executive staff.[19] The result was a cooperative relationship between the National Theatre and the Ghana Concert Party Union, which reflected both Rawlings's mandate of inclusiveness and the Union's desire to alleviate the financial plight of its members. On November 11, 1994, the Theatre and the Union came together to launch a fortnightly variety event—including live band music, stand-up comedy, and plays (now farcical, now melodramatic, now full of pathos)—that they called the Concert Party Show.

THE KEYSOAP CONCERT PARTY: NEOLIBERAL REFORMS AND THE POPULAR THEATER REVIVAL

At the beginning of the concert party revival, public interest was so small that the organizers' colleagues, family, and friends comprised the bulk of the shows' audiences. The Concert Party Union and the National Theatre nonetheless did their best to publicize the event, even going so far as to offer a free Guinness beverage to attendees.[20] This situation began to change when the Theatre secured coverage from its sister state-run institution, Ghana Television. After Concert Party Show performances began to be aired every weekend, a large public following quickly developed, leading to a dramatic increase in the size of the event's live audiences. The concert party performances were soon moved from the smaller, open-air "Folks Place" stage of the National Theatre to the Main Hall of the complex. However, the expanding popularity of the show also contributed to strains on the Theatre's budget. Wiring and lightbulbs alone cost 25 percent of the Theatre's gate proceeds in the 1995 financial year.[21] Far

The view from stage right of the open-air theater space called the Folks Place in the Ghana National Theatre complex in Accra. Courtesy of the author, July 2001.

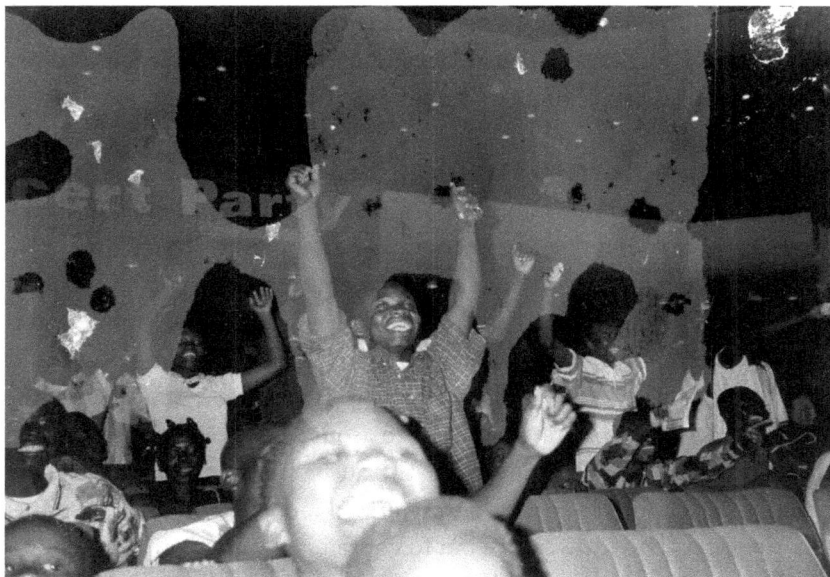

A typically raucous concert party audience cheering a performance inside the Main Hall of the Ghana National Theatre complex. Courtesy of the author, July 2001.

from expanding the National Theatre's subsidies to keep pace with this growing public interest, the Rawlings regime began to eye the shows as a liability in its bid to appease the neoliberal policy demands of Western investors. Increasingly, the government-funded performances were seen as a visible example of the overinflated public sector maligned by international finance institutions.

Starting around 1987, the Rawlings regime, goaded by international pressures, had begun a wholesale divestiture of numerous state-owned enterprises, many of which had lingered more or less untouched since the time of Ghana's independence. The range of the affected industries was broad—from paint, paper, liquor, steel, and sugar production, to farming, fishing, construction, mining, and hospitality services. The inauguration of the National Theatre building in 1992 and the emphasis placed upon funding the Theatre's cultural program were in many ways anomalies. As such, they helped to reassure the public that the regime was still dedicated to supporting the health of the community despite widespread concerns about the effects of neoliberalism. Perhaps unsurprisingly, however, as the imperatives of the tumultuous 1992 elections receded, the National Theatre increasingly found itself sharing the fate of other state-owned enterprises. Program managers faced decreased funding levels and political pressures to find nongovernment revenue sources. In 1995, just as the concert party revival was gaining momentum, the Theatre issued a revised mission statement that emphasized efficiency, profitability, and "customer-oriented programming"—in effect, taking its cues from the language of corporate management rather than public service.[22]

The colonial history of Ghana and the enduring strength of the post-independence social compact meant that the divestiture of public enterprises to the private sector remained an extremely controversial topic. This was especially true in Ghana's artistic community. The effect of the Theatre's new mission statement was to arouse "great alarm and trepidation" from critics who argued that the authenticity of African culture could never be sustained under a privatized model.[23] However, the Theatre managers had little choice but to contend with the regime's policy if they wanted to maintain a full cultural program. From 1995 onward, the managers increasingly embraced neoliberal rhetoric and actively sought corporate sponsorship. To alleviate concerns, they insisted that privatized funding would have no effect on the content of Theatre shows, which would remain committed to authentic cultural production. In fact, during this period, the Theatre aligned itself even more closely to the pro-African cultural ideals of the Nkrumah era, at least in a rhetorical sense. The program managers suggested that Western-style modernization should not be allowed to undermine "the inherent reverence for culture and tradition."[24] It seemed that the more the program came under the influence of corporate sponsorship, the louder and more strident became this emphasis on traditional authenticity.

The Concert Party Show turned into a central site for the Theatre to enact this ideal of privately sponsored cultural production (and to thereby validate the regime's neoliberal policy directives). This was only partly by design. The soaring popularity and cost of the show pushed it to the forefront of the Theatre's budgetary concerns and thus prompted the need for rapid action. Ultimately, the National Theatre established a joint sponsorship of the Concert Party Show with Unilever Ghana, the local subsidiary of an Anglo-Dutch multinational conglomerate with a long history of operations in the country. At the time of the concert party revival, Unilever was conducting an intensive marketing campaign for its Keysoap brand of multipurpose cleaner. The company was quick to seize upon the fresh opportunity offered by cultural sponsorship. In return for funding the show, Unilever required that Keysoap be mentioned by the concert party performers and used in their performances and that the production be renamed "the Keysoap Concert Party Show." This new manifestation of the concert party was inaugurated with a "mega-launch" in July 1995.

TRADITION AND PROGRESS: KEYSOAP, THE CONCERT PARTY, AND A LEGITIMATING MYTH

It is not immediately clear how using Keysoap as a prop in Concert Party Shows conformed to the National Theatre's rhetoric of authentic, traditional African culture. The context finally offered, at least in the realms of corporate fantasy, was that Keysoap was itself a part of Ghana's national traditions. Indeed, the product has a long history in the country, having first arrived during the pre-independence era as an import marketed by Britain's United Africa Company. Unilever began to produce the soap locally when it opened a factory in Ghana in 1963. This endeavor was cut short by a declining economy, but in the 1980s, local production resumed, and the company began to make aggressive efforts to corner the market. A Keysoap advertising campaign with the slogan "Many Years Ago" was first initiated in the late 1980s. In a typical television spot, a grainy, black-and-white image of an elderly woman near a clothesline is shown, while the lyrics "Longest-lasting Keysoap, the tradition goes on!" are sung. The woman picks up and smells a bar of Keysoap, smiles, and hands it to another woman, presumably her daughter, who is washing clothes in a basin of soapsuds. The image then turns sepia. The younger woman also smells the soap, smiles, and hands it to a young woman, presumably *her* daughter. The image turns to color. Finally, the young woman who is holding the soap smells it, smiles, and says, "Keysoap served my mother well, as it did for my mother's mother. Today it still meets my needs." She turns to a smiling child by her side and adds, "As I know it will do for my children."

With these ads, Unilever began to spin a narrative of "tradition" around its Keysoap product, an image of durability that was linked to the supposedly long-lasting qualities of the soap itself. The sponsorship of Ghanaian cultural traditions was therefore a perfect addition to the product's image. Eric Hobsbawm defined "traditions" as practices, either arising organically or consciously invented, that "inculcate certain values and norms of behavior by repetition, which automatically implies continuity with the past." The "long-lasting Keysoap" campaign is a paradigmatic example of an artfully invented tradition in Hobsbawm's sense, in which something that would not usually be considered culturally significant—the brand of a cleaning product—is intentionally bestowed with a timeless, normative aura.[25] Unilever's story about Keysoap thus had a certain congruence with the mission of the National Theatre: The sponsor could benefit from a perceived similarity, or consistency in sense-making, between Unilever's marketing efforts and the goal of reviving cultural traditions. For its part, the Theatre seemed willing to adopt this dubious logic. The corporate sponsor, Theatre managers explained, was not merely a profit-seeking enterprise but also a vibrant and authentic participant in Ghana's cultural history.

Theatre official William Addo presented a more controversial view of this relationship when he compared changing the Concert Party Show's name to the way a bride changes her last name to her husband's when she marries. Describing the negotiations between the National Theatre and Unilever, Addo said, "We told them, 'Well, if you want to get married, then let us talk. Bring the dowry, and then . . . you can call her Mrs. and she can acquire your identity.'"[26] As if to underscore the unequal relationship in this marriage of convenience, in June 1997, the Keysoap Concert Party literally dramatized Addo's metaphor. In a featured play, an African chief offers his daughter to whoever can perform her marriage rites "in the traditional way." One suitor offers money, a second offers alcohol, and a third offers cloth. The chief rejects them all. The fourth suitor, Gyamfi, obtains a giant bar of Keysoap from the heavens and offers it to the princess, assuring her "of a cleaner, healthier, and better life." Satisfied that Gyamfi has properly followed "tradition," the chief blesses their marriage.

This play can be interpreted as a rather straightforward exposition of the relationship between the Theatre and Unilever. The chief—a presumed custodian of cultural heritage—can be seen as a representation of the Theatre. The daughter—the object of interest—can be interpreted as the Concert Party Show. In Gyamfi, the successful suitor, we find a representative of Unilever the Keysoap-maker. The play seems to suggest that the mechanisms by which private sponsors purchase an interest in the shaping of culture is entirely in alignment with African traditions. Shamelessly, the play appropriates a central Akan/Asante legend in which a priest, Anokye, delivered a golden stool from the skies as a symbol of the Asante Confederacy's unity and the soul of its power. It also makes reference to Akan marriage rituals in which the groom often gives the bride's family a "thanks gift" (*aseda*)—usually a small token such as jewelry, handkerchiefs, hair oil, perfumes, mirrors, and so forth. Whether or not these traditions are appropriate analogies for the role of Keysoap in the Concert Party Show—or for that matter, whether or not they are traditions worthy of uncritical veneration—is a question that the production managers chose to disregard. Indeed, Unilever's desire to present Keysoap as an eternal and unquestionable tradition seemed to rub off on the way in which the National Theatre approached cultural forms. The concert party, which had always been a scrappy, innovative, entrepreneurial, hybrid genre fully engaged with modern social and political issues, be-came increasingly portrayed as a fixed, time-honored, and archaic ritual to be contemplated with detachment. In essence, the Theatre's traditions and performers were to be observed and manipulated by contemporary players such as Unilever, rather than be engaged with as the autonomous carriers of a modern and important message delivered from the past to the present.

Transforming living traditions into dead consumer products cleared the way for new messages to be attached to these cultural forms. The brand identity of Keysoap was one of these messages, as was the benevolent role of corporate players in the community. Many of the new messages attached to the concert party revival took the form of what corporate sponsors called "progressivism"—a paternalistic outlook on social de-velopment that emphasized "responsible" behavior on the part of ordi-nary citizens, while remaining firmly within the neoliberal paradigm and refusing to question the role of economic inequalities in creating suf-fering. Unilever had long been crafting such a narrative to legitimize its transnational profit-seeking activities. As early as the 1950s, the company had presented itself as "an enlightened firm with social responsibility and concern for public affairs" and as "a force for progress in the world."[27] As a result of the company's activities, its promoters emphasized, "hygiene and personal care [have become] commonplace" throughout the world, and nutritional values have increased.[28] Unilever's Ghana-based subsidiary likewise presented its business model in terms of social development—emphasizing the importance of "being responsible to the needs of the community in which one operates" and showing "strong commitment to the social and economic development of the country."[29] Such an outlook, of course, could also be perceived as a direct continuation of the "civilizing mission" through which colonial powers justified their economic exploita-tion in earlier eras.

In practical terms, the new focus on "progressivism" meant that The-atre acts were required to include themes such as AIDS awareness, envi-ronmental protection, family planning, and civic responsibility as part of their shows. These unequivocal messages of personal responsibility sharply diverged from the concert party's typically lighthearted and po-litically satirical approach. The changes distinctly altered the character

of concert party plays by asking performers to place the responsibility for
social problems on the shoulders of the ordinary citizens in the audience.
In addition, the messages were profoundly tied to affirmations of neoliberal culture and the promotion of sponsored products. For example, the
National Theatre soon developed a touring extension of the Concert Party
Show, which in a somewhat over-the-top adoption of corporate language,
was labeled the "Direct Consumer Contact Program."[30] This effort was
generally targeted at rural areas that had not yet been saturated by television providers and other advertising media. Unilever chose the locations,
and the Theatre would then direct a concert party troupe to visit the area
and perform sketches linking Unilever products to progressive outcomes
in the community. The troupe would set up alongside a truck containing
Unilever products, attract people with music, and then perform acts related to the products for sale, hawking them as vital elements of hygiene,
environmental sanitation, and nutritional health. National Theatre official
Ako Tetteh insisted that such a show was a reasonable balance of cultural,
progressive, and commercial objectives:

> We don't mention Keysoap until the tail end of the play. For twenty
> minutes they [performers] talk about the environment, sanitation, how
> to wash yourself, and all kinds of things, before they come to tell you, "If
> you've heard that all these things must be done, then use Keysoap. . . . If
> you are going to do it [brush your teeth], then use Pepsodent [a Unilever
> brand toothpaste]."

To drive his point home, Ako Tetteh added that although the Theatre
might be helping Unilever to sell its products, this was only a secondary
consideration in relation to the Theatre's primary goal of "educating" the
masses.[31]

The emphasis that the Theatre and Unilever placed on messages of
"progressive" responsibility thus helped to counteract concerns about
the commercialization of the concert party revival. In the larger political arena, these progressive messages were part of a strategy to reassure
voters that the privatization/divestiture of public enterprises was not in
conflict with the good of the community. In the more immediate environment, Theatre managers also used "progressivism" to reassure performers that the increasingly commercialized atmosphere of the show was
not an adulteration or co-option of their art but rather a path to greater

Unilever even sold Keysoap in the lobby of the National Theatre.
Courtesy of the author, July 2001.

social dignity. Theatre managers took pains to convince the Concert Party Union, in particular, that these new requirements would help to raise the image and status of the genre (and thereby help to improve the plight of impoverished performers). They also explained that participating in the commercialized and "progressive" programming would give a new image to concert party performers, elevating their status and overriding the social prejudices that the tradition had long faced. No longer vagabonds and purveyors of anarchic, frivolous, "low-class" entertainment, concert party performers would now be given their proper due as paragons of both cultural tradition and social progress:

> For any performer to be able to perform at that National Theatre and be projected on national television, that is the ultimate. . . . Now, these performers can walk with their chest out; they have regained their respectability.[32]

A central part of this image makeover was the Theatre's effort to shift the focus of concert party performances to "things that are relevant to the society."[33] This required performers to be "selective with their acts on

"Projecting" concert party performers "on national television."
Courtesy of the author, July 2001.

stage"—in particular, by replacing tomfoolery and pointed political satire
with responsible messages about civic duty.[34]

"WHO-IS-WHO": THE CONCERT PARTY UNION
FROM ACCOMMODATION TO CONFRONTATION

Within just three years, the National Theatre's concert party revival
had grown from a small and sparsely attended show at the "Folks Place"
to a televised, corporate-sponsored centerpiece of neoliberal "progressivism." How did the performers and the Concert Party Union feel about
these developments? First, there is no doubt that the Union was from
the start very accommodating of the changes proposed by the Theatre.
The initial forays of incorporating Keysoap into performances and shifting to "socially relevant" messages were accepted largely without protest.
Anything that might help to revitalize the tradition was seen as worthy
of attempting. The Union was slightly more hesitant about shifting the
performance venue from the outdoors "Folks Place" to the plush, 1,500-
seat Main Hall of the Theatre complex. One of the hallmarks of concert
party theater had always been its appeal to the country's rural peasantry
and urban underclass. The uncouthness and rambunctious participation
of these audiences had become integral to the format of the shows. The
Union expressed concerns that the upscale atmosphere of the Main Hall
would prove unfriendly to lower-class audiences, stifling the expressive
spectatorship and audience-performer rapport that had always been a
defining part of the concert party experience. These concerns notwith-
standing, the Union ultimately agreed that the show could be moved to
the Main Hall when bad weather and expanding audiences called for it.

The most striking of the Union's accommodations to the National Theatre format was its temporary suspension of the financial interests that had
long driven concert party work. As a state-run institution with severe budgetary constraints, the Theatre made it clear that it was not in a position
to pay a significant amount of money for concert party performances. By
providing logistical support and publicity, however, the Theatre could help
performers to regain their footing and develop a greater public following.
The Concert Party Union embraced this arrangement, in effect putting

its members' long-established commercial interests on hold. According to one performer, when the troupe members could not afford transportation, they would walk to Theatre rehearsals, believing that in the long run their "toils would not be in vain."[35] During the early years of the concert party revival, the performers made do with token payments out of the Theatre's gate proceeds—when there were any—embracing the hope that their efforts would create a path to a brighter future. When this future did ultimately come to pass, performers believed that they deserved to receive a larger share of the windfall from the Theatre's sponsorship arrangement with Unilever. The Theatre demurred, so in late 1997, money issues led to the first major conflict in the relationship between the Concert Party Union and the Theatre.

Explaining his side of the disagreement, Union secretary Kenneth Quarshie said that even when patronage for the Concert Party Shows began to increase in 1995, troupes still received only a paltry ₵20,000 per appearance (about US$17, divided among twelve to fifteen performers), while trusting in the Theatre's assurances that "all will be well one day." Quarshie said that any time the Union brought up the issue of compensation, the Theatre would speak of "better things to come" once the show obtained a sponsor. Yet, when the sponsorship did arrive, the increase in remuneration was "insignificant." In 1997 troupes received between ₵60,000 and ₵100,000 (between approximately US$30 and US$50). When the Union demanded details about the show's finances, it learned that gate fees for a full house brought ₵1,500,000 per show, while Unilever's sponsorship contribution approached ₵6,000,000. The Union also learned that the Theatre's contract with Unilever stipulated performer allowances for rehearsals, transport, refreshment, and costumes, none of which they had received. Incensed with these revelations, the Union decided to target its protest at the show's 1997 season finale, an intertroupe competition dubbed the "Who-Is-Who" championship. The Union demanded that, in return for members' participation in the show, each troupe in the final rounds of the championship should receive ₵300,000 for every level of qualification. The Union also demanded ₵500,000 separately, for itself, to be delivered at the end of the competition.[36]

The Theatre refused to meet these demands on the grounds that it could not afford it and that the Union's insistence of a direct payment to itself

was improper. Theatre official William Addo maintained that the Concert
Party Show's production costs had increased commensurately with its
proceeds, so there was no actual windfall to share with the performers.[37]
Regardless of the merits of these arguments, the specific form that the
Theatre's rebuttal took reveals the depth of its changing relationship to the
Union. In the original revival collaboration, the Theatre and the Union
had acted as equal partners, with the understanding that they would co-
operatively manage the affairs of the show. Union Secretary Quarshie insisted on this status as a full collaborator and co-promoter. He pointed to
the publicity materials for the revival, which read, "Ghana National Theatre and the Ghana Concert Party Union present . . ." and asserted that
the Union should be treated as a founding partner in the endeavor. The
Theatre, however, rejected that status and pointed out that the Union
was not an official party to its agreement with Unilever. Quarshie reluctantly admitted that this was in fact the case. However, he lamented that
the performers had "endured all these hardships" in the belief that they
were equal partners, while the National Theatre had acted in bad faith
by shutting Union representatives out of management decisions after the
endeavor became financially successful.[38]

Unimpressed by the Theatre's justifications, the Union called upon
concert party performers to suspend their participation in the show until better financial terms could be negotiated. The Theatre, however, refused to negotiate. Addo said, "I put my foot down seriously, and I told
them, well you can go . . . if you want to go, you can go."[39] The Union did
ultimately "go"; it severed its relationship with the Theatre and instead
teamed up with Brismen, an advertising company, to start a rival show
at the Accra Arts Center. The new collaboration attracted sponsorship
from Ghana Brewery's Star Beer and negotiated a broadcasting contract
with TV3, a private television network. However, without the high levels
of publicity and joint state/corporate sponsorship enjoyed by the Theatre,
this production proved to be unsustainable. It folded after just one season,
effectively diminishing the influence of the Concert Party Union. Keysoap's brand manager, Anthony Ebo Spio, triumphantly pointed out that
the name recognition between the concert party and Keysoap had become
so strong that other sponsors were unlikely to find it worthwhile to try to
create a new brand association. He said, "One thing that you cannot take

away from the concert party is that people know it as Keysoap Concert Party."[40] The National Theatre found that it could continue its Concert Party Shows using performers who were no longer beholden to the Union and who had nowhere else to turn. Having become fully disempowered hired hands, performers were never again in a position to question the Theatre managers' decisions.

KING KARO, THEATRICAL REALISM, AND THE CONSTRAINTS OF THE "PROGRESSIVE" STAGE

After the Union's departure, the Theatre and Unilever had free rein to expand their vision of the concert party revival, complete with product placement and themes of social responsibility. With even stricter regulations than before, performers who wanted to audition for the show were limited to representations that suited the sponsors' interpretations of development and progress. One performance group whose members lived through these tightening constraints was the King Karo Concert Party Troupe. This troupe had originally participated in the Union's boycott of Theatre shows, but after its founder King Karo's death in 1999 and the failure of the rival Union-Brismen effort, the performers found themselves nearly destitute. As the troupe teetered toward dissolution, the remaining members elected to return and participate in the Keysoap show at the National Theatre.[41]

Initially, some members of the King Karo troupe supported the "progressive" imperative in the Theatre's content restrictions. They believed it was a way to speak out against alarming trends in contemporary Ghana. One said, "Today you hear they've murdered this person, that a little kid has been sexually abused; another day you hear someone has been burgled." The troupe members said that it was necessary for performers to create awareness of these problems and to "advise the nation against the things that might destroy it." Therefore, performers could not, in good conscience, simply do whatever they liked in their plays. Others emphasized that with a greater exposure to "a wider and more critical audience," including "top government officials," concert party troupes had to be constrained to act more responsibly. Echoing the rhetoric of National Theatre officials, troupe members indicated that these limitations enhanced the respectability of their art. Troupe leader Joe Boy insisted that his group would not stage "any play for airing that does not contain something educative."[42] The performers also recognized that the inclusion of moral lessons was not in conflict with long-standing concert party practice. Especially since the 1950s, the popular theater had always tried to show people the "correct" way to live, and nearly all concert party plays ended with an instructive, proverb-laden musical number. Classics such as "Wusum Brɔde a Sum Kwadu" ("If You Plant Plantain, Plant Banana Too"), "Mma W'anyi Mber Obi N'adze" ("Don't Covet Your Neighbor's Possessions"), "Kakaiku's Siesie W'akyir Ansaana Ewu" ("Make a Will Before You Die"), and "Egyankaba" ("Orphan") included warnings against favoritism, covetousness, rootlessness, and the ill treatment of housemaids.

Despite these reassurances, the increasing didacticism and commercialism of the required messages, and the fact that they were formally imposed from outside, were troubling constraints for the performers. The moral messages of earlier concert party plays had been strongly marked by ambivalence and unpredictability, a feature of the Anansesɛm ethos that provided much of the identity and entertainment value of concert party performance. For example, a play might express admiration for foreign lifestyles but then ridicule characters who are enamored with items from overseas. It might tout farming as an honest and laudable occupation, yet portray peasants as simpletons and oafs. It might portray trendy urban entertainment as frivolous but then shamelessly exploit audiences' appetite for it. Often, just at the moment that a concert party play seems ready to make its point, it suddenly detours into confusing and complicated scenes that obscure the very moral lesson it is trying to teach.

The performers were happy to embrace messages of social responsibility in their plays, but their artistic impulse was to treat these messages with a significant degree of trickster-inspired ambiguity. They were unhappy with how the show's sponsors had made auditions into a disciplining tool to strip the concert party acts down to one-dimensional, *unequivocally* "progressive" themes. This insistence on weeding out nuance and complexity in favor of ideological forcefulness, including the endless plugging of soap products on stage, struck at the very heart of the concert party aesthetic and politic. As a result, many acts would satisfy the Theatre with an unequivocal message at auditions but then fall back into puns and satire during their live performances. This led to a kind of artistic guerrilla warfare in which Theatre and company officials used every power at their disposal to pressure the troupes into responsibility, while performers covered themselves in an aura of ambiguity, disavowal, and popular appeal. The stronger a troupe's popular following, the more risky it was for officials to censure them and risk the audience's displeasure.

By 1998, the end-of-season "Who-Is-Who" competition had come to provide the sponsors with a partial solution to their dilemma. The organizers simply made an unequivocally progressive theme one of the judging criteria. Success in the end-of-season competition was strongly linked to financial compensation and other prizes (such as retail quantities of Key-soap) that might be awarded to performers. Therefore, the manipulation of the judging standards could provide an effective disincentive against thematic ambivalence in the plays that the performers developed throughout the course of the season. The sponsors took these requirements even further in 1999 when they decided to use the judging to formally discourage any "supernatural" elements in the plays. Concert party performance typically eschews the elements of theatrical realism—verisimilitude, cause and effect, and narrative cohesion—in favor of a more anarchic aesthetic laced with "mercurial and miraculous changes of fortune."[43] The result is typically byzantine plot twists that often involve the intervention of supernatural figures from African, Christian, and Islamic folklore. The revival's sponsors had long been dissatisfied with this aspect of the genre, which they regarded as irresponsible fantasy. As National Theatre official William Addo explained, such fantastical devices undermined the message that audiences are responsible for solving their own problems.[44] Theatre official Ako Tetteh further elaborated this concern, saying:

> What need is there to portray ghosts and spirits in our plays? People must take responsibility for their actions. Ghosts . . . do not solve problems for anybody. Where do we see ghosts, where do we see spirits, where do we see angels? [We should] make people realize they have to help themselves and Ghana. . . . We want plays that are current and social; we don't want ghosts and that kind of thing.[45]

Performers strongly objected to this purge, but after the "realism" mandate was added to the end-of-season judging standards, it became very difficult to resist.

The King Karo troupe was the first of the concert party acts to be penalized for staging "spiritual things." For the 2000 competition, the troupe put on a play in which a village suffers a power vacuum after its chief dies. The village elders ask the Queen Mother to organize the installment of a new chief, as is her customary duty. She installs her own son, even though her nephew is rightful heir, and meanwhile seeks a powerful death charm to eliminate the nephew. Fortunately, the Queen Mother's sister and nephew, who are pious people, encounter the death charm during their prayers in the form of a ferocious giant eagle and are able to summon a powerful angel to eliminate it in a spectacular spiritual battle. The Queen Mother, angry about the failure of her death charm, lashes out at everyone in the village by poisoning its river. However, her unsuspecting grandson catches a fish in the river and makes soup with it, which he shares with the Queen Mother and her son. The villains die, victims of their own poison, and the nephew is rightfully made chief.

The director of this play, who goes by the name Ice Water, recalled painfully that despite an overwhelmingly positive response from audiences, the play came in last place when the judges announced their scores. The King Karo troupe members believed the judges were biased. Ice Water insisted that to his recollection, Theatre officials had never raised any objection to the spiritual elements of the play prior to the judging. He explained—perhaps with a bit of equivocation—that the play expressed a realistic, progressive message encouraging audiences to observe due process and refrain from postelection violence in Ghana's fledgling democracy. Another troupe member, Asantewa Botwe, insisted that bad spirits *do* exist and asserted that the play realistically dramatized prevailing beliefs. Powerless in the face of a constraining mandate that did not really make sense to them, many members of the troupe consoled themselves with the belief (as a result of rumors they had heard) that they were a casualty of a certain Theatre official's amorous involvement with a member of a competing act. Being able to accuse the Theatre and its judging process of ulterior motives allowed them to vent their displeasure at constraints that they were otherwise powerless to challenge.[46]

"AN ACTOR MUST LOOK BRIGHT":
SKIN BLEACHING AND (DIS)EMPOWERMENT

In 2001, while the King Karo troupe channeled their disappointment into preparing for the new season's "Who-Is-Who" competition, the sponsors added yet another judging criterion to the contest. Whereas the previous criteria targeted dramatic form and content, this new addition was focused on performers' corporeal bodies: Judges must penalize troupes whose members had "bleached" skin. The practice of skin bleaching is a worldwide phenomenon that goes back to the colonial construction of racial privilege. It involves the application of hydroquinone creams, steroid gels, and/or mercuric soaps to lighten the color of the skin. This "beautification" practice, however, can be harmful. According to a pamphlet published by the Ghana Skin Foundation, skin bleaching can destroy the skin's suppleness, reduce its defenses against fungal infections, prevent surgical stitches from staying in place, disrupt the functioning of the nervous system, and even lead to renal failure and cancer. Skin bleaching was a high-profile topic in Ghana at the turn of the millennium, as dermatologist Dr. Edmund Delle saw his twenty-five-year campaign against the practice culminate in the establishment of the Ghana Skin Foundation. Prominent personalities such as Ghana's dark-complexioned first lady, Nana Agyemang-Rawlings, spoke out in support of the Foundation's work and criticized skin bleaching as something practiced only by racially/culturally self-denigrating subjects.[47]

The antibleaching campaign had unsettling implications for Unilever. The company's India subsidiary had in 1978 launched a cream called "Fair and Lovely," which was touted as "the leader in women's lightening skincare." Up until the 2000s, ads for this cream typically showed a depressed, lonely woman who, once she starts using this product, suddenly obtains a boyfriend, a new job, or an otherwise brighter future because of her fairer complexion.[48] The growing momentum of the antibleaching campaign in Ghana meant that Unilever was sparing no effort to disassociate itself from such products or from any connotation that its products might be used for such purposes. Therefore, in 2001, the sponsor requested that the Theatre take steps to curb bleaching among concert party performers. This was seen as a proactive step to avoid any possible link between the

Keysoap brand and artificially lightened skin, a connection that might threaten the company's "progressive" image. The Theatre officials rapidly complied. As one concert party manager explained, "The show comes on television and is watched by 2 to 3 million people every Saturday. What kind of message would we be sending—that it is good to bleach your skin?"[49] In retrospect, it seemed obvious that the practice of skin bleaching might be antithetical to the Theatre's mandate of promoting authentic, pro-African culture. However, this only became an issue after the anti-bleaching movement began to threaten the sponsors' image.

Many of the King Karo troupe members admitted to bleaching their skin at some point in their lives. Troupe leader Joe Boy said he had bleached his skin for the same reason the show's sponsors were against it: "Once you become a TV star, everyone who sees you . . . looks at your appearance." Like the show's sponsors, Boy saw an advantage to modifying his public image; it just wasn't the image the sponsors wanted. Although Boy was well aware of the dangers of bleaching, he felt it had an overall positive value. He said lighter skin makes one "attractive" and "lifts one up" so "when one is seen, one is respected." No doubt, many people think bleaching their skin can help them meet the mate of their dreams or find a great job. For Boy, the visibility inherent in his profession created a particularly strong desire to maximize the commodity potential of his appearance. In his words, "An actor must look bright."[50]

To concert party performers such as Joe Boy, bleaching was seen as a means of controlling one's own destiny. The appearance of one's skin was viewed as a form of personal value over which the performers had at least some amount of control, a site of potential (albeit questionable) empowerment that stood in contrast to their growing disenfranchisement in all other aspects of their artistic careers. Indeed, even those members of the King Karo troupe who preferred not to bleach their skin agreed that the Theatre's prohibition of this activity strongly overreached into performers' private lives and circumscribed their control over their own economic well-being. The performers argued that they should be free to manage their appearance however they saw fit. This insistence on the right to bleach one's own skin is a fascinating counterpoint to the "progressive" messages of social responsibility mandated by the show's sponsors. The performers, confronting ever-tightening artistic constraints and

narrowing horizons of self-determination, clung stubbornly to this harmful and degrading practice as one of their few remaining spheres of personal agency. They acknowledged that within the historical constraints of
racial privilege, lightening one's skin could in fact be a way of enhancing
one's social capital. Meanwhile, the imperative of "personal responsibility" handed down from the sponsors suddenly required that performers
must abandon the practice. The mandate constrained the agency of the
performers, while simultaneously placing accountability squarely on their
shoulders, insisting that the performers absorb any personal losses that
they might incur either in acquiescing to or in resisting this demand. At
the same time, the mandate was intended to prevent the culpability of corporate managers who for many years had cynically profited by exploiting
the empowering underside of skin bleaching.

AFUTUO NSAKRA ONIPA GYE SƐ NSƆ-HWƐ

For the 2001 "Who-Is-Who" competition, the King Karo troupe put on
a play titled *Afutuo Nsakra Onipa Gye Sɛ Nsɔ-Hwɛ* (*Advice Does Not Make
a Person Change, Only Trial and Ordeal Do*). The performers studiously
examined the competition's judging requirements and took steps to improve their chances of winning. Troupe members cast in the play were to
discontinue any skin-bleaching practices. All reluctantly did so, although
Joe Boy planned to refrain only temporarily. The troupe also removed
all supernatural characters from the play, even though they believed it
would make the play much less enjoyable. Finally, whereas the previous
year's play had only vaguely alluded to a social development theme, *Afutuo* was constructed to be much more direct. Throughout the play, the
troupe presented several clear messages about national-communal pride
and disease prevention, in accordance with the imperatives set down by
the competition's sponsors.

Afutuo has thirteen characters. The principal ones are businesswoman,
Ma Red; her daughter, Asantewa; and her neighbor, Akyere. The others characters are the town drunk, Katawire; Ma Red's son, Fine Boy;
her business assistant, Tapo; a local government representative, Assemblyman; Assemblyman's Wife; Nurse; Doctor; Schoolteacher; and two

elders, Obaapanyin and Abusuapanyin. The plot of the play revolves around a health epidemic that has beset Assemblyman's area of jurisdiction. After his wife asks him to find a cure, Assemblyman invites Doctor and Nurse to a community meeting and learns from them that the epidemic is a mix of malaria, cholera, and typhoid fever, resulting from unhygienic practices in the community. Assemblyman asks Ma Red to help mobilize a community volunteer effort to improve sanitation. However, Ma Red declines this request, saying that her small business keeps her too occupied to be able to help out. Akyere, disapproving of Ma Red's lack of community spirit, declares that her refusal is actually a blessing: Ma Red can hardly keep her own house clean, much less encourage others to do so. Akyere volunteers in Ma Red's place.

One day, Ma Red receives a visit from Katawire, the town drunk, who tells her what Akyere is saying about her behind her back. Meanwhile, Ma Red's daughter, Asantewa, keeps complaining about how the dumpsters at the community dumpsite are too high. Ma Red tells Asantewa to just dump their trash anywhere. Akyere tries to stop Asantewa from littering,

Ma Red's daughter, Asantewa (left), tells off Akyere (right) for trying to stop her from littering, while Katawire, the town drunk, intervenes. Ma Red is second from the left. Courtesy of the author, September 2001.

which leads to an altercation in which Ma Red accuses Akyere of assaulting her daughter. The scene then shifts to a clinic, where Doctor and Nurse are getting ready to receive patients. Tapo, Ma Red's business assistant, totters in, complaining of pain in his side. Katawire follows, complaining that he vomits after every meal. Then, Ma Red's son, Fine Boy, rushes in, carrying a comatose Asantewa and crying for help. Nurse rushes Asantewa into an examining room as Fine Boy explains to Doctor that Ma Red is away on a business trip and that her daughter has vomited several times. Later, Ma Red arrives at the hospital, only to learn that Asantewa has died. Ma Red and Fine Boy leave the clinic in tears (PURL 4.1).

While Ma Red is in mourning, she begins to suspect that Akyere had cast an evil spell on Asantewa. In her mix of fury and grief, she gets nauseous and dizzy and feels stomach pain. Schoolteacher, visiting to offer condolences, finds Ma Red in agony and calls for help. Her responsible neighbor, Akyere, comes to her aid. Together, they carry Ma Red to the clinic. Meanwhile Assemblyman is receiving the elders Obaapanyin and Abusuapanyin at his home. When they learn that Ma Red is sick, they rush to the clinic, where, much to their relief, they find that Ma Red, Tapo, and Katawire have all recovered. Doctor explains that Ma Red and her daughter both had cholera, Tapo had malaria, and Katawire had typhoid fever, all of which would have been preventable if they had just taken his precautions. Ma Red thanks Akyere for helping her to the clinic and asks for forgiveness. She resolves, thenceforth, to keep her surroundings clean, to volunteer regularly, and to donate money to the community. Doctor reiterates his health recommendations and adds, "Advice does not make a person change, only trial and ordeal do" (PURL 4.2).

To accommodate the "progressive" themes required by the show's sponsors, *Afutuo* offers an abundance of specific advice. Doctor and Nurse provide health and sanitation tips in all of their scenes. The play drives home the point that these concerns are of practical importance to the national community, with a directness that was absent in the troupe's more allegorical approach the previous year. The geographical vagueness of the unnamed Ghanaian community represented in the play indicates that its concerns are applicable throughout the country. The Assemblyman, the first to appear on stage, enters singing a call-and-response song focused on the needs of the nation:

ASSEMBLYMAN: My brothers and sisters of this country,

CHORUS: Will this nation recover?

ASSEMBLYMAN: When ailments abound,

CHORUS: Will this nation recover?

ASSEMBLYMAN: When life's constraints abound,

ALL: This nation will recover only by our own efforts![51] (PURL 4.1)

At the end of the play, the entire community gathers onstage for a final musical number:

Think of this nation, Ghana is your very own
Think of this nation; don't say you're not part of it! (PURL 4.2)

Together, the songs suggest that the community's "ailments" should not be regarded as isolated events but as the makings of a national malady. And the source of this malady is the failure of Ghana's people to take responsibility and pitch in for the good of the whole.

As the wayward protagonist whose misdeeds incite calamity, Ma Red sees herself as an exception to progressive expectations. Refusing to behave responsibly, she puts her own enjoyment ahead of the health of the entire community. When Ma Red first appears onstage, she sings a song that introduces her character in this light:

Let me have my play, my play, oh my play,
Let me have my play, for tomorrow I'll be gone from this world.
Whatever a person does, people will criticize it,
Whatever a person does, people will criticize, humanity's children, eh!
Let me have my play, my play, oh my play,
Let me have my play, for tomorrow I'll be gone from this world! (PURL 4.1)

Ma Red then reveals that some in the community vilify her because of the "small wealth" she has accumulated. She admits that this is why she declined Assemblyman's request: She is not interested in sacrificing her precious time for a community that will not countenance her material ambitions. In response, the more dutiful members of the community increasingly censure Ma Red and Asantewa for their "insolence."

In light of Ma Red's distaste for her community, her casual instructions to her daughter to just dump their household trash wherever she can, and her refusal of Assemblyman's request to be a volunteer, she is shown to be a disrespectful, thumb-nosing, and money-centered woman who, because of her financial autonomy, sees no reason to care about others' needs. As a result, she becomes a viral force inimical to the cohesion and progress of the ailing community. In a very straightforward sense, then, *Afutuo* preaches that the ailing nation cannot recover or develop if individuals such as Ma Red act in ways that make them pariahs. Ma Red learns the hard way—her daughter's death and contracting malaria—that no one is immune from malady and that isolating oneself is not a protection from contagious illness. In the end, she comes to understand that her own actions (not Akyere's spell) were what killed her daughter and that taking personal responsibility is the key to progress.

THE LIMITS OF ADVICE: VICARIOUSNESS, VOICE, AND THE TRICKSTER'S DOUBLENESS

"Ma Red" was not only the name of a character in the play, but it was also the name by which the other actors and fans called the actress (Linda) who played that part. King Karo members usually assigned nicknames to new members as a form of initiation. After taking on the name, the members would use it as a means of developing their theatrical persona, answering to the name both onstage and off. In July 2001, Ma Red explained to me what this naming meant:

> There is no difference between Ma Red and Linda, but because of the concert party work I do, one can speak of a certain difference. . . . Now Ma Red is known all over Ghana. . . . The things Ma Red is able to do today, Linda could not do. Ma Red is able to speak on television for the masses to see, so that wherever I pass, everyone realizes "that's Ma Red coming!" The things Linda did, however, were never seen by the masses.[52]

Linda's reference to "Linda" in the past tense and to "Ma Red" in the present tense conveys the sense that initiation into concert party work had transformed Linda into Ma Red, the woman who is now seen on television and does things that "Linda could not do." In my discussions with Ma Red, I felt that she was asking me to think of the offstage star actress and her onstage character as two different but closely linked personas—each a replication and transmutation of the more ordinary Linda.

The character development at the King Karo rehearsals clarified this concept. The performers began their plays with very basic descriptions ("a renegade, a rich woman," in the case of Ma Red in *Afutuo*). They then built on these descriptions organically by drawing from aspects of their everyday lives. This endeavor of character-building extended far beyond the sort of preparation-by-emotional-recall that is used, for example, in the Stanislavski system of acting; it was a direct *bricolage*, in which characters and their stories were built out of personal experiences. Catherine Cole has previously reflected on this same aspect of concert party theater, describing performers' ability to cook up "one's signature character out of ingredients readily at hand." As Cole has shown, this process is one aspect of the concert party's affinity with the Anansesɛm performance tradition.[53] Following in the footsteps of traditional trickster-storytellers, the performers of the King Karo troupe distilled available props, personal experiences, and relayed stories into complex and formidable characters that embodied their own actual and imagined—and sometimes *aspirational*—identities. In *Afutuo*, for example, the character Ma Red has obtained a significant degree of financial success through (unsurprisingly) her business of selling soap. However, Ma Red, the actress, also promotes soap during the course of her concert party work, while Linda, the non-actress, maintains a retail business in which she, yet again, makes a living by selling soap. In essence, the character that Linda created on the concert party stage is a direct manifestation of her personal experiences and economic aspirations—and quite possibly of her anxieties surrounding those aspirations.

The history of women in concert party work adds yet another layer of significance to the story of Ma Red. In earlier decades, the rootless life and vagabond status of concert party performers meant that a woman who embraced the profession was generally presumed to be one of "those-who-move-about-in-order-to-eat" (basically, a prostitute, or at least sexually "loose").[54] Disparaging views about the moral rectitude of female performers continues to linger into the present day, with the result that these women, even more so than their male counterparts, are eager to defend their autonomy by holding down "day jobs." King Karo actresses

Ma Red (center) with two other members of the King Karo
troupe at an evening rehearsal of *Afutuo*.
Courtesy of the author, July 2001.

were no exception. Troupe member Asantewa (she uses her actual name
for her character in *Afutuo*) is a hairdressing apprentice. She explained,
"If I don't learn a trade beside theater work, it will affect me. A woman
must have her own trade; if you have three [trades] and one does not help
you, the other will." Charlotte (who plays Assemblyman's Wife in *Afutuo*)
even insisted that the author record the interview at her market stall so it
"doesn't appear as if concert party women don't have a real job to do." In

a profession still lowly esteemed, actresses bore a particular onus to make and to *be seen* making another income.

At the same time, however, the female performers had to confront the likelihood that financial success would also be regarded as threatening or socially inappropriate. Women have a long history of involvement in small-scale market enterprises in Ghana, but historically their prospects have been constrained by the broad patriarchal contours of society and the need to depend on male patronage and goodwill. This situation began to improve somewhat from the 1970s onward. However, anxieties about single and/or young women's growing wealth, autonomy, and assertiveness fueled misogynist reactions that maligned the character of financially independent women and sought to keep them "in their place."[55] In *Afutuo*, Ma Red's status as a single, independent, and financially successful soap merchant flies in the face of this hostility. In her opening song, Ma Red declares, "Let me have my play," asserting her right to independence and her refusal to be defined by the terms of her detractors. Linda explained, with more than a hint of admiration, that "Ma Red does whatever she likes despite what everybody says." This defiant and celebratory aspect of Ma Red complicates the miscreant status to which the play's overtly "progressive" message confines her, giving voice to the social aspirations and frustrations of women who can relate to Ma Red's disaffection.

The character of Ma Red in *Afutuo* contains a further layer of meaning, a sort of inside joke and subtle defiance against the constraints imposed by the Concert Party Show's sponsors. Ice Water explained that Linda was called "Ma Red" because of her full-bodied appearance and light skin tone, both of which were regarded as artistic assets. Linda confirmed this: "After I started concert party work, people looked at my body and my skin color and called me Ma Red." The troupe members were careful to emphasize that Linda's lighter skin color was natural and not cosmetically obtained. Because of this, Ma Red's character could convey the performers' continuing conviction that there is a link between socioeconomic status and a lighter skin tone without being subject to the Theatre's censorship of skin bleaching. By casting Ma Red as the affluent purveyor of Keysoap in the play, the troupe effectively disputed the sponsors' message that skin bleaching is disempowering. At the same time, they completely undermined Unilever's attempt to disassociate their product from lighter skin colorations in the Concert Party Show.

Through their play *Afutuo,* the King Karo troupe thus managed to enact humorous and spirited elements of ambivalence, despite the overwhelming social and financial pressures that constrained their performance. Beyond its dutiful avoidance of supernatural agency and its explicitly progressive themes, the play harbored a surreptitious, vicarious realm of meaning and identification in which performers expressed complex and unsanctioned truths. The character of Ma Red took on a form of doubleness, embodying both positive and negative messages, expressing a complex dialectic between hegemony and resistance, and blurring the lines between community needs and individual aspirations. For the members of the King Karo troupe, she became both a way to satisfy the sponsors' imposed themes and to express their own countervailing aspirations. This trickster maneuver undermined the unequivocal messages of an imposed "progressivism" in which ordinary citizens are told to be responsible and curtail their aspirations, while the national divestment of public enterprises and the larger structures of wealth concentration remain unquestioned.

Even the title of the play indicates this ambivalence. In one sense, *Advice Does Not Make a Person Change, Only Trial and Ordeal Do* can be read as a weary and hollow dictate, moralizing about Ma Red's need to suffer before learning to rein in her ambition. Alternatively, however, and more in line with the unpredictable aesthetic of the concert party tradition, the proverb-title can be understood as a critique of the corporate sponsors' obsession with pure didacticism. True progress, the play's title seems to suggest, must come from honest experience, interaction, and personal investment, not from an image-driven obsession with "progressive" themes. In the context of their concert party art, the performers seem to be insisting that it is the audience's connection to the world of the play that makes a difference—not the overtly imposed messages, the performers' skin tones, or the presence or absence of supernatural beings. By offering multiple, nuanced possibilities of identification in their play, the members of the King Karo troupe gave expression to Ananse's impulse to both support and subvert—to promote something, then undercut it; to teach a lesson, and then undermine it. King Karo did not advance beyond the preliminary rounds of the 2001 "Who-Is-Who" competition with *Afutuo*. In their effort, however, they revealed that the peculiarly disjunctive style of concert party theater was still alive at the turn of the millennium and was still providing an anarchic counterpoint within the teeth of corporate-institutional power.

5

⌘

In the House of Stories

Village Aspirations and Heritage Tourism

THIS CHAPTER EXAMINES the intersection between Anansesɛm performance and heritage tourism in neoliberal Ghana. As mentioned before,
the 1990s saw a rise in popular trepidation about the Ghanaian government's divestiture of state-owned enterprises and its courtship of foreign direct investment. Public concerns about external influences in the
government and fears of foreign profiteering detracted from the political legitimacy of J. J. Rawlings's administration. In order to undermine
and confuse this opposition, the neoliberal regime sought to co-opt the
stylistic rhetoric of pan-African cultural revival, which previously had
been a feature of the anti-colonial movement. One aspect of this strategy
of cultural legitimation was that the Rawlings regime began to strongly
promote international black heritage tourism in Ghana, thereby making
foreign involvement in the country appear less offensive. The regime proposed (in partnership with foreign investors) that the development of the
country's tourism industry, including the associated hotels, resorts, transportation, and infrastructure projects, could be tied to courting African
diaspora tourists who would return to Ghana to experience "traditional"
sites and cultural events.

One site that was celebrated as a potential destination for heritage
tourism was the village of Ekumfi-Atwia. This rural community obtained some renown in the late 1960s as the location of experiments in
modernist theater conducted by the famous Ghanaian dramatist Efua
Sutherland. Interest in Ekumfi-Atwia had largely dissipated during the

1970s and 1980s, however, so an influx of international tourism under the Rawlings regime promised a new socioeconomic lease on life for the community theater project, as well as for the village as a whole. Unfortunately, the revitalization efforts provided few of the promised benefits, and they came at a steep cultural cost as performers were compelled to reinterpret their storytelling tradition and repackage it for the consumption of tourists within a market-centered promotional narrative. The theater performances in Ekumfi-Atwia were given the name *kodzi* (the term for traditional Anansesɛm storytelling in the language of the Fante ethnic group, as discussed in chapter 2). However, these performances are better understood as a *staged* re-presentation of Anansesɛm. Sutherland's community theater project had always been conceptualized as a modernist/ experimental reworking of traditional storytelling practices, one in which scripted (i.e., rehearsed and stage-directed) elements predominated over the spontaneity and fully open participation that characterize traditional Anansesɛm. In 1999, under the guise of heritage tourism, the kodzi performances in Ekumfi-Atwia were more carefully orchestrated and constrained, even as the self-conscious context of avant-garde modernism was downplayed and the difference from traditional practice became more obscure. One day, however, a young woman from the village wandered onstage in the middle of a staged kodzi performance—a spontaneous incident that caused visible anxiety among the participants in this supposedly spontaneous community event. This unscripted arrival of an interloper in the midst of a staged version of Anansesɛm can be seen as a resurgence of the uncontainable legacy of the trickster.

A RURAL BACKWATER: THE HISTORY OF A VILLAGE'S MARGINALIZATION

The community of Ekumfi-Atwia is located in what is known today as the Central Region of Ghana, occupying the middle portion of the country's coastline. The occupants of the region were part of a great fourteenth-century migration out of the Bono Kingdom that once existed to the north of the area. These migrants were called the *Fante*—literally "the half that broke away"—because large numbers of them separated from the kingdom and headed south toward the coast. A mere century later, the areas near Ekumfi-Atwia began to feel the effects of European mercantile exploits. In the calm, sheltered bays of the coastline, the Portuguese, Swedish, Danish, Dutch, British, and Prussian fortune-seekers built forts and castles and quarreled over territorial rights. The Fante states, which were gradually developing into a unified coalition with a strong military presence, enjoyed a key role in the early Euro-African trade. They acted as middlemen in the commerce between the Europeans and the African interior, extracting rents and taxes from European merchants. Ultimately, however, the Fante fell more and more under British jurisdiction because they appealed to the foreigners for help in their battles against the neighboring Dutch-allied Asante Kingdom. By the late nineteenth century, Britain held full administrative rule over Fante lands and had defeated its rivals throughout the region, basically controlling the entire area that forms the current country of Ghana.

The circumstances of British colonial administration meant that select coastal cities were protected, developed, and exploited as centers of trade. On Ghana's central coastline, for example, the city of Cape Coast became a time-honored British enclave. A center of colonial administration, it soon boasted numerous mission schools and a modern public infrastructure. It was home to an established community of Western-educated Africans who were familiar with European languages and the specialized idioms of transatlantic commerce. Trained and obedient locals worked in trade-related jobs as deckhands, stevedores, interpreters, soldiers, clerks, and buying agents, while a few African elites held profitable positions as lawyers and merchants. The stereotypical Cape Coast African was an "Anglo Fante," a self-styled *krakyeni* (educated man), who adopted Eurocentric conceits of urbanity, while donning tailored suits and ten-guinea hats, or in the case of women, petticoats, chemises, and elegant footwear. In contrast, the nearby village of Ekumfi-Atwia was almost completely ostracized. Located a mere thirty-five miles northeast of Cape Coast, it was a landlocked community of subsistence farmers with little mineral wealth and thus a very low priority for colonial infrastructure investment. It was seen as the domain of unruly peasants—the *efurantamfo* (cloth wearers) who labored on farms and lived in the roughness of unrefined nativism.[1] By the start of the twentieth century, many Cape Coasters saw themselves as vastly superior to Africans living in villages such as Ekumfi-Atwia and viewed these rural inhabitants through the lens of their distance from the supposedly civilizing centers of Euro-Christian influence.

Ekumfi-Atwia remained sparsely populated at the time of Ghana's independence, consisting of no more than a few hundred residents who eked out a subsistence living and only occasionally traveled to nearby cities to sell some of the corn they grew on their farms. The almost complete lack of modern infrastructure in the village reinforced its image as an undeveloped backwater in the shadow of Cape Coast. Ghanaian academic and performer Sandy Arkhurst described his impressions upon visiting the area during the 1960s:

> Several sections of the regional capital [Cape Coast] had been built to impress and to provide comfort. The streets were wide and clean. Modern architecture, well-kept lawns and hedges, constant power-supply and ever-flowing water taps, several educational institutions and shopping centers were the hallmarks of Cape Coast.

Ekumfi-Atwia, however, provided a contrast that was "sharp as day and night":

> The buildings were close to each other, haphazardly arranged and interspaced with gullies caused by erosion, creating an unsightly artificial drainage system under some houses with the threats of sudden collapse of the wall. A rocky dirt road led to and around the village. The houses had roofs made of a combination of thatch, debris, and rotting roofing sheets. . . . Small bathrooms were seen with house drains developing into virtually stagnant, meandering offensive pools, which were left to breed mosquitoes.

Arkhurst adds that the only source of water in the village was a stream and that the city had no sewage disposal system, schools, or modern health facilities.[2]

THE HOUSE THAT EKUMFI-ATWIA BUILT: COMMUNITY MOBILIZATION AND MODERNIST EXPERIMENTATION

In the early 1960s, Nana Okoampa Baah IV ascended to the chieftaincy of the village of Ekumfi-Atwia. Finding herself the leader of a community immobilized by years of neglect and marginalization, Nana Baah tried to motivate the citizens to escape their poverty by embracing the spirit of independence and taking "matters into their own hands."[3] Nana Baah had previously gained a reputation throughout the region for her radio shows on Akan folklore, which featured her remarkable singing voice and her dexterity with proverbs, storytelling, and other oratorical skills. Fortuitously, one of her fans was the dramatist Efua Sutherland, and they became close friends. When Sutherland visited Nana Baah in Ekumfi-Atwia, she saw the chief participating in a spectacular folkloric procession. The dramatist soon became fascinated with the rich culture of oral storytelling that she encountered in the village, as well as its reenergized spirit of self-help. Sutherland would later recount that she "was so struck with that village" that she felt compelled to incorporate the experience into her artistic work.[4]

Sutherland was one of the principle playwrights of the Ghana National Theatre Movement during the 1950s and 1960s. As discussed in chapter 4, the movement sought to promote a modern and politically conscious art that could help Africans take pride in their native traditions and liberate themselves from internalized European discourses. Sutherland and her colleagues wanted to escape from Euro-centric representations and outlooks—in particular the assumptions of black cultural inferiority and the European ethos of competitive individualism—but these artists did not see themselves as traditionalists. Instead, they presented their work as part of the modernist avant-garde and sought to articulate an autochthonous African modernity that would be different from, but on par with, Europe's. In Ekumfi-Atwia, Sutherland found a source of inspiration for her explorations into community-oriented, non-European theater—and eventually a laboratory for enacting these modernist experiments.

Throughout her career, Sutherland had envisioned the creation of new African theater buildings as a tangible expression of her artistic goals. She was convinced that the proper studio design, based on traditional Ghanaian architecture, could be a vital part of offering a community-oriented and African-centric theatrical experience.[5] By 1960, Sutherland had obtained funding to create such a space in the Ghanaian capital of Accra. Drawing on her understanding that the central "courtyards" of traditional African homes are a focal point of creative activity and a crucible of community interaction, she developed a circular theater with a central stage, a building that she called the Ghana Experimental Drama Studio. Though satisfied with this achievement, by the late 1960s, Sutherland was determined to move her artistic experiments out of the country's metropolitan capital and into the cultural heartland. Thus, she headed for Ekumfi-Atwia, where local storytelling traditions and other folkloric riches remained vital enough to inspire and ground her modernist theatrical experiments. Sutherland asked Nana Baah if they could build a new theater together so Sutherland could collaborate with local performers. The chief welcomed this vision and even expanded it. Having already mobilized her people to build a new local school, Nana Baah suggested that the theater could be a similarly inspirational achievement. Sutherland and Nana Baah envisioned the structure as a community meeting center that would host a wide range of events and activities, from artistic productions to ceremonies, wakes, and official village gatherings.

Despite their enthusiasm for the project, Sutherland and Nana Baah knew that its success would depend on the villagers' willingness to get involved. After many years of being scorned by Westernized, urban Africans, the rural residents had a strong distrust for their interference in local affairs. Sutherland acknowledged the legitimacy of these suspicions, noting that city dwellers often come to study or profit from rural life but "much like Europeans, rarely remain to build and create." In fact, on her first day in the village, one resident remarked with suspicion, "What is this fine lady doing walking on our pebbles?"[6] It took more than fifty visits to the community with a team of college theater students from Accra before the villagers finally admitted to Sutherland that they had not been completely honest with her and were only recently beginning to believe her intentions were sincere. Once they decided to invest in the enterprise, however, the villagers wholeheartedly poured their enthusiasm into it, choosing a site for the building at the center of the community and providing labor to help complete its construction. As with Sutherland's Accra studio, the Kodzidan was designed as a circular auditorium with a stepped-down center stage, modeled after traditional African compound houses with their central community areas. Unlike standard European designs, this theater was deliberately constructed to encourage a sense of audience involvement and proximity with the performers on the stage.

One day, Sutherland overheard a local woman calling the project "Kodzidan," which means "the house of stories." That is how the theater got its name.

Sutherland put a great deal of thought into how she could combine traditional storytelling practices with modern theater. She wanted to draw strongly from traditional Anansesɛm practices such as *mboguo,* a convention in which audience members have the opportunity to interrupt and displace the primary storyteller by contributing their own performances and commentary. However, she recognized that the chaotic and open-ended nature of traditional Anansesɛm practice would not sit well with modern sensibilities—including her own artistic aspirations toward avant-garde compactness and technical precision. Furthermore, the leisurely pace and irregular timing of village Anansesɛm would be difficult if not impossible to extend to the larger theatrical audiences that she hoped to attract. Thus, Sutherland sought to transform and update conventional African aesthetics into a modern format, not to merely replicate the leisurely storytelling practices of village life, "where nobody cares how long you wait for the drummer while he has his bath."[7] In her Kodzidan productions Sutherland worked to retain the sense of excitement and community participation of traditional Anansesɛm but also to adapt these practices so they entailed less randomness and operated within a fixed time frame.

In order to enact this modernized version of Anansesɛm, Sutherland established a trained cadre of villagers in Ekumfi-Atwia, who rehearsed their planned "interruptions" of the primary storyteller. Described as "specialist performers," these locals were tasked with acting as an interface between conventional village practices and the expectations of modern audiences. They provided planned disruptions of the storytelling narrative and encouraged other audience members to share in their scripted songs and dances. Thus, the theater audiences were not full Anansesɛm participants in the conventional sense, but they did have the opportunity to engage with the trappings of an alternative African tradition that was radically distinct from European-derived performance expectations. If improvisation and audience participation are the hallmarks of Anansesɛm practice, then the Kodzidan experiment should be viewed as relying on the *impression* of Anansesɛm. Like magic shows in which audiences members are aware of the illusion but are there to enjoy the sleight of hand, these modernist experiments were effective due to the artifice of apparent randomness and scripted audience participation.

Nonetheless, it would be inaccurate to regard Sutherland's kodzi theater as a misappropriation of village traditions. Her modernist experiments at the Kodzidan were conducted in the spirit of full and patient collaboration with local performers and with the goal of enhancing the village's independence and self-sufficiency. Most important, these performances were not exploitative activities designed to enrich external profiteers, nor did they act to cannibalize, obscure, or eliminate more traditional folkloric forms. Instead, the modernist kodzi theater empowered local performers to share their traditions with a broader audience, while the profits from the endeavor were retained locally and reinvested in the community. Performance and folklore theorists have long recognized that living cultural traditions are never "pure" or stagnant and that it is inappropriate to confine villages like Ekumfi-Atwia to an idealized, ahistorical cultural position.[8] This is especially true when the villagers themselves aspire to more contemporary lifestyles and modes of expression.

In Ekumfi-Atwia, the local community came to unapologetically celebrate the Kodzidan as a collaborative product and to regard the modernist performances as just as valuable and authentic as traditional Anansesɛm. Linking their activities in the "house of stories" to the larger narratives of independence and African empowerment, they saw the theater as an opportunity to mobilize against their socioeconomic marginalization. The Kodzidan project helped to shift the image of Ekumfi-Atwia from an "undeveloped backwater" to a reservoir of alternative African values. In the process, the community was able to attract the kind of attention and infrastructure development that it had long been denied under the colonial regime. In 1967, Ekumfi-Atwia even became the subject of an American documentary film, *Araba: The Village Story*. Commentators noted the transformative effect that this local empowerment had for the community. In 1968, for example, E. O. Akyea wrote:

> A co-operative store started in the village as a result of performances.... A new block of buildings is being added to the school to make it more presentable. Atwia has become the "eye" of villages around, and a few of the young men in Accra have returned to inject some new life into the village.[9]

In subsequent years, Ekumfi-Atwia received government assistance to help combat a measles epidemic. The community also obtained pipe-borne water, additional funding for educational programs, and technical assistance to help local farmers grow pineapples.

A DIFFERENT STORY: THE KODZIDAN IN THE ERA OF NEOLIBERALISM

Roughly thirty years later, in July 1999, the Kodzidan conducted a special storytelling session for a visiting group of African Americans, which the author was fortunate enough to attend. At that time, the village's particular brand of modernist-inspired kodzi was rarely presented. Ghana's sharp economic downturn and political instability from the 1970s through the 1980s had all but eliminated public support for the project, and despite the promises of Rawlings's heritage tourism agenda, the village had seen little benefit. The draw of new urban jobs along with declining opportunities in Ekumfi-Atwia had lured away most of the local labor force, including many of the specialist performers. Efua Sutherland died in 1994, and celebrated storyteller chief Nana Baah Okoampah IV died in 1998, leaving the Kodzidan at a standstill.

The group of African Americans had traveled to Ghana for the First International Storytelling Conference (FISC). The main organizers of the conference were two African American storytellers: Therese Folkes Plair, a teacher from Westchester, New York, and Melissa Heckler, a school librarian from Croton, New York. Local support was provided by Esi Sutherland-Addy and the poet-folklorist Kofi Anyidoho, who at the time was the head of the English department at the University of Ghana. The goal of the FISC was to affirm the cultural ties between Ghanaians and the far-flung members of the African diaspora, particularly African Americans. In the conference information packet, the organizers described the event as a cultural gathering that would "celebrate and honor the oral collective history of people of African descent." Ekumfi-Atwia, a prominent destination in the group's itinerary, was described as a village "known for its rich oral traditions," and the recently deceased village chief was portrayed as "ardently dedicated to the preservation" of African culture.[10]

It was surprising to see the frequent references in the conference literature to the Kodzidan as a place where attendees could experience a "preserved" and "perpetual" African storytelling tradition. In effect, the Kodzidan's original goals of modernist theatrical experimentation and local development were completely omitted in favor of portrayal of the village as a timeless source of traditional Anansesεm. It is doubtful that the conference participants had any exceptionally naive illusions about the timeless "authenticity" of their cultural engagements in Africa.[11] It is interesting, however, how the narratives of African-centric modernity and rural development that were so central to the original creation of the Kodzidan were now deemed irrelevant.

The group arrived by bus at Ekumfi-Atwia in the late afternoon. A crowd of locals had gathered by a pile of timber logs on the outskirts of the village—singing, waving cloths, and moving around in a feet-shuffling dance of welcome. They approached the bus en masse and led the group to the Kodzidan. No doubt this aura of traditional authenticity that camouflaged a staged and originally avant-garde theatrical performance was related to Rawlings's promotion of heritage tourism.

Throughout the 1990s, Ghanaian cultural programs such as the Kodzidan had shifted their outlook. They were scrambling to reimage themselves in ways that would appeal to international visitors and foreign investors. The attitudes promoted by the regime had filtered down throughout Ghanaian society and become relevant for any cultural performers who hoped to attract funding and public attention. And the shape of these attitudes was one that positioned African culture as politically inert—a timeless tradition to be observed, preserved, and stylistically appreciated but not seen as directly relevant to modern institutions (in other words, exactly the opposite of what the Kodzidan's founders had in mind).

A TWO-STEP SHUFFLE: THE POTENTIALS AND PROBLEMS OF FOREIGN DIRECT INVESTMENT

Today, foreign direct investment (FDI) is one of the largest sources of external financing for developing countries. As a category of investment, it describes situations in which an organization or individual with

residency in one country establishes a lasting financial interest in a business enterprise that is registered in a different country.[12] Those who support FDI argue that it creates local employment opportunities and enables
the transfer of resources, knowledge, and skills into less-developed parts
of the world, while helping to integrate the host country into the international economy. Skeptics, in contrast, regard FDI as a form of neocolonial
exploitation in which foreign interests control the development process
for the sake of their own profit, while eroding public safety nets and exerting an undue influence over the domestic policies of local governments.
Regardless of these concerns, the global prevalence of FDI increased tre-
mendously throughout the 1980s and 1990s, from US$58 billion in 1985 to
US$1.4 trillion in 2000. In sub-Saharan Africa, the annual inflow of FDI
rose from an average of US$1.3 billion during the 1980s to US$4.3 billion
during the 1990s.[13]

These increases in FDI reflected the neoliberal policy changes that were
enacted during the 1980s and 1990s by many African regimes, including
the Rawlings regime in Ghana. By reducing economic regulations, remov-
ing legal barriers against the repatriation of profits to other countries, offering tax breaks to large investors, and divesting numerous state-owned
enterprises into the private sector, African governments scrambled to
make their countries more appealing to foreign capital. The regimes also
struggled to overcome the historic European image of Africa that broadly
associates the entire continent with civil unrest and disorder, hastening
to reassure investors that their countries could now provide a stable and
welcoming climate in which profits would flow.[14] In practice, this often
meant brutally subduing local opposition, as was the case during Ghana's
Kum-me-preko protests (discussed in chapter 3). Despite these efforts,
neoliberal African regimes faced an uphill battle to both convince investors that they could find stable returns in Africa and convince local populations to accept the influx of foreign capital.

It is a basic fact that Africa does not have a history of comfortably
accepting FDI. Deep-seated sentiments against foreign investment are
rooted in the history, ideology, and politics of the colonial era and the subsequent African independence movements. The historical association that
Africans perceive between foreign economic investment and exploitative
foreign political control was heightened by the top-down manner in which

neoliberal policy changes were enacted during the 1980s. Many Africans
continue to hold firmly to the moral belief that their leaders should be
protecting the local economy and taking a proactive role in helping to
provide for the common welfare, rather than forcing unpopular economic
policies onto the population. Even as African regimes turned increasingly
toward the short-term fix of foreign capital, many prominent political figures remained "unrepentant" state-centrists or, at best, unwilling converts
to economic liberalism. There remained a strong belief in Africa that FDI
was exploitative—that it created a strongly uneven playing field in which
domestic enterprises would be unable to compete, leaving Africans in
a position of dependency as the benefits of their labors went to enrich
foreign profiteers.[15]

Ghana is a paradigmatic case of the torturous relationship that many
African countries have had with foreign direct investment. Even during
the post-independence Nkrumah years, when the narratives of economic
protection and African-centrism were at their height, the government surreptitiously attempted to entice foreign capital into the country. Ghana's
first premier offered a ten-year tax holiday to international investors, and
his Capital Investment Act of 1963 provided a variety of additional incentives.[16] In contrast, after the right-leaning NLC military coup deposed
Nkrumah, its leaders struggled to further expand the role of FDI due to
widespread public resistance. The resurgence of socialist-based programs
under Colonel Acheampong's regime in the mid-1970s led to the seizure of
existing foreign assets in the country—and yet even that government soon
found itself returning to international capital, quietly enacting incentives
in 1973 and 1975 in an attempt to lure investors back.

And so it went, in a kind of back-and-forth, two-step shuffle, as governments tried to balance the value of ready cash from investors against
the long-term issues of economic dependency and public unrest. Rawlings himself, prior to the 1980s, had often expressed a radical suspicion
of foreign capital.[17] After consolidating power, however, he proceeded to
enact some of the most far-reaching economic policy changes in Ghana's
history, opening the country to FDI and ultimately selling off the majority
of state-owned enterprises to foreign investors (as is discussed in more
detail in chapter 1). In 1994, the regime established an official agency,
the Ghana Investment Promotion Center, which was dedicated solely to

informing international financiers about the now-comprehensive array of tax incentives, duty exemptions, and investment guarantees that the country offered to help ensure that money would flow readily into—and out of—the country.

A NEW SECTOR ARISES: THE GROWTH OF TOURISM AND THE QUANDARY OF FDI LEGITIMATION

As the Rawlings regime steadfastly pursued its agenda of economic liberalization during the 1980s and 1990s, the country's tourism sector began to emerge as a principle locus of foreign investment. This was not surprising; in a global context, tourism is one of the world's major industries, surpassed only by petroleum and vehicle production in terms of its economic impact at that time. By 1995, it generated more jobs worldwide than any other industry.[18] The international market prices for Ghana's traditional commodity exports had declined steeply throughout the 1970s and 1980s, but the worldwide tourism industry continued to expand, offering an alternative source of revenue. Furthermore, Ghana's tourism potential was significantly undeveloped. The country's earlier regimes had made some effort to invest in extravagant hotels and related facilities, but years of political and economic instability had brought tourism prospects to a virtual standstill. This left plenty of room for foreign investors to step in and create a growth industry—as long as Rawlings could convince potential investors and tourists that Ghana was a desirable destination.

The year 1985 was a remarkable turning point for tourism development in Ghana. In that year, Rawlings's military regime identified tourism as one of its four priority areas and enacted a policy specifically calling for foreign investment in hotels and resorts. Deteriorating tourist facilities that once operated at a loss under government management were auctioned off to international companies, which quickly began to renovate them to contemporary standards. Meanwhile, the government removed foreign currency exchange controls, resulting in a drastic devaluation of the Ghanaian cedi. This decimated the purchasing power of local earners, much to their chagrin, but at the same time it made Ghana a more affordable destination for international travelers. The regime established a

Ministry of Tourism to oversee and promote development as the industry quickly expanded to become the fastest-growing sector of the country's economy. Tourist arrivals to Ghana increased from a mere 85,000 in 1985 to 325,400 in 1997, raising receipts from $20 million to $266 million over the twelve-year period.[19]

Despite this economic growth, the regime was confronted with a skeptical public that remained largely unconvinced that the changes were in the best interest of Ghana's people. In some ways, the tourist industry acted as a visible symbol of the influx of foreign interests, as well as foreign capital, into the country. Various analysts and stakeholders attempted to navigate these concerns, often expressing both excitement and trepidation as they enacted the old "two-step shuffle" of the country's ambivalent relationship with FDI. On one hand, it was frequently noted that FDI inflows for tourism continued to lag behind the amounts that Ghana could potentially absorb based on the projected growth of the industry. Some described the current FDI as "woefully inadequate," insisting that it must be encouraged with even more tax rebates and incentives for foreign investors.[20] On the other hand, industry analysts bemoaned that much of the profit from these endeavors was "leaking"—that is, being repatriated out of the country by foreign stakeholders—and that local employees continued to receive poor remuneration.[21] One analyst, epitomizing this shuffle, stated:

> Given the increasing rate of foreign ownership to tourist and other infrastructure, there is a real danger of most of the gains from tourism being repatriated out of the country. . . . While any radical steps at retaining tourism earnings [i.e., regulating the outflow of profits] will go against the very principles of encouraging foreign investments, failure to implement policies of income retention will ultimately harm the very objective of promoting tourism as a vehicle for earning foreign currency.[22]

In other words, Ghanaians found themselves as economic hostages in relation to foreign investment. Any attempt to regulate the industry so that its benefits would be fairly shared by locals would result in financially powerful backers withdrawing their support.

Like other neoliberal African leaders, Rawlings had to work hard, both at boosting the confidence of external investors and at overcoming (or at least appeasing) the entrenched local objections against FDI. As late as 1990, when most of his economic reforms had already been enacted, Rawlings made the following recalcitrant remark:

> But I am obliged to state and to emphasize that we cannot tolerate foreign investors who think that because Ghana is a small developing nation, they can arrogantly throw their weight around, bribe petty functionaries to cut corners with regard to necessary producers, or even combine a little profitable gold or diamond smuggling with their business trips.[23]

Rawlings's neoliberal agenda—and, in particular, his concessions to domestic policy changes demanded by the International Monetary Fund and the World Bank—exposed him to charges of prioritizing foreign interests above the needs and desires of Ghanaians. He was left struggling to find ways to continue the two-step shuffle, to acknowledge local disaffection even as he continued to work at attracting foreign capital. We have seen in previous chapters how Rawlings turned to a stylistic appropriation of African-centric cultural rhetoric in order to undermine and confuse opponents of his Western-looking economic agenda. As the tourism economy grew to be a central locus of foreign investment in Ghana, it was natural that this cultural rhetoric should extend to forging a link between the growth of tourism and the honoring of African traditions.

"BACK TO AFRICA": HERITAGE TOURISM AND THE BLACK DIASPORA

Starting in the late 1980s, heritage, or "roots"-related, travel emerged as a key element in Ghana's development strategy. This heritage tourism occurs in the context of a long history of literal and virtual returns to the continent by Africans in the diaspora. From the 1700s on, African Americans such as Prince Hall, Paul Cuffe, Daniel Coker, John Russwurm, Martin Delany, and Marcus Garvey expressed a longing for Africa and devised various resettlement schemes in the hopes of return. In addition to providing a sense of identity and belonging in the midst of a society that denied their humanity, the idea of Africa was held by these luminaries as a place where they would finally have the opportunity to live comfortably among equals. This was not a naive or idle dream but rather a politically trenchant conviction that by pooling together the political and economic strength of black people both within and outside of Africa, they could speed the destruction of American slavery, negate ideas of black inferiority, and put an end to European imperial occupation and exploitation.

Efforts were also made on the other side of the Atlantic to facilitate African Americans' return to the continent. In 1913, Chief Alfred Sam of the Gold Coast (now Ghana) saw an opportunity for a commercial sea venture to ferry black Americans back to Africa. He organized large camp-style meetings in Oklahoma, where he portrayed West Africa as a haven where blacks could live a life of freedom and urged them to buy passage there by purchasing stock in his company. Sixty people traveled with Sam to the Gold Coast, though the problems they encountered there prevented 500 others who had been planning to do the same from taking the journey.[24] Such shady adventures aside, it is important to note that there was a very sincere interest among black Africans for forging political and cultural connections with the members of the diaspora. In the early twentieth century, Ghanaian newspapers began to publish feature articles on leading African American entertainers, reporting on developments in the Harlem Renaissance and covering the careers of Paul Robeson, Louis Armstrong, Coleman Hawkins, Ethel Waters, and Noble Sissle. Colonial Ghanaians were interested in studying and emulating black American artists, especially as African opposition against the European authorities began to solidify. Ghanaian newspapers published editorials on discrimination laws in England and stories about the economic exploitation of blacks in the United States and the West Indies. They connected Jim Crow laws in the United States and the color bar in England to the subjugation of Africans locally. Ghanaians obtained insights about the larger black world from publications deemed seditious by colonial authorities, such as the Paris-based *Negro Worker* and Marcus Garvey's *Negro World*.[25]

Correspondingly, the independence movements in Africa were celebrated by black-owned newspapers in the diaspora, which ran features on the newly independent African states. Ghana in particular held a special place in the African American imagination as a symbol of black self-worth and political accomplishment. The *Pittsburgh Courier* carried a full schedule of Ghana's independence celebrations. Its articles described a mutual admiration between African Americans and Ghanaians, while pointing out that the "ancestors of most American Negroes" came from the region of West Africa and that the new nation of Ghana was a "spearhead for the liberation of black Africa."[26] The *Chicago Defender* likewise noted that it was from Ghana "that slaves in chains were brought to America" and predicted that "someday black men from Ghana may stand before the UN and plead the case for American Negroes and be the cause for their winning complete equality."[27] American newspapers also published reports of prominent African Americans who traveled to participate in Ghana's celebrations, including Ralph Bunche, Martin Luther King Jr., and Adam Clayton Powell. One paper even held an essay contest with an all-expense-paid trip to Ghana as the prize.[28]

Interest in traveling to Ghana—for a vacation or to live there permanently—swelled in the United States during the Nkrumah years. This was fueled in part by the Ghanaian premier's frequent visits to the United States. Nkrumah felt a strong connection with black Americans, having lived in the United States from 1935 to 1945, where he studied and then taught at the historically black Lincoln University. In return, the premier's charisma and conviction made a deep impression on many African Americans. In 1958, Nkrumah arrived in Harlem and was greeted by a 10,000-strong crowd who lined the streets and cheered him as he rode past in an open car decked with Ghana's colors and accompanied by a forty-five-piece brass band. Nkrumah invited teachers, technicians, lawyers, doctors, engineers, artists, activists, and entrepreneurs from the United States to come to Africa and help with postcolonial reconstruction. His influence, and that of black-owned newspapers, inspired numerous African Americans to make the journey across the Atlantic. Unfortunately, this historical moment vanished amid the 1966 coup that deposed Nkrumah and the subsequent decades of political and economic turmoil. It was not until Rawlings's neoliberal tourism incentives in the 1980s and 1990s that African Americans would once again start to visit Ghana in significant numbers.

In the Rawlings era, the return to Africa was perhaps unavoidably infused with a subtly different tone, in comparison with the political optimism of the 1960s. Although the same histories, images, and cultural benchmarks remained as motivating factors, this cultural heritage in Africa was now permeated more with an aura of the past rather than the future. Visitors were primarily drawn by the European forts and castles built between the fifteenth and eighteenth centuries along Ghana's coastline. Notorious for the dungeons in which the Europeans held slaves before they were shipped to the New World, these structures are now sites of somber memories that can still evoke pride in the resilience and survival of black ancestors.[29] Basically, they are sites of pilgrimage. As one African American emigrant put it, returning to the dungeons is "a necessary act of self-realization" because "the spirits of the diaspora are somehow tied to these historic structures."[30]

Within the modern neoliberal economy, such attractions become the supply side of tourism. They translate into economic value. Therefore, when Ghana began to court the African diaspora to its shores, it presented opportunities for pilgrimage with a mind—at least partly—to the much-needed currency that these visits would bring into the country. Basically, the country deployed a "neoliberal pan-Africanism," made up of discourses of slavery and emancipation that recalled Africa and the African diaspora's shared heritage to, among other things, attract foreign investment in Ghana's increasingly market-centered economy.[31] Tourism is a competitive market that calls for the strategic leveraging of one's attractions. Of the forty or so remaining colonial forts in West Africa, twenty-nine are in Ghana (three as UNESCO-designated World Heritage Sites), making them one of the most comparatively advantageous tourist attractions in the country. Their draw spills over and intermingles with other, somewhat less-competitive, sites such as architectural commemorations to Ghana's independence, mausoleums and memorials of pan-African figures, and cultural events such as festivals, concerts, and theater.

Rawlings, along with a host of international investors, used these sites to intentionally leverage the cultural-historical bond between Ghana and the diaspora for economic purposes. The African diaspora was, in Rawlings's words, "a force to reckon with."[32] It had purchasing power, and, perhaps just as important, it could provide international validation and a cultural justification for Rawlings's tourism development projects. Thus, the emphasis on heritage tourism in the Rawlings regime was at least a three-level strategy. One level was to affirm the diaspora's rightful sense of kinship with Africa and thereby bring money and international affirmation to the country. A second, more cynical level, however, was to confirm to foreign investors that neoliberal Ghana could tap into a broad international tourist base and thereby provide a steady return in corporate profits. Finally, at the third level, through his stylistic show of cultural pan-Africanism, Rawlings sought to give foreign investment a more palatable face in order to quell prevailing trepidations about alien control over the Ghanaian economy.

"UNITING THE AFRICAN FAMILY": FROM PANAFEST TO FISC

Ghana's renewed appeal to the African diaspora culminated in the Pan-African Historical Festival (PANAFEST), a veritable showcase of cultural heritage that has been held every two years since 1992. The festival attracts large numbers of international visitors to the country and features a heavy emphasis on traditional customs and practices. Tours are conducted to the old European forts and castles, especially at Cape Coast and Elmina. The event also encompasses rituals of connection and commemoration, such as candlelight processions, nondenominational church services, traditional rites of reunion, and wreath-laying ceremonies. After helping to inaugurate PANAFEST in 1992, Rawlings embarked on an ongoing quest to identify his administration with the theme of international black unity. In 1993, in a speech before the assembly of the fifty-two nations of the Organization of African Unity (OAU), he described the African diaspora as people who "possess a genuine commitment to . . . [Africa's] development." Rawlings proposed that representatives from the diaspora should be granted observer status at the OAU and should be allowed to contribute to discussions of African economic issues.[33]

In 1995, Rawlings traveled to the United States to receive an honorary degree from Lincoln University in what, by then, had become one of his many acts of following in Nkrumah's footsteps. The president of Lincoln University, Niara Sudarkasa, confirmed this explicitly, stating that Rawlings "has effectively taken the mantle" of Nkrumah in Ghana.[34] In that spirit, Rawlings also visited Harlem, where he affirmed the legacy of Nkrumah as a cultural bond between the Ghanaian state and black America. In Harlem, Rawlings promised that he would give African Americans legal right-of-abode in Ghana so they could "feel in the very soul that Africa is indeed" their mother continent. He noted, however, that black Americans should only visit Ghana if they have money or skills to offer; otherwise, they "would only contribute to Africa's poverty."[35] Rawlings went on to attend a gala night in Los Angeles, where the artists Michael Jackson, Stevie Wonder, and Isaac Hayes performed. He told the audience, consisting mostly of Californian businesspeople and financiers, that he would welcome their interest in Ghana's mining, manufacturing, agriculture, and tourism sectors.

In the years that followed, Rawlings's courtship of the diaspora continued to gain steam. In 1997, he attended a celebration of Emancipation Day in Jamaica, a commemoration of the August 1, 1834, liberation of slaves in the British colonies. On his return, Rawlings issued a directive that beginning that year, Emancipation Day would be celebrated in Ghana as well. The celebration would be under the auspices of the Ministry of Tourism, and the Actors Guild and the National Dance Ensemble would perform reenactments of the slaving raids that had taken place for centuries. In May 1999, Rawlings hosted the Fifth African–African American Summit in Accra. Explicitly described as a "business and investment promotion exercise," this gathering hosted over 7,000 participants. Along with Rawlings and twelve other African heads of state, the summit was attended by U.S. Secretary of Labor Alexis Herman, black activist Jesse Jackson, former ambassador to the UN and ex-mayor of Atlanta Andrew Young, Nation of Islam Minister Louis Farrakhan, leader of the Black Caucus of American Mayors Wellington Webb, and many other black mayors and ministers.[36] The conference focused on international investment and the development of the agricultural, telecommunications, finance, energy, and tourism sectors in Africa. One outgrowth of this meeting was the inauguration of the People's Investment Fund for Africa, a financial vehicle for Americans to purchase an interest in small-business operations in Ghana and other African countries. Another result was a partnership between Ghana's Ministry of Tourism and the U.S. State of Georgia's Department of Industry, Trade, and Tourism, to combine their efforts in promoting black heritage travel across the Atlantic.

Barely a month after Ghana hosted the African–African American Summit, the First International Storytelling Conference was held. The organizers of the conference had timed the event to correspond with Ghana's peak tourism period (July to August) so the American delegates would be able to participate in Ghana's Emancipation Day and PANAFEST celebrations. The FISC itinerary also included pilgrimages to the coastal forts at Elmina and Cape Coast, a visit to the historical kente-weaving town at Bonwire, nubility ceremonies at Ejisu and Krobo-Odumase, and, finally, an African storytelling performance at the Kodzidan in Ekumfi-Atwia. The African tales described in the following sections were included.

THE STORIES OF EKUMFI-ATWIA

It is dusk in the village of Ekumfi-Atwia. Modest fluorescent lights on the walls combine with the brighter bulbs of a video crew to illuminate the Kodzidan. In the central arena of this community theater, the storyteller, a woman of about fifty-five years, sways elegantly to the rhythm of the song she is singing. She wears a blue wax-print *kaba* blouse, a matching ankle-length skirt, a waist-wrap patterned with a bright brown motif, and dangling gold earrings. She wields a carved wooden staff that is red from its base upward and blue at the top; mounted on it is the red-painted carving of a spider. She shares the stage with a younger man who is wearing a brown outfit. He plays castanets on his fingers and dances as he leads the surrounding audience in a rousing chorus of greeting and welcome. Soon the chorus ends (PURL 5.1). The man returns to his position in the audience, and the storytelling commences:

> STORYTELLER: Ananse stories are not to be believed.
>
> AUDIENCE: They are to be received for keeping.

The place grows quiet. The storyteller, looking around, announces her tale—"how women's co-wife rivalry came into the world." Upon her announcement, a short, baldheaded elder, likely in his midsixties, steps out of the audience and raises a tune. He walks to the stage and is joined by three others as they lead the throng in a chorus. Finally, the stage clears except for the storyteller, who begins:

> Once upon a time, a certain man lived with his wife, Abena, with whom he had been married for thirty years without issue. Then one day the man, a hunter, brought home an antelope he had killed in his hunt. He cut and

prepared the meat, but saved one thigh and hung it on the kitchen wall, where it stayed days after the couple had finished eating the rest of the meat.

A cry issues from somewhere in the audience. A young man, about twenty-five, dashes onto the stage. He wears brown trousers and a white shirt with rolled-up long sleeves; he has white powder on his face. For a minute or so, he leaps about acrobatically in the manner of one trying to catch an intruding lizard, and then he exits to the audience's applause (PURL 5.2). After patiently waiting through this interruption, the storyteller continues:

> The couple discovered that an unidentified helper was doing the household chores and fixing breakfast for them. The hunter, therefore, decided to keep a nightly vigil to find out the identity of this anonymous benefactor.

The man with the finger castanets now returns to the stage and interrupts the storyteller with a song. He leads the audience in another chorus, this one addressing an unknown woman named Mansa:

> MAN WITH CASTANETS: Ei! Mansa! Keep tight-lipped! Keep tight-lipped, Mansa!

He exits the stage after the song ends (PURL 5.3).

> STORYTELLER: The hunter discovered, much to his amazement, that it was the antelope-thigh he had hung on the wall that turned into a beautiful woman and did the morning chores. As this antelope-thigh woman worked in the house, she looked around now and then to see if either the hunter or Abena was present.

The storyteller leans out and looks pointedly to the left and to the right, miming the antelope-thigh woman's movement. She begins a song, and the audience joins in with the chorus.

> STORYTELLER (singing): My eyes are cast to this side, my ears are cast to that side; I check to see if the owners are coming. (She then resumes her narration.) The hunter came out of hiding. Caught, the antelope-thigh woman explained that she had been doing the chores out of sympathy for the couple, who had no one to help them about the house. The hunter, struck by her beauty, begged her to stay human and to be his junior wife. The antelope-thigh woman refused the request, saying that

she was afraid the hunter would not be able to keep her animal origins
a secret.

INTERJECTION FROM AUDIENCE: Were you there?

STORYTELLER: Indeed, I was present! (*She continues after laughter in the
crowd clears.*) The antelope-thigh woman finally agreed to the hunter's
proposal upon his promise of secrecy.

A loud moan issues from someone in the audience. A bare-chested man
with white markings on his skin, a cover-cloth around his waist, and a
rag on his head staggers into the central arena, scratching himself in the
manner of one afflicted with a terrible itch. He initiates a chorus with the
audience, during which he does an amusing body-scratch dance, running
his fingers over his loins and backside. Overwhelmed by the itch, he strips
off his cover-cloth to reveal an absurd set of underwear: a thin, red cloth
over a ragged loincloth, both over dark, worn-out trousers. He dashes out
of the arena, leaving the audience rocking with laughter (PURL 5.4). The
storyteller resumes her performance:

> The hunter announced to his wife, Abena, that the young woman would be
> staying with them. Abena grew displeased, particularly when the hunter
> started dishing out a significant share of their property to the newcomer.
> Abena demanded to know from whence this new wife had come. The
> hunter, contrary to his earlier promise of secrecy to the antelope-thigh
> woman, disclosed her animal origins to his wife.

A young man, likely in his midtwenties, calls out frantically and runs into
the arena. He tells the audience that he was traveling with a chief but got
lost. He requests directions. Someone in the audience suggests that the
young man must answer a riddle in exchange for directions. The man
hesitates, saying that riddles must not be performed gratuitously, but eventually he obliges, asking to be given timely warning should the audience
see the chief approaching. He then draws out an orange stick and, beating
rhythmically on both ends, poses the riddle:

> Consumer-of-waters, Spirit-sea, Consumer-of-waters
> If you cannot handle chieftaincy
> Then resign! Resign! Resign!
> For chieftaincy is a harsh experience.

The man launches into a rhythmic chorus with the audience, all the time dancing in the arena. Then, in a manner suggesting that the chief has come into sight, he dashes offstage (PURL 5.5). The storyteller continues:

> One day, while sweeping the house, the antelope-thigh woman happened to brush Abena's foot with her broom. In the ensuing dispute, Abena called the young woman "a mere antelope thigh."

The storyteller initiates a chorus with the audience, singing Abena's words: "I happened to discover, she is nothing but an antelope's thigh." After the song ends, she continues:

> The new wife, realizing the hunter's betrayal, turned back into an antelope's thigh. Displeased, the hunter scolded Abena, declaring, "You women and your marital rivalry, you will never be rid of it!" And that is how co-wife rivalry came into the world! (PURL 5.6)

Having completed her tale, the storyteller steps aside, and an extended session of music and dance commences.

Ultimately another man, about thirty-five years old and dressed in cloth draped around one shoulder, receives the carved staff with the spider motif (an indication that he is next in line for telling a story). As the music and dance come to a close, he announces, "I am going to tell a story about why Oweah, the tree bear, cries out over the treachery of woman." At this, a jovial murmur of protest issues from some in the audience. He ignores them and, with a grin, sets out to begin his performance. But before he can get started, a man from the audience enters the arena with the greeting "Agoo!," and the entire audience responds, "Ameee!" The interloper is dressed in fine cloth and a turban-like headpiece, and he strides with the gravitas of an important elder. A teenage girl follows him, carrying his chair.

> MAN: What's going on here?
>
> AUDIENCE: We are telling stories!
>
> MAN: Good. I'll join you, then!

He begins a call-and-response song with the audience, in which he is endlessly dissatisfied with wherever the teenager places his chair:

> MAN: Child, bearer of my chair . . .
>
> AUDIENCE: Place it here (*she puts it down*).

MAN (*pointing somewhere else*): Place it there! Place it there!

AUDIENCE: Place it there (*she puts it down where the man directed*).

MAN (*pointing somewhere else*): Place it here! Place it here!

This continues until the interloper and his hapless chair-bearer have worked their way completely out of the arena (PURL 5.7). The new storyteller now begins his narration.

> STORYTELLER: All the animals of the forest gathered together and made an agreement to publicly disclose their secret *mmrane* [an identity-poem; a personal accolade extended into poetry] so that their poem may be recited in memoriam on the occasion of their death. However, Oweah the tree bear refused to make the disclosure, not even to his own wife.
>
> INTERJECTION FROM AUDIENCE: What was her name?
>
> STORYTELLER: Aba 'Weah. And many times Aba 'Weah asked Oweah to disclose his mmrane to her, each time without success. She tried hard, begged and coaxed, until Owea finally promised the disclosure to her alone.

At this point the storyteller recites Oweah's private accolade:

> Simpi, Simpi, Simpi Akwa. It is at the brink of day, Simpi Akwa
> Oweah, Kofi Ampong, thick-skinned, hardy one
> I say, I hide above, speaking for the nation to hear
> Give some service to Chief 'Kow
> For Owea has flown up unto the trees!

The storyteller then continues with her narration:

> Unbeknownst to Oweah, his wife had asked Hare, the sharp-eared messenger drummer for all the animals, to eavesdrop upon the disclosure. So at the next meeting of animals, when Oweah still refused to disclose his mmrane, Hare asked for a drum and then recited the secret poem for all to hear in drum language.

Just when the storyteller is about to perform the results of Hare's revelation, a young man steps out of the audience into the arena. "Make way for the Chief!" he cries. "I am a chief from Asante-land. Make way for the Chief!" This sets the audience to laughing, as chiefs usually have path-clearing heralds and do not personally announce their own royalty.

Moreover, Asante royalty are known for their luxuriant apparel and accoutrements, but this man wears flip-flops and the plain cloth of a commoner. As the contradiction between his claim to royalty and his drab appearance becomes comically obvious, he begins to sing:

> MAN: Poverty has ravaged me!
>
> AUDIENCE: Poverty has ravaged me!

It quickly becomes apparent that even this modest attire is borrowed. An audience member walks in and claims his flip-flops, while the rest resume the chorus, "Poverty has ravished me!" Another steps into the arena and claims his handkerchief. Yet another walks in and claims the very cloth on his back, resulting in a struggle in which the mendicant chief is stripped to his undershorts. He runs out of the space to the delight of the audience, especially the children in the front seats (PURL 5.8). Finally, the storyteller returns to his narrative:

> Realizing his wife's betrayal, a very upset Owea decided to hide away on a huge tree nearby. As he climbed up, he met Osebo, the leopard, who tried to grab him but merely detached his tail. Finding his tail detached, and regretting his wife's betrayal, Owea shook his head and cried, "Oh, the treachery of woman!"[37]

A round of music begins, and somewhere in the middle of it, a woman with an extended headscarf, a white-powdered face, a padding-accentuated backside, and a walking stick walks slowly onto the stage. (This is a typical comic representation of "Nana Abrewa," the centuries-old woman who frequently appears in Anansesɛm and whose oddity often belies her wisdom.)

> NANA ABREWA: My entire family is already dead.

Her comic facial expressions and vocal exaggerations set the audience laughing at what would otherwise be a horribly sad announcement. The old woman then starts calling out for her son, Kwarteng, whom she apparently believes is in the audience, all the while singing and receiving an audience response:

> NANA ABREWA: Kwarteng! Death does not make you sad?
>
> AUDIENCE: Kwarteng...

NANA ABREWA: Death does not make you sad?

AUDIENCE: Kwarteng!

As she sings, she makes motions as if she is repeatedly scooping water into a basket. Several women, one after the other, emerge to announce to her that Kwarteng is in fact dead, but Nana Abrewa appears hard of hearing, can't understand what they are saying, and continues to call out for her son. Finally, one of the women gets the message across to her and she wails, comically.

NANA ABREWA: My child, Kwarteng, is dead! (PURL 5.9)

A round of music and dance, with general audience participation, ends the set of stories performed by Ekumfi-Atwia for the visitors.

THE RETURN OF THE TRICKSTER

As the preceding performance was taking place, a subordinate drama played out, at first almost unnoticed by some in the audience. While the first storyteller spoke about the antelope-thigh woman's discovery, a young girl from the village, no more than five years old, walked into the central arena. The storyteller continued on with her performance, paying little attention to the girl. However, a few elderly locals in the front row attempted to shoo her away from the stage. The girl stood and observed the storyteller, seemingly oblivious to the subtle commotion that she was causing. Several elders looked discomfited by her breach of protocol and her attempts to draw attention to herself in the middle of the performance! Were her actions deliberate? Ignoring the elders who were trying to wave her off, the girl commenced to wander leisurely across the stage, making herself more visible. Then, as suddenly as she had walked into the arena, she was gone, merging back to the audience and watching the storytelling as if nothing had happened.

To appreciate the girl's actions, however, we must remember that the spirit of Anansesɛm is one of continual narrative revision and multivocal creativity. It is a tradition in which social expectations and authorial definitions are always open to question. The fanciful mboguo interruptions that were presented by the villagers in the preceding performance are *apparently* anarchic and transgressive examples of this kind of narrative interruption; however, being mostly rehearsed, they are in some sense dead examples. The young girl's spontaneous walk across the stage, in contrast, is an organic, living example of mboguo. It created an ironic and revealing counterpoint against the expectations of the event's participants and caused at least some of us to reevaluate our ongoing narrative. It revealed the ways in which we had given ourselves over to an illusion of improvisation and full participation. As such, the author looks at this young girl's interruption as a reemergence of the original, chaotic spirit of the Anansesem tradition in the midst of the forces that attempted to pacify and confine it.

If Anansesem is an embodiment of the spider-trickster's open-endedness and multivocal spirit, then the Kodzidan created by Efua Sutherland and the villagers of Ekumfi-Atwia during the 1960s was a reasonable attempt to engage with this spirit in an innovative, forward-looking, and collaborative fashion. The static, historical-preservationist framework that was later overwritten onto this theater for the purposes of neoliberal tourism was something else entirely. It leaned much more strongly toward a univocal, externally imposed narrative that sought to constrain and objectify the spirit of Ananse as an economic commodity. Seeking to capture the trickster in this fashion is a risky venture, to say the least. Ananse is a ceaselessly countervailing force that eternally reaffirms the open-endedness of life. The impulse of this spirit can always find new ways to transcend the stale constrictions of attempted ideological closure and remind us, as William Hynes said, that "every construct is constructed."[38]

What else can we take away from this young girl's actions? One factor that has limited our dialogue about the circular traffic of history and memory between African and African diaspora cultures is that the inescapable economic dimensions of this engagement sometimes take on the quality of an untouchable subject—as if perhaps the genuine interest in our shared cultural heritage is somehow rendered insincere by an association with material interests. Paula Ebron has addressed the uneasy place of commerce in discussions about heritage, explaining that it is all too easy to fall into "a utopic vision . . . that one could go back to someplace outside the economic system." Perhaps, she suggests, it is time to remind ourselves of the intertwined relationship between culture and economy and to confront difficult questions about how our shared cultural goals and consciousness-raising can be better reflected in our commercial strategies.[39]

It is important to recognize that the people of Ekumfi-Atwia were not passive subjects blindly forced into the historical-preservationist framework. They embraced this paradigm because they believed that it was the best way to attract the interest of international visitors. Tourism in Ghana relies on the enthusiastic participation of the private sector, and by the late 1990s, many local enterprises were actively seeking to carve out a niche in the industry. There continues to be a slow-growing but recognizable trend of African communities becoming aware of the benefits of tourism and working to develop local attractions at least partly on their own initiatives. (Some of the most active examples of this work are in the areas of ecotourism and natural crafts—villages specializing in kente fabrics, woodcarvings, and similar items.) Although they often lack the promotional resources that are available to large, internationally funded endeavors, many local communities have been able to support livelihoods from small and micro-tourism businesses and have funded community projects out of the proceeds from tourist trade.[40]

Nonetheless, even local entrepreneurial tourism will always be constrained by the intersections of agency between locals and visitors—and between micro- and macro-economic interests. Just as Africa competes with the rest of the world for foreign direct investment and Ghana competes with other West African countries for heritage tourists, Ekumfi-Atwia competes with other communities throughout Ghana that might hold an attraction for international visitors. In these market dynamics, it is almost always the case that the more economically marginal entities must make way for the interests and presumptions of those with purchasing power. In the case of heritage tourism, this often means curtailing any unsettling or potentially disruptive aspects of one's cultural commodities and being careful to position them in a way that will render them harmlessly distant and confined in the historical-preservationist sense. It was, after all, no external authority or investor who attempted to remove the young girl from the Kodzidan stage; it was the villagers themselves who nervously tried to shoo her away. Seeking a new socioeconomic lease on life through heritage tourism, the performers and other individuals of

Ekumfi-Atwia had no incentive to make the experimentally modified nature of Kodzidan storytelling obvious to the visiting FISC delegates. Instead, they chose to embrace the preservationist frame with their own masquerade—until the spirit of the trickster returned to seek its revenge and expose their commercial strategy.

The people of Ekumfi-Atwia were not the only participants with economic interests at stake in this performance. When the FISC conference was promoted to potential attendees, it was partly on the basis that gainful employment opportunities exist for storytellers in American schools, libraries, churches, and business venues. Thus, participation in the conference could provide the delegates with artistic sources and cultural capital for leveraging storytelling abilities into "career choices that will help pay sustainable wages" in the United States.[41] These commercial aspects of cultural exchange should not be hidden. Doing so only leads us further into the trap of a competitive scarcity mindset in which the truly transformative potential of African cultural heritage is effaced. Refraining from talking about the economics of the situation only prevents us from addressing vital questions about patterns of commerce in neoliberal Africa and the manner in which our cultural resources are being developed. Fortunately, there are many hopeful and empowering possibilities within the range of community-initiated tourist activity. These alternatives can provide a more meaningful intercultural experience to visitors and hosts alike, as well as a greater integration of tourism with the socioeconomic development goals of African communities. Exploring these possibilities requires only the capacity to look beyond the larger, well-funded neoliberal alternatives, and it is primarily just a matter of knowledge-resources and political will.

Finally, let's go back to the role of the trickster in this endeavor. We have seen how neoliberal ideology "went native" in the case of the Rawlings's regime, appropriating local African imaginaries to provide legitimacy for unpopular economic policies. Scholars like Jemima Pierre and Bayo Holsey recognize the underbelly of "nativized" neoliberalism in the kind of narratives that heritage tourism privileged in Ghana. Pierre maintains that global neoliberal economic restructuring diminishes postcolonial African states' control over their own economies, yet heritage tourism discourses in Ghana do not emphasize this historical reality. Rather, they focus on a "distinctly *diaspora* experience" of slavery and emancipation. The result, she notes, is a silence on (neo)colonial exploitation in Africa.[42] Holsey observes that the old Atlantic order was oppressive indeed; it made African rulers and merchants alike inescapable conscripts in the slave trade. However, she insists that it must be seen as part of a broader history of exploitation that includes (neo)colonial forms and whose effects not only continue but are not easily overcome. She is concerned that in the neoliberal economy, the Ghanaian nationalist and heritage tourism narratives tend to be romantic tales of triumph and achievement and call for protest narratives that critique contemporary forms of exploitation.[43]

If we understand the transformation of African cultural performances in this context—seeing the shift from an active, modernizing approach to a historical-preservationist framework as a kind of cultural "capture" by neoliberal forces—and if we can understand that the immediate possibilities of countering oppression often lie in surreptitious embodied forms of resistance, then we can again appreciate a young girl's walk across a small stage in the village of Ekumfi-Atwia as a profound challenge to the legitimating narratives of market fundamentalism. Somewhere between her apparent childish naivety and her seemingly purposeful naughtiness lay the "infra-politics" of the trickster ethos—the unquenchable need to thwart the limitations of totalizing ideology.[44] Arriving unheralded in the arena, she seemed to have a message for the visitors: "There is more to Africa than what you see here." Scholars have recognized that the culturally ubiquitous figure of the trickster exceeds its folkloric representations. More than a specific persona, the trickster is a counterhegemonic *ethos* embodied in the disposition of actual historic subjects who respond artistically and politically to material and ideological constraints. Thus, this young girl's walk across the Kodzidan stage was something more than a little girl's walk. It was a spider walk.

Conclusion

We have seen how J. J. Rawlings's government attempted to co-opt gyimi, concert party, and kodzi—three different cultural performance genres that are rooted in the stylistic tradition of Anansesem. Performers in these genres were profoundly constrained by the institutional policies of the regime as it sought to use African cultural traditions to sway Ghanaian public opinion in favor of the neoliberal government. Ever since the independence era, traditional African cultural values have been associated with resistance against economic exploitation on the continent. By intervening in these social outlooks, the regime sought to appease or confuse the opposition and to establish political legitimacy for its unpopular economic policies. However, although Rawlings's legitimation project constrained the range of cultural and artistic expression available to the performers of these co-opted genres, the trickster ethos of their performance traditions helped them to creatively overcome these constraints.

LEGITIMATING ECONOMIC POLICY CHANGES AND MANAGING PUBLIC TREPIDATION

We saw early in the book that Africans are strongly influenced by the legacy of economic exploitation and by the alternative social compact that arose as African countries achieved their independence. Derived from Africans' experiences under colonialism and supported by structuralist development theories, this moral outlook held that political regimes should be accountable for ensuring the common welfare. Chapter 1 described Kwame Nkrumah's articulation of these arguments in the Ghanaian context—his view that colonialism had bequeathed to Africa a distorted, nonmanufacturing economy that is overdependent on primary exports, starved of modern knowhow, and used as a dumping ground for overpriced foreign goods. The post-independence regime established a protectionist, interventionist state in order to shelter nascent domestic industries and to help ensure a fair distribution of wealth.

Nkrumah also believed that the economic exploitation of Africa had a corollary in the repression of African culture. He grounded his political and economic agenda in an appeal to the "African Personality"—an authentic, nonexploitative, community-oriented outlook that was posited as an alternative to European-style capitalism. By drawing on this "African Personality," Nkrumah and other post-independence leaders believed they could create an alternative form of modernity, wedding what is valuable from Africa's cultural past to the forward-looking potential of modern society. They sought to develop a pan-African cultural identity that would be wider than ethnic and national affiliations, believing that this could lead the continent into a new era of strength, prosperity, and power. Nkrumah's pan-Africanism (see chapter 4) spurred the emergence of a National Theatre Movement in Ghana that involved notable playwrights such as Efua Sutherland, Joe de Graft, and Michael Dei-Anang. His pan-African outlooks also extended to the black diaspora, helping to inspire civil rights leaders in the United States and elsewhere, and in turn drawing strength from the support of these far-flung communities.

In the early years after independence, Nkrumah's state-centered investments produced respectable rates of economic growth, while his distributive policies helped to ensure that this prosperity would be widely shared. The result was an era of great political optimism that sustained the public's confidence in an alternative, community-oriented African modernity. This era was to be short-lived, however, as unsustainable rates of public investment began to take their toll on the country, followed by Nkrumah's violent overthrow and the worldwide energy crises of the 1970s. Ghana entered into a downward spiral of political and economic chaos, while vital social and economic infrastructure depreciated and suffering increased among much of the country's population. During this time, the pan-African cultural initiatives of the Nkrumah years lost much of their national priority. Those that relied strongly on the state-centered model, such as Efua Sutherland's modernist theater experiment in Ekumfi-Atwia, fell rapidly into decline. Others that maintained a more robust popular commercial base, such as the concert party theater, continued to thrive for a while longer, before eventually succumbing to the growing economic depression.

Despite the failing ability of the state to provide for the general welfare, Ghanaians' belief that their government *should* ensure prosperity (and provide patronage for African cultural initiatives) remained strong. Nkrumah's exile diminished neither the belief in the social compact nor the view of the state as the central locus of community development. Furthermore, the heavy infrastructure investment and overall economic surplus of the post-independence years had led Ghanaians to expect drastic and immediate improvements in their conditions. Governments that were unwilling or unable to meet these impossible expectations were overthrown one by one, in a kind of "musical chairs" routine of civilian and military regimes. As the economic crisis deepened, these same expectations of rapid material improvement led Ghanaian regimes to increasingly look outward for infusions of foreign capital, despite long-held misgivings about external control and exploitation. A paradigmatic transformation was enacted in the 1980s when the Rawlings government bowed to the policy mandates of international finance institutions in exchange for an influx of borrowed money. These changes included a wholesale abandonment of public welfare programs and state-owned enterprises, as well as the elimination of restrictions on the repatriation of profits out of the country. This neoliberal program also failed to provide instant plenitude for the country; in fact, it led to an even greater reduction in the standard of living for many Ghanaians, while marking an explicit breach of the protectionist social compact (see chapter 1).

Rawlings's military regime was able to maintain its unpopular economic agenda during the 1980s through a combination of charisma, sheer political inertia, and a harsh crackdown on the opposition. Ghana fell into a "culture of silence," in which would-be dissidents were quickly branded as security threats and disappeared into the maw of the system.

Nonetheless, resistance against the military government grew steadily both within the country and among external investors, who were concerned about the negative image created by the strong-arm tactics of the regime. In a remarkable sleight of hand, Rawlings came up with an inventive strategy for maintaining his administration's hegemony in the midst of this growing displeasure. He retired from the military and announced that he would hold open elections, thereby reinventing himself and taking credit for the return to multiparty democracy that his regime had long resisted. At the same time, he initiated a publicity blitzkrieg in which he sought to co-opt the pan-African cultural legacy of Kwame Nkrumah in order to bolster his charismatic image among the electorate. In a process fraught with accusations of fraud and threats, Rawlings managed to hold onto power as an elected president within Ghana's new constitutional order.

Ghanaians' resistance against externally mandated policy changes remained high, however, and the government frequently revealed its less-than-sincere adoption of democratic values and pan-African ideology. Rawlings's ongoing neoliberal agenda continued to produce flash points and protests—as was the case with his drastic restructuring of the tax code to shift burdens away from businesses and onto consumers, a move that was decried both for its economic effects and for the manner in which the bill was preemptively enacted with little parliamentary or public media debate (see chapter 3). When the resulting Kum-me-preko demonstrations were violently dispersed, in contradiction to the supposed constitutional guarantee of public dissent, many opponents argued that the new Rawlings regime was much different from the old one. In chapter 4, we saw another anxiety that emerged around the regime's divestiture of the National Theatre and its consequent sponsorship by the Unilever Corporation. Many Ghanaians perceived the divestment as a betrayal of Nkrumah's legacy and selling out the spirit of African culture to international profiteers.

Nonetheless, throughout the 1990s and into the millennial decade, Rawlings managed to undermine or at least confuse the opposition by enacting a stylistic appropriation of pan-African rhetoric. This cultural imagery allowed the regime to suggest that it was holding to the forms of the postcolonial social compact, even as it enacted policy changes

that produced alarm and trepidation. This marked the onset of a new
liberal-democratic era, in which public discontent was managed increasingly through spin and manipulation, rather than by outright violence
and fear. The turn to liberal democracy forced Rawlings to look for ever
more sophisticated ways of managing discontent and placed a premium
on the cultural strategies of ideological legitimation. The various ways in
which the Rawlings government deployed these culture strategies reveal
the "affective and embodied [one might say, the performative] dimensions
of state authority."[1] In the wake of the Kum-me-preko violence, Rawlings
sought to secure a public endorsement from Ghana's top gyimi comedian,
Bishop-Bob Okalla, in order to help redeem his reputation among Okalla's
rural, working-class, and urban-underclass fans. We saw how the managers of the National Theatre attempted to use the Keysoap Concert Party
Show as a way of reassuring an anxious public that corporate sponsorship
was compatible with the revival of African cultural traditions. Finally, we
saw how an emphasis on heritage tourism allowed the regime to give a
less objectionable face to the growing role of foreign direct investment in
Ghana's economy.

NEGOTIATING THE CONSTRAINTS:
MANIFESTATIONS OF THE TRICKSTER ETHOS

Rawlings's co-option of African traditions placed constraints upon performers' art and aspirations and largely negated the socially transformative
potential that had been attributed to these traditions during the independence era. Thus, Bishop-Bob Okalla's popular appeal was based around
his slippery and humorous capacity to play upon multiple meanings and
ambiguity. His entrance into the political fray as part of Rawlings's legitimation project, however, threatened to reduce him to an unequivocally
polarizing figure and thereby led to a sense of disenchantment among his
fan base. The pressures of corporate sponsorship mandated that concert
party performers shift from their traditionally lighthearted, ambiguous,
and satirical aesthetic to a more formal, didactic, and marketing-oriented
approach. The pressures of the neoliberal tourism industry forced cultural
performers at Ekumfi-Atwia to downplay their developmental aspirations

and the modernist/experimental nature of the Kodzidan. In their hopes of attracting the attention of international visitors and the support of tourism development initiatives, these performers had to recast their art as a backward-looking, "preserved" tradition.

The trickster storytelling ethos from which gyimi, concert party, and kodzi are derived provided resources that helped performers to subvert this attempted political co-option. We saw in chapter 2 that the Ghanaian trickster ethos is a wily, counterhegemonic tradition in which resistance against social domination is firmly entrenched. The spider-trickster Ananse—the traditional "owner of the stories"—is a fundamentally ambiguous and anomalous character. The inherent doubleness of Ananse straddles the counterpoised sectors of the heavens and the earth, humanity and animality, and creativity and treachery. This doubleness is politically significant in that it allows those who adopt the mantle of the trickster to maneuver around social constraints and to avoid being pinned down as they supply a steady stream of contradiction, undermining the unequivocal hegemony that power seeks to impose. While it is possible to view the trickster as a "permitted iconoclast" or social relief valve, we should not let this authoritarian perspective hide the fact that Ananse's anarchic potential is never fully contained. The trickster ethos acts as a reservoir and a resource of opposition, and its ambiguity always has the potential to give expression to marginalized and/or constrained voices. By embodying this ethos, however, storytellers in the tradition of Anansesɛm embrace a disordering social logic in which ideological closure is rejected in favor of creative, forward-looking, and multivocal possibilities.

In chapter 3, we saw that Bishop-Bob Okalla invoked the trickster ethos to introduce uncertainty into the minds of his audience members about how seriously they should take his endorsement of Rawlings's political campaign. While continuing to enact the political theater into which Rawlings had recruited him, Okalla inserted contextual hints that this political endorsement might—possibly—be a broader form of the dubious, sarcastic praise and backhanded compliments that were part of his comedy routines. He left it unclear as to whether he was reshaping his routine to endorse Rawlings or reshaping his endorsement so it looked like it was part of his act. Thus, his performance drew on the ambiguity of his trickster reputation and created a contradiction onto which his fans could posit their own interpretations. Demonstrating the trickster's ability to spin complex webs of deception, he was able to evade the clear partisanship demanded by the neoliberal regime and to retain his reputation for artistic sophistication and satirical doubleness. Okalla emerged intact and with room to maneuver—able to navigate among powerful interests, while still remaining true to his fans and his performance tradition.

In chapter 4, we saw how the King Karo Concert Party Troupe also enacted the trickster ethos in the face of overwhelming social and financial pressures. The divestiture of the National Theatre to corporate sponsors left the troupe members struggling with demands to incorporate commercial marketing into their performances and to replace the whimsical, ambivalent aspects of their routines with an unequivocal promotional agenda. The Theatre's partial divestiture—a result of the government's continued regard of it as a strategic enterprise, exemplified the fact that for all its rhetoric of *government minimus,* the "signature dynamics of neoliberalism" remain dependent on the capacity of state apparatuses to "make and enforce rules, as well as delimit the rulemaking of others."[2] The Theatre's relationship with the concert party is a prime example of how such state control capabilities extend beyond outright force to include those grounded in proactive disciplinary techniques.[3] In response to the pressures that divestiture wrought, the King Karo troupe presented a play that met the sponsors' rules on a superficial level, while harboring surreptitious layers of affect, meaning, and identification just below the surface. The character of Ma Red became an embodiment of trickster ambiguity, laden with both positive and negative messages, expressing both the sponsors' demands and a stubborn refusal to accede to those demands. Although Ma Red was ultimately chastised in the play's narrative, the celebratory status and loving attention that was focused on her told a different, unsanctioned story. Through this ambivalence of representation, the King Karo troupe was able to retain the peculiarly disjunctive style of concert party theater, while giving voice to Ananse's impulse to simultaneously promote and undercut moral lessons.

Finally, in chapter 5, we saw how the trickster ethos emerged in the actions of a young girl who walked into the arena during a heritage performance at the Kodzidan in Ekumfi-Atwia. In a context where Anansesεm performance had become staged and almost antiquated due to the perceived expectations of African diaspora tourists, this unscripted interruption revealed the illusion and reminded the participants of the difference between a preserved tradition and a living one. The scripted "interruptions" of audience members during this performance offered a passable and delightful reinterpretation of village Anansesɛm, but the originally forward-looking and modernist/experimental intention of these endeavors had become lost under the false rhetoric of traditionalism. The girl's intrusion, in contrast, was more than a theatrical simulacrum of Anansesɛm's improvisation and open participation. Embodying Ananse's ceaselessly self-reinventing ethos of multivocality and narrative revision, the girl revealed the ultimate failure of power to confine the chaotic potential of the trickster. In doing so, she exposed the neoliberal appropriations of African cultural heritage for what they are: the artificial reflections of a living ethos.

TRICKSTER PERFORMANCE AS "TECHNIQUE": SOME THEORETICAL AND METHODOLOGICAL CONSIDERATIONS

The examples in this book demonstrate that performances rooted in the spider trickster tradition are, by that fact, political. They have the capacity to deploy the trickster's "ethos"—the ambiguity that gives expression to marginalized and/or constrained voices and therefore serves as a resource of tactful opposition—to navigate and negotiate the constraining teeth of power. Spider Ananse is always trying to make the connection between his words and actions and their meanings/intentions ambivalent. As a model of political engagement, this tendency of the spider disposes "trickster performers" (i.e., those of cultural performance traditions rooted in the trickster) to prevaricate the nature of their relationship to dominant social forces. Performers' rootedness in the trickster's "doubleness" therefore positions them to navigate and negotiate the constraints of domination even when they cannot overthrow the domineering forces.

Beyond its argument that Ghanaian cultural performances of the spider trickster tradition bear an inherent political potential, this book makes a theoretical intervention in performance studies. This intervention centers on the Schechner theory in the Introduction, which states that performance exists as an unresolved dialectic tension between two basic kinds of expression. This, if we recall, is more or less the idea that it is unclear whether performance represents a performer's true personality and intentions (it is indicative) or is purely an act (i.e., in a subjunctive or "as if" mode). Very likely, Ananse's essential tendency to render the meanings and intentions of his words and actions ambivalent makes this spider trickster ethos a perfect embodiment of that dialectic tension. In presenting performers who draw on this ethos to navigate/negotiate the constraints of dominant social forces, the examples in this book show that the unresolved dialectic tension is something more than what Schechner describes: something more than a *mode* of performance. They reveal that this tension may also be a *technique:* a procedure and proficiency that performers deploy, not simply to engage with domination but also to survive that typically precarious engagement.

Other theoretical insights about improvisation can be drawn when one considers the essential ambivalence of performance, especially of *trickster* performance, as a technique of political engagement. Judith Hamera's (see the Introduction) theory of technique links performance with sociality in that it generates (and is generated by) a shared idiom—a "discursive matrix"—partly because its repeatability, memorability, and represent-ability make performance legible and intelligible. Technique in this sense is an embodied and historically embedded but future-minded "archive" of personal and institutional memories that makes performances (and the bodies that deliver these performances) readable/reproducible in relationship to time and place. What did trickster performance, as the fountainhead of an ambivalence-oriented technique of political engagement, make readable and reproducible in millennial Ghana? The three cases in this book show that under the constraints of neoliberal legitimation, trickster performance allowed for the reproduction and readability of a double-ness under which marginalized and constrained voices could find expression and cover.

The cases, in essence, help us to see how improvisational "tactics," are reproduced when anything from specialized cultural performances to quotidian practices are constrained under domination. Tactics, social theorist Michel de Certeau maintains, are the improvisational and contingent forms of creative resistance to the strategies—the imposed set of relations—that structures of power present.[4] As a technique of political engagement, each of the three cultural performances in this book exemplified tactics in the form of the spider trickster's doubleness. This technique was particularly important in millennial Ghana, where, as neoliberal economic austerity undermined the state allocation of resources, the real terms of democratic participation were "both reduced and obscured" alongside the heightening of the rhetoric of democratization.[5] Compelled and constrained but not wholly determined by the legitimation strategies of a neoliberal regime, these cultural performances enabled the makeshift maneuvering of those constraints.

THE LOCAL NEGOTIATION OF NEOLIBERALISM:
AN INFRA-POLITICAL CONTESTATION

Each of the stories in this book can be summed up as a tale of neoliberal ideology imposing upon the moral outlook that informed postindependence African states and the resilience of the African trickster ethos in thwarting this ideological co-option. While neoliberalism trades upon the ideal of free-flowing capital in an unregulated global market, it does not actually involve the retraction of the governing state. In reality, neoliberalism relies upon *activist* and *interventionist* states that enforce its competitive ethos and aggressively militate against the alternative goals of compassionate and community-oriented collaboration. The paradox of the neoliberal state's interventionism is a result of the way in which market fundamentalism and the "commodification of everything" operate in denial of the actual cultural bonds and personal interdependence that allow society to function. In order to dominate this cultural fabric and repress the moral and community-oriented drive toward economic justice, neoliberalism relies upon a massive bureaucratic propaganda machine and militarized state apparatus. The tendency of neoliberal states to teeter on the edge of authoritarianism reveals the conflicted and contradictory relationship that market ideology has with the ideals of individual freedom, democracy, and self-sufficiency.[6] Thus, maintaining the popular legitimacy of the neoliberal state is always a difficult proposition, especially among populations who have historically been confined to the margins of this socioeconomic system.

Due to the cultural richness of the actual world, proponents of neoliberalism must find ways to enforce and legitimate their ideologies within local contexts. In the United States, neoliberalism "captured" a long-standing cultural valorization of rugged individualism to serve as its legitimating framework. Arguments about the virtues of individual liberty provided (and continue to provide) the primary justification for unregulated markets in the United States. In its insatiable need for expansion, however, this ideology of market fundamentalism had to adjust to the differing social fabrics and local histories of diverse global environments.[7] Brenda Chalfin notes that neoliberalism's unfolding in Ghana is not just "a simple pattern of the export of pretested models from . . . advanced capitalism's core to its periphery." Rather, Ghana demonstrates "how specific national paths of neoliberal reform actually inflect global models, to shape their replication and ongoing dissemination."[8] We have seen how in Ghana, neoliberalism gradually adapted to the local climate by co-opting the cultural legacy of pan-African nationalism to act as its legitimating framework. As in the United States and elsewhere, neoliberalism in Ghana could not simply be maintained by force but instead came to rely on a moral language to explain why market-centered outlooks are superior to other forms of socioeconomic organization. Unlike the United States, however, Ghanaian regimes did not invoke an appeal to individualism but rather to social solidarity and cultural revival as the primary legitimating mythology for their economic policies. We have seen how Rawlings and other proponents of neoliberalism took great pains to associate their policy shifts with pan-African ideologies and arguments about social development. They did not negate Ghanaians' belief in the social contract and public welfare programs but rather co-opted these values and attached them, somewhat questionably, to the neoliberal privatization project. In this sense, the central legitimating narrative of neoliberalism in Ghana was nearly the opposite of the individual-freedom justifications that predominate in Western countries.

This is not to say that these legitimating narratives were absolute or uniform; discourses of individual liberty do circulate among some of neoliberalism's proponents in Ghana, just as certain forms of social development narrative do circulate around neoliberalism in particular U.S. contexts (increasingly so, in the current era of globalization). As a general trend, however, the legacy of Rawlings's regime is a testament to the ability of market fundamentalism to "go native" by co-opting the cultural imaginary of local environments. In this part of West Africa, neoliberalism embedded itself in a national context defined by the legacy of the anti-colonial social compact and spun a legitimating narrative around itself by laying claim to those same cultural values. Whether it was recruiting a popular comedian to buttress Rawlings's image as a man of the people, reframing concert party shows as a progressive tradition to justify the divestiture of the National Theatre, or encouraging African heritage tourism to help ease concerns about foreign direct investment, the neoliberal regime was compelled to demonstrate a commitment to African culture and community welfare as its principal justification for its drastic policy changes.

It is useful, then, to reiterate what the examples in this book suggest: that the rise of the neoliberal state in Ghana has not eroded the cultural foundations and moral outlooks that characterized the early post-independence state but has only been circuitously appended onto those aspirations. In a Western context, neoliberal ideology has long been hostile to the rhetoric of social solidarity, but in Ghana, it has now legitimated itself on the moral premises of those very same values. I disagree with the view that African leaders have abandoned moral premises for technocratic ones—a view that has been forcefully articulated in recent years by James Ferguson and other scholars. Ferguson has noted that in the 1950s and 1960s, many African leaders justified socialist-leaning policies by linking economic production and prosperity to a moral social order. Producing and sharing material wealth was seen as a morally just cause, while accumulating wealth without producing or sharing was seen as immoral. Socialism and state-centered policies were consciously linked to solidarity and community, while market-centered policies were linked to selfishness, exploitation, and individual acquisitiveness. Ferguson argues that in turning to neoliberal reforms, African leaders abandoned these moral premises for an "economistic language of international technocracy," shifting economic policy into the technical context of efficiency, pragmatism, and fiscal prudence.[9]

Ferguson and others have argued that the supposed neutrality of neoliberalism's "technical façade" masks more profound appeals in the realm of social philosophy—ideological presuppositions about the nobility of financial success, the inviolate rights of individuals, the sanctity of private property, and the value of personal freedom.[10] According to Ferguson, "The morality of the market denies its own status as a morality, presenting itself as mere technique."[11] The author suggests, however, that, at least in millennial Ghana, the language of neoliberalism presented the market as a morality. It appealed to the same community-based morality that framed the earlier, protectionist-oriented state. While the seductive glory of individual freedom can account for part of neoliberalism's allure, the legitimation of economic reforms in Ghana also—and perhaps more prominently—involved an attempt to link these policies to a more durable social compact that emphasized cultural foundations and the long-term good of the community.[12] For example, in the Keysoap Concert Party Show, corporate investment in what had begun as a state-sponsored cultural-aesthetic revival was used to demonstrate the purportedly responsible nature of the Unilever corporation, appealing not to individualist aspirations but rather to the ethos of community health, development, and cultural authenticity. In the performances discussed in this book, the moral terms of the post-independence social compact were rearticulated as a supposed foundation of neoliberal reforms, rather than its antithesis.

This brings us back to the role of cultural performance in providing support and/or opposition to particular paradigms of socioeconomic power. The legitimation of power relies strongly upon the appropriation and manipulation of cultural symbols as a means of urging political subjects to act in desired ways. We might say that by co-opting the moral language of the postcolonial social compact, Rawlings engaged in a political sleight of hand—a trick in its own right—that sought to constrain Ghana's cultural landscape and re-present neoliberal paradigms in deceptively familiar, autochthonous, local-moral terms. However, nonelite actors can also reconstruct symbols for purposes that may not align with those of the dominant regime. The trickster-inspired responses to neoliberal legitimation described in this book indicate that cultural creativity remains a deep reservoir of counterhegemonic potential. Within the broad range of practices that can be considered political opposition, the trickster ethos occupies a unique territory. It does not provide a definitive counternarrative to power but rather an endless process of recursive contradiction and ambiguity. In doing so, however, it negates one of the central principles of social dominance: the establishment of ideological closure. The ultimate goal of trickster contestations is not so much to repudiate neoliberalism as it is to interrupt its ascendency, raise questions about its negative potential, and reposition it as one of many possible voices within an ongoing dialogue. By creating such openness, however, one might suggest that these interventions strike at the very heart of market fundamentalism, which like all totalitarian ideologies is predicated upon the absence of dialogue.

The subversive performances described in this book involve what James C. Scott calls "infra-politics"—indirect and furtive engagements with dominant ideas and structures.[13] As such, they are limited in the scope of their individual repercussions. However, if a radical act is defined as a confrontation with the root cause of a problem (rather than just a response to its symptoms), then the trickster contestations described in this book can truly be considered radical interventions.[14] By exposing the legitimizing narratives of neoliberalism, they draw attention to the fundamental cause of the constraints placed upon Ghanaian society. Furthermore, by embodying the very principle of contradiction against the prospect of narrative closure, they refute the fundamental aspiration of power to eliminate multivocal dialogue and dissent. They reveal contradictions in areas where power cannot admit of contradiction and give continuing voice to unsanctioned outlooks. Thus, we should not underestimate the ongoing political impact of the trickster ethos and the performance traditions that are grounded in it. The machinations of a global political economy rely upon countless stories of local acquiescence. In millennial Ghana, where trickster performers confronted the constraints of neoliberal legitimation, these "spiders of the market" wove a crafty tale of contradiction in which alternatives to market fundamentalism could be envisioned.

NOTES

INTRODUCTION

1. For an explanation of IFI conditionalities, see Akonor, *Africa and IMF Conditionality;* Killick, *Aid and the Political Economy of Policy Change,* 6; and Mosley, *Development Finance and Policy Reform,* 129. Literature on the politics of Ghana's reforms includes Gyimah-Boadi and Johnson, "PNDC and Organized Labor"; Gyimah-Boadi and Jeffries, "Political Economy of Reform"; Herbst, *Politics of Reform in Ghana;* Hutchful, *Ghana's Adjustment Experience;* and Rothchild, *Ghana.*

2. The concept of "cultural performances" has been defined in different ways, but its most basic meaning is temporarily and spatially framed expressive behavior, usually in a subjunctive mode (i.e., "acting"), that involves display and follows a more or less structured order of activities. In Milton Singer's descriptive and conservative view, cultural performances are discrete, concretized, observable units of social structure (Singer, *Traditional India,* xii–xiii; Singer, *When a Great Tradition Modernizes,* 71). Victor Turner, in contrast, has argued that cultural performances are not merely concrete implementations of culture but consist more broadly of all the reflexive and active ways in which individuals engage with cultural traditions (V. Turner, *Anthropology of Performance,* 23–24, 39–42, 123).

3. The terms *gyimi, kodzi,* and *Anansesɛm,* along with other African phrases transliterated and translated throughout this book, are derived from the various dialects of the Akan language. The transliteration system used here follows the unified Akan language orthography developed by the Bureau of Ghana Languages (Akan Orthography Committee, *Writing of Akan*).

4. The discussion here draws strongly on Rachel Turner's interpretation of neoliberalism as a social ideology (*Neo-liberal Ideology,* 7–11). Nevertheless, the author shares the view of others who rightly address the more pragmatic aspects of neoliberalism as a "theory of political economic practices" (Harvey, *Brief History of Neoliberalism,* 2); a "distinctive political economic philosophy" (Peck and Tickell, "Conceptualizing Neoliberalism," 28); and an "agenda of economic and social transformation" (Connell, "Understanding Neoliberalism," 2).

5. Harvey, *Brief History of Neoliberalism,* 2, 64–66; R. Turner, *Neo-liberal Ideology,* 4–5, 119–32.

6. The influence of neoliberal think tanks on leaders of powerful Western countries during the 1980s, especially in the United States and the United Kingdom, is addressed by R. Turner (*Neo-liberal Ideology*, 96–97, 106–7, 160); Peck and Tickell ("Conceptualizing Neoliberalism," 38–48); Plehwe and Walpen ("Between Network and Complex Organization," 40–44); and Harvey (*Brief History of Neoliberalism*, 44). As early as 1978, Celso Furtado called IFIS a "U.S.-serving control instrument over the economic and financial policies of other countries" ("Post-national Capitalism," 6). More recently, Ngaire Woods noted that "the political preferences of the United States and other industrialized countries provide a strong bottom line or outer structural constraint in which the IMF and World Bank work" (*Globalizers*, 4). Walden Bello's *Dark Victory* also links Reagan and IFIS as co-conspirators in a regime of domination. For a quick overview of the shifts in IFIS' funding focus at various times in their history, see Sachs, "Growth in Africa," 20.

7. See Mkandawire and Soludo, *Our Continent, Our Future*, 12; and Killick, *Development Economics in Action*, 17–21. Influential structuralist development economists of the time include the Nobel laureates Sir William A. Lewis and K. G. Myrdal, as well as A. O. Hirschman, R. Prebisch, Tibor de Scitovsky, and Hans W. Singer. The ideas of Prebisch and Singer, often bundled together as the "Prebisch-Singer thesis," are also foundational to dependency theory. Paul A. Baran, Andre Gunder Frank, and Paul Sweezy gave dependency theory a Marxian perspective. Other influential dependency theorists include Walter Rodney, Theotonio Dos Santos, Immanuel Wallerstein, and Samir Amin.

8. See Beckman, "Empowerment or Repression?," 96–97.

9. African countries' fall from economic growth to collapse is often mentioned in the literature about structural adjustment on the continent, usually as a preamble or justification for the institution of neoliberal reforms. See, for instance, Herbst, *Politics of Reform*, 17–37; Hutchful, *Ghana's Adjustment Experience*, 1–52; Mkandawire and Soludo, *Our Continent, Our Future*, 1–22; and Sahn, Dorosh, and Younger, *Structural Adjustment Reconsidered*, 1–8.

10. Mensah, *Understanding Economic Reforms in Africa*, 4.

11. Beckman, "Empowerment or Repression?," 97. More specific descriptions of IFI reform proposals can be found in Mkandawire and Soludo, *Our Continent, Our Future*, 40–48; Sahn, Dorosh, and Younger, *Structural Adjustment Reconsidered*, 4; and "Sisters in the Wood," *The Economist*.

12. Beckman, "Empowerment or Repression?," 97; Campbell and Loxley, *Structural Adjustment in Africa*, 4–5; Mkandawire and Soludo, *Our Continent, Our Future*, 70–74; Abouharb and Cingranelli, *Human Rights and Structural Adjustment*, 231–32.

13. Leitner, Peck, and Sheppard, *Contesting Neoliberalism*, 1–2, 4. See also Comaroff and Comaroff, "Millennial Capitalism," 14–15; Comaroff and Comaroff, "Afro-Modernity and the Neo-World Order," 345; and Greenhouse, *Ethnographies of Neoliberalism*, 2.

14. Cole, *Ghana's Concert Party Theatre*, 79, 113, 125, 151. See also Bame, *Come to Laugh*, 10; and Sutherland, *Original Bob*.

15. As columnist Basiru Adam explained, in Ghana, "to refer to a comedian as a fool is . . . a firm approval of his mastery of the art of making others laugh at their own follies" ("Ghana Regains Her 'Fool' Sense of Humor," n.p.).

16. Cole, *Ghana's Concert Party Theatre*, 109. See also Bame, *Come to Laugh*, 10; and Barber, Collins, and Ricard, *West African Popular Theatre*, 7, 11.

17. National Theatre of Ghana, *Corporate Plan*, iv.

18. The Fante and the Asante are two of the several ethno-linguistic communities that make up the Akan people. Fantes are concentrated along the southwestern coast of Ghana, and

their Akan dialect includes some words that are different from the language of Asantes and other Akan subgroups.

19. Sutherland, *Marriage of Anansewa and Edufa,* 5.

20. For more on the improvisatory and participatory character of Anansesɛm and the reworking of the tradition in the Kodzidan at Ekumfi-Atwia, see Akyea, "Atwia Ekumfi Kodzidan," 82–84; Arkhurst, "Kodzidan," 165–74; Donkor, "Kodzidan Mboguw," 38–46; and Jeyifo, "When Anansegoro Begins to Grow," 24–37.

21. See Bruner, "Tourism in Ghana," 300.

22. See Barker, *Political Legitimacy and the State,* 11; R. Cohen, "Introduction," 18; Coicaud, *Legitimacy and Politics,* 10, 26, 31; Fabienne, "Political Legitimacy"; and Gilley, "Meaning and Measure of State Legitimacy," 501–3.

23. A. Cohen, *Politics of Elite Culture;* Kurtz, *Political Anthropology,* 35–36; Merelman, "Dramaturgy of Politics," 216.

24. Edelman, *Symbolic Uses of Politics,* 11.

25. Conquergood, "Beyond the Text," 47.

26. Turner, *Anthropology of Performance,* 81.

27. Singer, *Man's Glossy Essence,* xii.

28. Schechner, *Performance Studies,* 22–23, 28–29; Schechner, *Between Theatre and Anthropology,* 35–116.

29. Hamera, *Dancing Communities,* 3–9, 19–25, 72–77.

30. Bhabha, *Location of Culture,* 146–49; Conquergood, "Beyond the Text," 47–48; Diamond, "Introduction," 5; Dolan, "Geographies of Learning," 419.

31. Diamond, "Introduction," 4.

32. Conquergood, "Power of Symbols," 11.

33. See Doty and Hynes, "Historical Overview of Theoretical Issues," 22–26; and Pelton, *Trickster in West Africa,* 5–10. The vast literature on trickster figures (not including folktale collections) also includes Hyde, *Trickster Makes This World;* Landay, *Madcaps, Screwballs, and Con Women;* Jurich, *Scheherazade's Sisters;* Reder and Morra, *Troubling Tricksters;* Reesman, *Trickster Lives;* and Roberts, *From Trickster to Badman.*

34. Pelton, *Trickster in West Africa,* 15.

35. Ibid., 14; see also Hynes and Doty, "Introducing the Fascinating," 6.

36. Schechner, *Between Theatre and Anthropology,* 6.

37. Pelton, *Trickster in West Africa,* 37; Hynes, "Inconclusive Conclusions," 211–12.

38. For an anthologized version of this story, see Rattray, *Akan-Ashanti Folk-Tales,* 106–9. Note that Rattray's translation of the figure's name as "Hates-to-Be-Contradicted," differs from the author's translation. In the Asante-Akan language, the name is *Kyiriakyinnyee,* combining the verb *kyiri* (hates) and the noun *akyinnyee* (contradiction). Thus, the author's translation, "Hates-Contradiction," is a more exact English rendering of the original meaning of the name.

39. Ibid., 4–6.

40. Roberts, *From Trickster to Badman,* 30–53.

41. Burton, *Afro-Creole,* 47–65.

42. The work in this summation includes Rattray, *Akan-Ashanti Folk-Tales;* Pelton, *Trickster in West Africa;* Tekpetey, "Kweku Ananse"; van Dyck, "Analytic Study of the Folktales"; Vescey, "Exception Who Proves the Rule"; and Yankah, "Question of Ananse." The dearth of contextualization in these analyses has led to a call from Margaret Drewal for a performance-studies approach to African folklore to highlight contingency and temporality ("Performance

Studies and African Folklore Research," 334). Sandra Richards has likewise argued that scholars should pay more attention to how African traditions change over time with the changing material conditions of their adherents ("Under the Trickster's Sign," 66). John Roberts extends Richards's call for a *materialist* contextualization (*From Trickster to Badman,* 30), but both Richards and Roberts again seem to ignore the *historical* context and development of trickster performances. One exception to this trend of decontextualization can be found in the work of Catherine Cole, who focuses on Ghanaian concert party theater as a development of traditional Anansesem from the 1920s through the 1960s. Cole argues that the growth of the concert party genre is a tribute to the resourcefulness of the trickster, who is "fantastically successful at exploiting opportunities," despite social and physical limitations (*Ghana's Concert Party Theatre,* 110). Cole describes this adaptation of Anansesem practice as a creative strategy of survival through which concert party performers were able to "negotiate the pragmatics of their lives" (117). Her work details the historical contexts of this materialistic creativity—the discouraging economic prospects that concert party performers and their audiences faced in Ghana from the 1920s through the 1950s.

43. Leitner, Peck, and Sheppard, *Contesting Neoliberalism,* 15. See also Plehwe, Walpen, and Neunhöffer, "Reconsidering Neoliberal Hegemony," 3; Slater, *Geopolitics and the Post-colonial,* 98; and Willis, Smith, and Stenning, *Social Justice and Neoliberalism,* 3.

44. See Ashcroft, Griffith, and Tiffin, *Postcolonial Studies,* 169.

45. See Slater, *Geopolitics and the Post-colonial,* 11, 85; Bargh, *Resistance,* 12–15; and Ashcroft, Griffith, and Tiffin, *Postcolonial Studies,* 148–49.

46. Scott, *Domination and the Arts of Resistance,* 70–107.

47. Comaroff and Comaroff, *Of Revelation and Revolution,* 1:22–30.

48. Ibid., 30. Similar ideas are developed by James C. Scott in his book *Weapons of the Weak.*

49. Michel de Certeau is referring to such subversion from within when he talks about the art of "making do," or styles of action that "intervene in a field which regulates them" (*Practice of Everyday Life,* 30).

50. The First International Storytelling Conference was organized by a committee of storytellers from New Rochelle, New York, comprised of Therese Folks Plair, Melissa Heckler, Maria Mitchell, and Donna Duckett. Their local Ghanaian counterparts were professors Esi Sutherland-Addy and Kofi Anyidoho of the University of Ghana, and Papa Baah of the Afrikan Folklore Organization.

51. Taylor, *Archive and the Repertoire,* 20.

52. Dwight Conquergood's publications about culture, performance, ethnography, and research praxis are all included in a book edited by E. Patrick Johnson (*Dwight Conquergood,* 16–264). For some of the specific ideas mentioned here, see in that book, Conquergood, "Rethinking Ethnography," 91–98; Conquergood, "Performing Cultures," 16–23; and Conquergood, "Performance Studies," 33. See also Madison, *Critical Ethnography,* 184–90; and Madison, "Co-performative Witnessing," 826–31, for excellent syntheses of Conquergood's ideas and practice of ethnography and for how his concept of co-performative witnessing fits into his overall ethnographic practice.

53. Madison, *Critical Ethnography,* 192.

54. This calls to mind Dwight Conquergood's observation ("Of Caravans and Carnivals," 27) that "performance privileges threshold-crossing, shape shifting, and boundary-violating figures" such as "tricksters."

55. For a critique of *scriptocentrism,* see Conquergood, "Performance Studies," 34–35.

56. See Madison's discussion of dialogic performance as a "political act" of "being there and with" others to excavate subjugated knowledge for the creation of alternative futures ("Co-performative Witnessing," 829).

57. Taylor, *Archive and the Repertoire*, 18.

1. FROM STATE TO MARKET

1. African opposition against colonial authority in the Gold Coast first crystalized during the late nineteenth century. At that time, the objections were mainly focused on the lack of institutional means for "native" opinion to influence colonial legislation. The first orga-nized vanguard of this opposition included Western-educated lawyers and merchants—the self-described African "intelligentsia"—along with some traditional chiefs. This opposition remained limited to fragmentary calls for legislative reform; it did not focus on larger issues of inequality and economic grievances and therefore failed to sustain any broad base of political support. Furthermore, the opposition was weakened by the co-option of many of the chiefs and intelligentsia into the colonial structure and by the chiefs' suspicion that the merchants and intelligentsia wanted to usurp the chiefs' traditional authority. This stalemate continued until the late 1940s, when ineffectual calls for reforming the colonial system began to be overtaken by the voices of populist leaders who wanted to eliminate colonialism altogether.

2. A more detailed discussion of the "veranda boys" and their role in the anti-colonial movement can be found in Apter, *Gold Coast in Transition*, 1:65–66; Austin, *Politics in Ghana*, 55; Genoud, *Nationalism and Economic Development in Ghana*; and Killick, *Development Economics in Action*, 34.

3. Rooney, *Kwame Nkrumah*, 68, 70, 77.

4. Nkrumah, as quoted by the *Ashanti Pioneer* on March 5, 1949, and cited by both Rooney, *Kwame Nkrumah*, 69; and Fitch and Oppenheimer, *Ghana*, 25.

5. Killick, *Development Economics in Action*, 35.

6. By 1954, Africans held 38 percent of appointments in the civil service, compared to 14 percent in 1949 (Gocking, *History of Ghana*, 99). For more information about the changes instituted by the Nkrumah government, see Gocking, *History of Ghana*, 118–22; and Rooney, *Kwame Nkrumah*, 120–25.

7. Genoud, *Nationalism*, 98.

8. Killick, *Development Economics*, 35.

9. Killick, *Development Economics*, 40. As this quote indicates, Nkrumah's economic plan was "socialist" by his own description. Some commentators have dismissed the earnestness or accuracy of the "socialist" label for various reasons, one of which is that many details of Nkrumah's plan were consistent with the ideas of structuralist development economics (SDE), a prominent branch of the field in the 1950s and 1960s. Roger Genoud argued that what was paraded as socialism in Nkrumah's official doctrine was merely "anti-colonial nationalism" by a different name (*Nationalism*, 219). Similarly, K. B. Asante insisted that Nkrumah "gave the impression" that his economic plans derived from socialist leanings when they were really just "dictated by Ghana's circumstances, experiences, and aspirations" (Asante, "Nkrumah and State Enterprises," 268–69). Fitch and Oppenheimer concluded that Nkrumah's willingness to share power with colonial authority during the 1951–1957 period indicates a lack of robust socialist commitment (*Ghana*, 83–84).

Despite these reservations, Nkrumah did undoubtedly take himself seriously as a social-ist in the Leninist-Marxist tradition. He frequently expressed indebtedness to socialist ideas in his writing, even prior to his entrance on the political stage. During the CPP's tenth anniversary celebration in 1959, he declared that the party would pursue "the creation of a welfare state based on African socialist principles" (Nkrumah, *I Speak of Freedom*, 163). In 1960, he called on Ghana's National Assembly to "acquire a socialist perspective and a socialist drive" (ibid., 208–9). In 1962, the CPP affirmed socialism as the party's foundational principle, stating that progress would only be achieved "by a rapid change in the socio-economic structure of the country" (Killick, *Development Economics*, 38–39). And at National Assembly debates in 1964, Nkrumah once again reaffirmed his regime's aim to "generate a socialist transformation of the economy."

In addition to these statements of ideological affiliation, it should be noted that after independence, Ghana began to shift its trading relationships away from the United States and Western European countries, increasingly striking deals with members of the "socialist bloc." While Western businesses demanded hard currency in exchange for manufactured products (often at exorbitant rates), the socialist bloc countries were more open to deals that would allow Ghana to pay for its investments over a period of years by supplying raw products (Jonah, "Nkrumah and the Decolonization," 337). This prospect of more equitable international trade arrangements strengthened Nkrumah's socialist outlook. He visited the USSR in 1961 and was so impressed with the modernization efforts he saw there that he decided to pattern Ghana's economic reconstruction after the Soviet model. Ghana's "seven-year development plan" was initiated shortly after Nkrumah's return from the Soviet Union; it took as its model the USSR's own seven-year plan, which had been launched in 1959.

10. Genoud, *Nationalism*, 98.

11. Nkrumah, *Consciencism*, 49–50, 74.

12. Nkrumah, *Neocolonialism*, xi.

13. Nkrumah, *Axioms of Kwame Nkrumah*, 3–4.

14. Ibid., 17.

15. For more about the suspected foreign involvement in the 1966 coup, see Mwakikagile, *Africa after Independence*, 146–51; and Blum, *Killing Hope*, 198–99.

16. Gocking, *History of Ghana*, 178.

17. Hutchful, *Ghana's Adjustment Experience*, 11.

18. For example, the NLC only managed to wholly divest three of the country's state-owned enterprises because public opinion thwarted their efforts. Their attempts to open the country to outside investment likewise ended up proceeding little further than a partial dismantlement of Nkrumah's import and licensing regulations. By 1971, forty-three out of the fifty-three enterprises that Nkrumah had set up remained unsold (Gyimah-Boadi, "State Enterprises Divestiture," 196; Gyimah Boadi and Jeffries, "Political Economy of Reform," 43; Herbst, *Politics of Reform*, 21–22; Killick, *Development Economics*, 313).

19. Osei, *Ghana*, 82.

20. Chazan, *Anatomy of Ghanaian Politics*, 181.

21. Shillington, *Ghana and the Rawlings Factor*, 44.

22. Oquaye, *Politics in Ghana, 1972–79*, 134; Yankah, *Trial of J. J. Rawlings*, 16.

23. The words of this popular ditty are from the author's recollection.

24. Osei, *Ghana*, 95.

25. Tribunals were to act on "evidence properly assembled," but they were not to be "fettered by technical rules . . . [that] perverted the course of justice and enabled criminals to go free." Kandeh, *Coups from Below*, 81.

26. *Workers Banner*, as cited by Yeebo, *Ghana*, 66.

27. Ray, *Ghana*, 19.

28. Ziorklui, *Ghana*, 522–30.

29. Quoted in Nugent, *Big Men, Small Boys*, 43; and Osei, *Ghana*, 103.

30. See Nugent, *Big Men, Small Boys*, 17; and Osei, *Ghana*, 105.

31. Yeebo, *Ghana*, 73. From the beginning, Rawlings's PNDC party was divided in its outlook as to whether revolution was supposed to flow from the top down or from the bottom up. For the most part, the party supported Rawlings's own view that the innate political ingenuity of the people should be given precedence. An "Interim National Coordinating Committee" was established to help organize the activities of the P/WDCs, but its mandate was limited to providing logistical support to the local organizations "without controlling them in any way" (Nugent, *Big Men, Small Boys*, 49–50). The relationship between local P/WDCs and the country's larger political structure was left intentionally vague on the premise that it would be inappropriate for the central government to prejudge the course in which "people's power" would eventually flow. The result was that there was little consensus about how the regime should or could react once P/WDCs did start to assume political initiative (see also Osei, *Ghana*, 105).

32. Yeebo, *Ghana*, 58.

33. Ibid., 116.

34. Kandeh, *Coups from Below*, 85.

35. Yeebo, *Ghana*, 123.

36. Chalfin, *Neoliberal Frontiers*, 14–15, 29. The term *revolutionary* was commonly used to refer to Ghana's reforms. See, for instance, United Nations, *World Economic Survey*, 174.

37. See Donkor, *Structural Adjustment and Mass Poverty*, 236; and Hutchful, "From 'Revolution' to Monetarism," 122.

38. Herbst, *Politics of Reform*, 45. However, Yeebo attributes this to the workers of the Ghana-Italian Petroleum Company (*Ghana*, 190).

39. Herbst, *Politics of Reform*, 48. For more on the history of Ghana's unions under the Rawlings regime, see Herbst's discussion (58–75) and Hutchful, *Ghana's Adjustment Experience*, 170–76.

40. Nkrumah's 1958 Industrial Relations Act and Preventive Detention Act allowed for the imprisonment without trial of any dissident whose activities the regime considered a threat to national security and stability. Later acts went on to severely restrict the freedom of the press (Gocking, *History of Ghana*, 123–24; Omari, *Kwame Nkrumah*, 179–89; Rooney, *Kwame Nkrumah*, 301). The right-leaning NLC regime that overthrew Nkrumah condoned lethal action against striking workers, and its Prohibition of Rumors Decree criminalized any statement that might cause "alarm and despondency . . . or disaffection against the NLC" (Pinkney, *Ghana under Military Rule, 1966–69*, 43). The Busia administration that followed the NLC banned the TUC. They also fired and arrested journalists of both the state and opposition press who criticized the regime (Gocking, *History of Ghana*, 159–60). The NRC/SMC government was the first to normalize informal acts of political violence to curtail dissent (Chazan, *Anatomy of Ghanaian Politics*, 235–70).

41. See Oquaye, *Politics in Ghana, 1982–1992*, 399–403.

42. Nugent, *Big Men, Small Boys*, 119–20.

43. Hutchful, *Ghana's Adjustment Experience*, 40–41.

44. Oquaye, *Politics in Ghana*, 488.

45. Shillington, *Ghana*, 171. See also Ninsin, *Civic Associations*, 70.

46. Nugent, *Big Men, Small Boys*, 200.

47. See Herbst, *Politics of Reform*, 73–74; Hutchful, *Ghana's Adjustment Experience*, 166–68; and Nugent, *Big Men, Small Boys*, 229. Rawlings's efforts to appropriate Nkrumah's mantle were likely motivated by his party's own opinion research, which indicated that a unified Nkrumahist opposition would be the greatest electoral threat to the regime (Haynes, "Ghana," 101–2). Fortunately for Rawlings, this threat was mitigated by the fragmentation of the Left into several squabbling factions. The Rawlings camp took no chances and moved to further dilute the socialist opposition by co-opting Nkrumahist rhetoric and, according to some, even co-opting the loyalty of Nkrumahist leaders. Opposition leader Kwaku Boateng, for example, resigned from the leftist National Congress Party in disgust after alleging that the party's other bosses had been bought off by Rawlings (Haynes, "Ghana," 102–4).

48. Yeebo, *Ghana*, 158.

49. Yeebo, *Ghana*, 158. See also Nugent, *Big Men, Small Boys*, 229; Hutchful, *Ghana's Adjustment Experience*, 166–68; and Herbst, *Politics of Reform*, 73–74.

50. Hutchful, *Ghana's Adjustment Experience*, 41.

51. Rawlings interview with the *People's Daily Graphic* on March 5, 1987, cited in Shillington, *Ghana*, 135.

52. Hutchful, *Ghana's Adjustment Experience*, 160.

53. Diamond, "Introduction: Political Culture and Democracy," 23; Hutchful, *Ghana's Adjustment Experience*, 199.

54. Bangura and Gibbon, "Adjustment, Authoritarianism," 11.

55. Beckman, "Empowerment or Repression?," 92.

56. Hutchful, *Ghana's Adjustment Experience*, 218.

57. Botchway, "President," 90.

58. Hutchful, *Ghana's Adjustment Experience*, 125, 215.

59. Ibid., 25–29.

60. de Certeau, *Practice of Everyday Life*, 66.

61. Haraway, *Simians, Cyborgs, and Women*, 4.

2. ONCE UPON A SPIDER

1. Sutherland, *Marriage of Anansewa*, v.

2. Bosman, *New and Accurate Description*, 322; Ellis, *Tsi-Speaking Peoples*, 339; Macdonald, *Gold Coast, Past and Present*, 46.

3. Guggisberg and Guggisberg, *We Two in West Africa*, 339.

4. All of the Anansesɛm stories in this chapter are the author's translations or renditions of popular Akan stories, each of which has been previously recorded in one or more textual sources. A variant of this story, titled "Wunni Biribi De Ma W'Ase A, Wommo No Koron" ("If You Don't Have Something for Your In-Law, You Do Not Charge Him or Her with Theft"), can be found in Ayeh, *Mmrehua*, 96–99. The use of the term *Ananse Kokuroko* here follows the version of the story recounted in *Mmrehua*.

5. Rattray, *Ashanti Proverbs*, 73; van Dyck, "Analytic Study," 108.

6. A version of the story in which Ananse retrieves Death's golden sandals, snuffbox, and whip appears as "Ananse the Daring Messenger," in Asihene, *Traditional Folk-Tales*, 55–57. Variants of the story in which Ananse weeds Nyame's nettle-infested farm include "Why It Is the Elders Say We Should Not Repeat Sleeping Mat Confidences" (Yankah, "Question of Ananse," 129–33); and "Be Pleased with What You Have" (Asihene, *Traditional Folk-Tales*, 61–62). Ananse decides which of Nyame's sons would be the better heir in "The Sky God

and Ananse" (Asihene, *Traditional Folk-Tales*, 251–52) and in "How It Came About that Men Commit Evil by Night" (Rattray, *Akan-Ashanti Folk-Tales*, 73–76). Ananse captures various creatures, including a pot full of bees, a python, a leopard, and a magical dwarf, in "How It Came About that the Sky-God's Stories Came to Be Known as 'Spider Stories'" (Rattray, *Akan-Ashanti Folk-Tales*, 55–59), in "The Origin of Spider Tales" (Asihene, *Traditional Folk-Tales*, 217–20), and in "How Stories Became Spider Stories" (van Dyck, "Analytical Study," 204–7). Finally, the trickster takes up Nyame's challenge to impregnate the wife of Akwasi-the-Jealous-One in "How Ananse Got Aso in Marriage" (Rattray, *Akan-Ashanti Folk-Tales*, 133–37).

7. See Yankah, "Question of Ananse," 139.

8. Ananse goes to bid good morning to Nyame in the story "We Do Not Leave an Elephant Behind to Go and Throw a Stone at Asrewa the Hen" (Rattray, *Akan-Ashanti Folk-Tales*, 269–70). He promises Nyame a beautiful maiden in exchange for the sky god's sacred sheep in "How It Came About that Many Diseases Came Among the Tribe" (ibid., 77–81). Ananse claims to be able to inexpensively cure Nyame's sick mother in "You Are as Wonderful as Ananse" (ibid., 265–66) and does the same in regard to Nyame's sick son in "How Ananse Escaped Death" (Asihene, *Traditional Folk-Tales*, 75–76).

9. The phrase "Ananse's wealth" is discussed in Sutherland, *Marriage of Anansewa*, v. For a short time, Ananse owns a farm that is so big that a sound at one end could not be heard at the other in "Why the Spider Lies on the Rafters" (Ayeh, *Mmrehua*, 79–82). Nyame's characterization of the trickster as a vagrant can be seen in "How It Came About that the Sky-God's Stories Came to Be Known as 'Spider Stories'" (Rattray, *Akan-Ashanti Folk-Tales*, 55–59).

10. Yankah, "Question of Ananse," 140. Yankah may overstate the case in saying that the two are "always" at cross-purposes—for example, there are no apparent conflicts between them in the popular story where Nyame sends Ananse to retrieve Death's golden possessions ("Ananse the Daring Messenger," in Asihene, *Traditional Folk-Tales*, 55–57). Nonetheless, it is no exaggeration to describe their special relationship as contentious.

11. Variants of this story include "How Incrimination and Injury-Causing Came into the World" (Yankah, "Question of Ananse," 3) and "Why the Creator Lives in the Sky" (van Dyck, "Analytical Study," 193–97).

12. The phrase "washer of the sky god's soul" indicates a sacred ritual office. See "How It Came About that Ananse the Spider Went Up on the Rafters" (Rattray, *Akan-Ashanti Folk-Tales*, 249); "Why It Is the Elders Say We Should Not Repeat Sleeping-Mat Confidences" (ibid., 129–32); and "How Ananse Got Aso in Marriage" (Rattray, *Akan-Ashanti Folk-Tales*, 133–37).

13. Barker, "Nyankopon," 158.

14. See Nketia, *Funeral Dirges*, 7; Yankah, "Question of Ananse," 145; and Tekpetey, "Kweku Ananse," 75.

15. Sutherland, *Marriage of Anansewa*, v.

16. See Vescey, "Exception Who Proves the Rule," 112.

17. A variant of this story titled "Sɛnea Ananse daadaa ɔbosomfoɔ bi gyee ne guan kodii" ("How Ananse Tricked a Priest Out of a Sheep to Make a Feast") can be found in Ayeh, *Mmrehua*, 16–17.

18. Yankah, "Question of Ananse," 10.

19. Jackson-Opoku, *River Where Blood Is Born*, 16.

20. Hynes, "Mapping the Characteristics," 34. Hynes appears to invoke a kind of Hegelian dialectic in which the trickster provides an overarching synthesis of opposites. From the author's experience, this seems to be a reasonable interpretation of Anansesɛm.

21. Ellis, *Tsi-Speaking Peoples,* 339. Compare this with the view presented in van Dyck, "Analytical Study," 106.

22. See van Dyck, "Analytical Study," 110–11; and Yankah, "Question of Ananse," 140.

23. Variants of this story include "M'awerɛfiri a ema mekae sɛ mikyi abete yi" ("It's My Forgetfulness that Made Me Say I'm Allergic to Cornmeal Pulp") in Ayeh, *Mrehua,* 6–7; and "Ananse and His Forgetfulness" in Asihene, *Traditional Folk-Tales,* 7–8.

24. British explorer H. H. Johnston, as cited in Barker, "Nyankopon and Ananse in Gold Coast Folklore," 158.

25. A variant of this story called "Ananse and the Donkey" can be found in Asihene, *Traditional Folk-Tales,* 31–32.

26. van Dyck, "Analytical Study," 109.

27. A variant of this story called "Why Spiders Have Small Waists" can be found in Asihene, *Traditional Folk-Tales,* 359–60.

28. The story of Ananse's baldness can be found in "How the Spider Got a Bald Head" (Rattray, *Akan-Ashanti Folk-Tales,* 119–23); "How Ananse Became Bald" (Asihene, *Traditional Folk-Tales,* 73–74); and "The Cause of Ananse's Baldness" (ibid., 153–54). The story of his flat shape is told in "How Ananse Became Flat-Shaped" (Yankah, "Question of Ananse," 3); and, with an alternative explanation, in "How It Came About that Ananse, the Spider, Went Up on the Rafters" (Rattray, *Akan-Ashanti Folk-Tales,* 249). See also "How It Came About that the Hinder Part of Kwaku Ananse, the Spider, Became Big, at the Expense of His Head, Which Became Small" (ibid., 67–71).

29. See "Why Ananse, the Spider, Runs When He Is on the Surface of the Water" (Rattray, *Akan-Ashanti Folk-Tales,* 139–41); and "Why Spiders Hide in Dark Corners" (Asihene, *Traditional Folk-Tales,* 363–64).

30. See "Nea Enti a Ananse taa nwene ne Ntontan Wo Abe mu" ("Why Ananse Often Weaves His Web in the Palm-Nut Tree") (Ayeh, *Mrehua,* 11–12); "Ananse Ne Preko Asem Bi" ("A Story about Ananse and Pig") (ibid., 32–33); "Nea Enti A Ananse Tare Dampare Ani" ("Why the Spider Lies on the Rafters") (ibid., 79–81); and "Why a Spider Hides on the Ceiling" (Asihene, *Traditional Folk-Tales,* 317–19).

31. Asihene, *Traditional Folk-Tales,* ii (emphasis added).

32. Yankah, "Question of Ananse," 141 (emphasis added).

33. See, for example, Pelton, *Trickster in West Africa,* 54–55; and Carroll, "Trickster as Selfish-Buffoon," 113–16.

34. The author agrees with Charles van Dyck, who insists that Ananse is "simultaneously human and spider" ("Analytical Study of the Folktales," 119). However, van Dyck's outlook seems to be that Ananse has *no* definitively preconceived human or spider identity and that individual storytellers are thus free to position him in any way they see fit. It is important to note that Ananse always possesses *both* forms and that he will therefore resist any attempt to identify him as one or the other.

35. Roberts, *From Trickster to Badman,* 24–29.

36. See Rattray, *Akan-Ashanti Folk-Tales,* ix–x.

37. Tekpetey, "Kweku Ananse," 81; Vescey, "Exception Who Proves the Rule," 119; van Dyck, "Analytical Study," 153–58.

38. van Dyck, "Analytical Study," 153–58.

39. Stott, *Comedy,* 35.

40. See Turner, *From Ritual to Theatre,* 44–45, 84; and *Dramas, Fields, and Metaphors,* 56, 256–57, 295.

41. See Metraux, "Trickster," 1123; Mills, "Gender of the Trick," 240; Poliner, "Exiled Creature," 16; Yankah, "Question of Ananse," 8; and Tekpetey, "Kweku Ananse," 8.

42. Examples of the diverse uses of *asɛm* can be seen in common expressions. *Asɛm* means "an utterance" in the phrase "asɛm a ɛnna aka nen" (that's what Mother said). It can be translated as "news" in the sentence "Esi sika a w'anya nansa yi de ɛyɛ asɛm pa" (Esi's newfound wealth is good news). It translates as "concern" in "Ofori adwuma a ɔbɛ yɛ de ɛyɛ n'asɛm, ɛnyɛ m'asɛm" (what occupation Ofori chooses is his own concern, not my concern). It means "situation" in the phrase "asɛm yi de yɛ yɛ no den?" (what are we to do about this situation?). It refers to a legal proceeding or "case" in the phrase "wɔ kyere no wie yɛ no wɔ de n'asɛm kɔ to ɔhene anim" (following his arrest, his case was brought before the chief).

43. Hyde, *Trickster Makes This World*, 17. For additional discussions of the trickster-as-storyteller, see Pelton, *Trickster in West Africa*, 20; and Tekpetey, "Kweku Ananse," 75–81.

44. Variants of this story include "How It Came About that the Sky-God's Stories Came to Be Known as 'Spider Stories'" (Rattray, *Akan-Ashanti Folk-Tales*, 55–59); "The Origin of Spider Tales" (Asihene, *Traditional Folktale*, 217–20); and "How Stories Became Spider Stories" (van Dyck, "Analytical Study," 204–7).

45. See Sutherland, *Marriage of Anansewa*, vi; Tekpetey, "Kweku Ananse," 75; Jablow, *Anthology of West African Folklore*, 30; and Cole, *Ghana's Concert Party*, 109.

46. See Sutherland, *Marriage of Anansewa*, vii.

47. A variant of this exchange is described in van Dyck, "Analytical Study," 18.

48. See Ayeh, *Mmrehua*, ix.

49. See van Dyck, "Analytical Study," 17.

50. The term for "believe" in Akan is *gye dzi* (Fante dialect) or *gye di*, which literally means "accept and consume." This metaphorical connection between eating and belief is part of an extended cultural analogy that occurs throughout the various Akan subgroups.

51. See Yankah, "Nana Kwame Ampadu," 138; and Rattray, *Akan-Ashanti Folk-Tales*, xii.

52. See Asihene, *Traditional Folk-Tales*, ii; Sutherland, *Marriage of Anansewa*, v; and Yankah, "Nana Ampadu," 138–39.

53. Rattray, *Akan-Ashanti Folk-Tales*, x.

54. Yeboa-Danqua, "Storytelling of the Akan," 34. See also Sutherland, *Marriage of Anansewa*, vi.

55. A variant of this exchange can be found in Sutherland, *Marriage of Anansewa*, vii.

56. A variant of this exchange is given in van Dyck, "Analytical Study," 96–97.

57. Variants of these statements can be found in van Dyck, "Analytical Study," 18; and Ayeh, *Mmrehua*, x.

58. An example of this kind of exchange is given in Ayeh, *Mmrehua*, x.

59. In his remarks on the ethos of the trickster, Lewis Hyde emphasizes the ambivalent truth-status of storytelling by citing Pablo Picasso's paradoxical statement "Art is a lie that tells the truth" (Hyde, *Trickster Makes This World*, 13).

3. SELLING THE PRESIDENT

This chapter is a revision of the author's article "Selling the President: Stand-Up Comedy and the Politricks of Indirection in Ghana." *Theatre Survey* 54, no. 2 (2013): 255–81.

1. For a more detailed discussion of the role of IFIs in mandating tax policy, see Stewart and Jogarajan, "International Monetary Fund."

2. Safo, "Kumepreko March," 12. For additional perspectives on the VAT protests, see Danso, "VAT Has Failed Hopelessly"; Owusu, "Workers Disrupt May Day"; Samwini,

"VAT"; "Hear the Workers Cry," *Ghanaian Chronicle;* and "VAT Takes Off Today," *Ghanaian Times.*

3. Opposition leaders in Ghana included hard-line leftists (who supported Rawlings's original coup but later felt betrayed by his switch to neoliberal policies), as well as more moderate "politicos" (who had long opposed Rawlings's authoritarian tendencies on the basis of liberal-democratic principles). The diverse perspectives of these opposition leaders made it difficult for them to organize a unified opposition party, and this contributed to Rawlings's victory in popular elections. For a fuller discussion of the political coalitions that developed in opposition to Rawlings, see Haynes, "Ghana"; Jonah, "Political Parties"; and Oquaye, *Politics in Ghana,* 297–357.

4. As Brenda Chalfin observed, although specialized military units and functions had been removed from the coercive apparatus of the state in Ghana's transition to democracy, they did not disappear but, rather, resurfaced in new guises (*Neoliberal Frontiers,* 126).

5. Alliance for Change, "Killers of May 11."

6. J. Taylor, "Some Unconstitutional Aspects," 5.

7. Starobin, "Politics as Theatre," 2103.

8. See Okyere, "President Cuts Sod."

9. Rawlings, "Foreword," n.p.

10. Rawlings, "Let's Go Forward Together," 6.

11. Ibid.

12. Fuseini and Okyere, "Mother of All Rallies," 1.

13. "President Grateful to Supporters," *Daily Graphic,* 1.

14. Schechner, *Performance Studies,* 22.

15. National Theatre of Ghana, "General Report on the Concert Party Show Sponsored by Key Soap: July–Sept 1995." This is an internal company report from the office of the National Theatre of Ghana.

16. For some of Okalla's press accolades, see Abdulai, "Comedy at National Theatre" and "Bob Okalla in Concert"; Alomele, "AAA and Okalla Meet" and "Bob Okalla at Concert Party"; and Crabbe, "Bob Okalla on Stage."

17. Yankah, "Leave Okalla Alone," 5.

18. See Yankah, *Speaking for the Chief,* 51, and "Nana Kwame Ampadu," 137.

19. "Thugs Threaten O. D. and Okalla," *Daily Graphic,* 1.

20. "Bob Okalla," *The Mirror,* 3.

21. Dadson, "Is Okalla Finished?," 11.

22. The Akan expression "te yie" in this song—like its English equivalent, "well seated"—is a phrase that can convey not only literal physical stability but also sociopolitical positioning and/or the possession of wealth. For a discussion of "Ebi Te Yie" and other recordings by Ampadu, see Yankah, "Nana Kwame Ampadu."

23. Ibid., 151.

24. Ibid.

25. See Bame, *Come to Laugh,* 10; and Collins, "Comic Opera in Ghana," 50.

26. Cole, *Ghana's Concert Party Theatre,* 79.

27. For North Americans, the blackface practices from which Johnson borrowed are emotionally charged representations associated with the continuing legacy of racism. However, at least by the available evidence, neither Ishmael Johnson nor subsequent "Bob" performers in Ghana were aware of the social impact of these kinds of racial representations in the

Americas. The concert party blackface tradition initiated by Johnson thus developed, at least for some decades, relatively independently of New World systems of signification. Today, the continuing tradition of "Bob" performances in Ghana has to be viewed in the light of this autonomous development, as well as through the lens of more recent transnational dialogues. See Cole, *Ghana's Concert Party,* 17.

28. Ibid., 125.

29. Crabbe, "Bob Okalla on Stage," 11.

30. This is the author's translation from a live performance by Okalla at Ghana's National Theatre, March 2000.

31. Ibid.

32. Sakyi-Addo, "Soap Wars," 1. For an extensive discussion of the political history of soap in Africa, see Burke, *Lifebuoy Men, Lux Women.*

33. Yankah, "Leave Okalla Alone," 5.

34. Scott, *Domination,* 137.

35. Yankah, "Leave Okalla Alone," 5.

36. J. Lartey, "NPP Exposes Bob Okalla"; Fuseini, "NPP Denies Harassing OD."

37. Some prominent examples include Ankrah, "Politics of Thuggery"; Kassim, "NDC Thugs Attack"; and O. Lartey, "Bloody Clash."

38. Zingaro, "Watch These Things."

39. This is the author's translation from a live performance by Okalla at Ghana's National Theatre in March 2000. The phrase "pastor-woman" is the author's translation of "osofo-maame," an Akan term that is used to refer to a female pastor of a church but also to the wife of a male pastor.

40. Boadu, "Clash of Women over Evangelist," 3. For a discussion of the moral legitimacy of comedic parodies of fake pastors in Ghana, see Shipley, "Comedians, Pastors, and the Miraculous," 523–52.

41. The "Glass and Bottle Church" is a standard part of Okalla's routine; he usually sings it as he is leaving the stage at the conclusion of his performance. The particular rendition given here is the author's translation of a live performance by Okalla at Ghana's National Theatre, July 2000.

42. See Akyeampong, *Drink, Power,* 12–19.

43. Ewusi, "Stop Bishop Okalla," 2.

44. Crabbe, "Bob Okalla on Stage," 11.

45. Mimesis is a process of imitation that creates an apparent or superficial correspondence, one that is based on similarity but not on identity. The "mimetic gap," then, refers to the lack of identity between an original and its imitation—in this case, the gap between the actual Bible and Okalla's book-that-looks-like-a-Bible. The mimetic gap—although real—is always a bit suspicious, because imitations are commonly seen as having an effect on the value or substance of the original. See Gebauer and Wulf, *Mimesis,* 317; Davis and Postlewait, "Theatricality," 12; and Taussig, *Mimesis and Alterity,* 52–59.

46. Linda Hutcheon (*Theory of Parody,* 40) distinguished between *travesty* and *parody* on the basis that the former always involves ridicule and belittling, while the later is more ambiguous and may or may not be interpreted as involving ridicule. In a similar vein, Margaret Rose (*Parody,* 51) writes that "most parody worthy of its name is ambivalent toward its target. This ambivalence may entail not only a mixture of criticism and sympathy for the parodied text but also the creative expansion of it into something new."

47. See Gates, *Signifying Monkey*, 56–57.

48. Jonas, *Ananse in the Great House*, 2.

49. Drewal, "State of Research," 10.

4. MA RED'S MANEUVERS

1. Hagan, "Nkrumah's Cultural Policy," 6–7. See also Sutherland, *Second Phase*, 45.

2. Ministry of Education and Culture, *Culture Policy in Ghana*, 9, 41.

3. Arthur, "Sessional Address," 287.

4. Whether the National Theatre Movement survived Nkrumah's overthrow at all has been a matter of debate. Some critics have argued that NTM rhetoric in the post-Nkrumah era romanticized and emphasized "tradition" in ways that artists with broader creative sensibilities found disagreeable (Halm, *Theatre and Ideology*, 185–95). Others have suggested that the NTM was "a ghost movement from the start" that lived only "in the dreams and rhetoric of its exponents" (Yirenkyi, "Kobina Sekyi," 40).

5. Constructed at a cost of US$20 million, the elegant edifice covered about 12,000 square meters and was said to appear, from a distance, like "a gigantic ship returning in victory from the Atlantic Ocean" (National Theatre of Ghana, *National Theatre in Retrospect*, 13).

6. Rawlings, "Enhancing," 108–9.

7. Cole, *Ghana's Concert Party Theatre*, 24; Agovi, "The Origins of Literary Theatre," 7.

8. See Agovi, "The Origins of Literary Theatre," 11–13; Edsman, *Lawyers*, 15; Kimble, *Political History*, 64; and Arhin, "Rank and Class," 17. See also Plageman, *Highlife Saturday Night*, 67–99, which, although contextualizing highlife music and dance, describes the same colonial social formation from which the concert party emerged.

9. Cole, *Ghana's Concert Party Theatre*, 68–69. In fact, one outcome of the educated elite's disfavor with popular expressive culture was the construction of youth recreation facilities. It was hoped that these clubs would turn these young people, described as "ruffians and criminals whose sole intention is illicit pleasure and self-gratifying debauchery" into disciplined, well-behaved citizens who fit the elite's own vision of social order and cultural progress (Plageman, *Highlife Saturday Night*, 74–83).

10. Cole, *Ghana's Concert Party*, 150.

11. Plageman, *Highlife Saturday Night*, 154–59.

12. David Dontoh, president of the Ghana Concert Party Union and former master of ceremonies of the Keysoap Concert Party Show, personal interview, February 2001.

13. See Barber, Collins, and Ricard, *West African Popular Theatre*, 70–71. The period from the 1940s to the time of independence was especially suitable for promoting the concert party to a paying audience because of the growth of commercialized leisure in the city of Accra. For a detailed discussion of commercialized leisure during those years, see Plageman, *Highlife Saturday Night*, 103–24.

14. Cole, *Ghana's Concert Party Theatre*, 89.

15. Barber, Collins, and Ricard, *West African Popular Theatre*, 59, 64. See a discussion of the promises and pitfalls of being a "bandsman" also in Plageman, *Highlife Saturday Night*, 183–212.

16. Ibid., 82.

17. Ibid., 78–81.

18. Ibid., 14.

19. Ama Buabeng, personal interview, March 2001. See also Buabeng and Sutherland-Addy, "Drama in Her Life," 69.

20. Anastasia Agbenyegah, former National Theatre official, personal interview, January 2001.

21. National Theatre, "Minutes of Key Soap Concert Party," 5.

22. National Theatre, *Corporate Plan,* 5.

23. Ibid., iv.

24. Ibid., vi.

25. Hobsbawm, "Inventing Traditions," 1. In 1996, Alex Appiah wrote a letter to the editor of Ghana's *Mirror* newspaper, titled "In Praise of Keysoap," suggesting that this invented narrative of symbolic value had gotten through to consumers. Appiah wrote, "I do not know how old Keysoap has been [*sic*] in Ghana, but . . . I am sure of one thing. It is more than 36 years." Appiah claimed that, as a child, his mother made him sell Keysoap to help pay for his education. He felt that there was a continuity in the quality and economy of the soap, explaining that it had always been "sufficient for everything": Children could wash clothes and bathe with it, the soap "formed rich lather just like [in] the present," and the product he remembers from his childhood looked "just like the present one in the market, except for a few changes here and there."

26. William Addo, personal interview, March 2001.

27. Jones, *Renewing Unilever,* 323–29.

28. Unilever Ghana Limited, "Balancing Profit with Responsible Corporate Behavior," http://www.unilever.com/aboutus/ourhistory/.

29. World Investment News Report on Unilever Ghana, "Report on Ghana: Enhancing Trade and Accruing Investment," http://www.winne.com/ghana4/to08.html.

30. Unilever Kenya had already developed a similar program in that country, and the efforts in Ghana were based on the Kenyan model (Ako Tetteh, National Theatre Official, personal interview, February 2001; Anthony Ebo Spio, Keysoap Brand Manager, personal interview, August 2001).

31. Ako Tetteh, personal interview, February 2001.

32. "Concert Parties," *Weekly Spectator,* 6.

33. Anastasia Agbenyegah, personal interview, January 2001.

34. "Actors, Comedians Update Techniques," *Ghanaian Times,* 3.

35. Bonsu, "Concert Party Fracas," 17.

36. Kenneth Quarshie, as quoted in Bonsu, "Concert Party Fracas," 17.

37. William Addo, as quoted in Bonsu, "Concert Party Fracas," 17.

38. Kenneth Quarshie, as quoted in Bonsu, "Concert Party Fracas," 17.

39. William Addo, personal interview, March 2001.

40. Anthony Ebo Spio, personal interview, August 2001.

41. Joe Boy supplied this information about the history of the King Karo Troupe in a personal interview, July 2001.

42. Group conversations with King Karo members, principally Linda Amoako, Asantewa Botchway, Miriam Donkor, Ivan Odartey Lamptey, and leader Joe Boy, June–July 2001.

43. Cole, *Ghana's Concert Party Theatre,* 151.

44. William Addo, personal interview, March 2001.

45. Private conversation with Ako Tetteh, July 2001.

46. James C. Scott (*Domination and the Arts of Resistance,* 145) observed that spreading rumors can often be a form of "insinuated" political resistance. In addition to providing a consoling logic and expressing group cohesion, rumors spread among disempowered and disgruntled persons can also be a way of contesting dominant ideologies that are perceived as unsatisfactory but cannot be directly challenged.

47. See Chisholm, "Fade to White."

48. Ray, "India's Unbearable Lightness of Being," n.p.; see also Leistikow, "Indian Women." Unilever discontinued two of their ads for this product after a campaign by the All India Democratic Women's Association compelled the Indian government to issue a notice to the company.

49. Private conversation with Ako Tetteh, July 2001.

50. Private conversation with Joe Boy, June 2001.

51. The author's translations from the play *Afutuo Nsakra Onipa Gye Sɛ Nsɔ-Hwɛ* are taken from the production's final dress rehearsal, conducted at the Accra Arts Center in September 2001.

52. Private conversation with Linda Amoako, July 2001.

53. Cole, *Ghana's Concert Party Theatre*, 84.

54. Cole, *Ghana's Concert Party Theatre*, 126; Buabeng and Sutherland-Addy, "Drama in Her Life," 73.

55. Hutchful, *Ghana's Adjustment Experience*, 22.

5. IN THE HOUSE OF STORIES

1. For more about colonial-era distinctions in African clothing, education, and mannerisms, see Essah, "Fashioning the Nation," 58–63; and Miescher, "Life Histories of Boakye Yiadom," 168–73.

2. Arkhurst, "Kodzidan," 169.

3. Ibid., 168.

4. July, *African Voice*, 78.

5. See July, *African Voice*, 76; and Wellington, "Architecture," 185.

6. See July, *African Voice*, 80; and a similar account in Arkhurst, "Kodzidan," 169.

7. De Graft, *Through a Film Darkly*, 3.

8. See Conquergood's characterization of culture as "an unfolding performative invention instead of a reified system, structure, or variable" ("Rethinking Ethnography," 190) or Drewal's advocacy for a paradigmatic shift in the study of culture from "structure to process" ("Performance Studies," 673; "State of Research," 3; *Yoruba Ritual*, 10).

9. Akyea, "Atwia Ekumfi Kodzidan," 83.

10. Plair and Heckler, *Goals of FISC*, n.p.

11. For more on the nuanced outlooks and experiences of "post-tourism" travelers, see Feifer, *Going Places*, 269–71; and MacCannell, "Staged Authenticity."

12. Organization for Economic Co-operation and Development, *Benchmark Definition*, 234–35.

13. Tsikata, Asante, and Gyasi, *Determinants of Foreign Direct Investment*, 8. See also Abdulai, *Sectoral Analysis*.

14. See United Nations Conference, *World Investment Report*, 8–9, 24–25; United Nations Conference, *Foreign Direct Investment*, 4–5; and Tsikata, Asante, and Gyasi, *Determinants of Foreign Direct Investment*, 16.

15. Some economic research suggests that these fears are well founded. See Oxfam International, *Emperor's New Clothes*, 17–18; Abdulai, *Sectoral Analysis*, section 8.0; Moss, Ramachandran, and Shah, *Is Africa's Skepticism of Foreign Capital Justified?*, 8; and Center for Research on Multinational Corporations, *Is Foreign Investment Good for Development?*, 3.

16. See Tsikata, Asante, and Gyasi, *Determinants of Foreign Direct Investment*, 2.

17. Ibid., 31–32.

18. Konadu-Agyemang, "Structural Adjustment Programs," 188. Also, tourism's position after oil and vehicle production is severally acknowledged. See, for instance, Asiedu, "Prospects," 11; Batta, *Tourism and the Environment,* 13; Brohman, "New Directions," 52; Colantonio and Potter, *Urban Tourism,* 25; and Steel, *Vulnerable Careers,* 4.

19. Ghana Tourist Board data in Konadu-Agyemang, "Structural Adjustment Programs," 190.

20. Asiedu, "Prospects," 20.

21. Asiedu, "Prospects," 22; Konadu-Agyemang, "Structural Adjustment Programs," 204; and Segbefia, "Community Approach to Tourism," 57–58, all raise concerns about "leakage."

22. Konadu-Agyemang, "Structural Adjustment Programs," 202.

23. Tsikata, Asante and Gyasi, *Determinants of Foreign Direct Investment,* 31.

24. For a detailed account of Chief Alfred Sam's attempt, see Bittle and Geis, *Longest Way Home;* and Field and Coletu, "Chief Sam Movement."

25. See Cole, *Ghana's Concert Party Theatre,* 32–34.

26. See "Celebration Highlights," *Pittsburgh Courier,* A7; "Ghanese Await Day," *Pittsburgh Courier,* A7; and "Ghana, Africa," *Pittsburgh Courier,* B4.

27. Payne, "Ghana Independence," 3.

28. "Ghana—A New African Nation," *Pittsburgh Courier,* A7.

29. For a similar contrast between Nkrumah-era and Rawlings-era pan-Africanism, see Pierre, *Predicament of Blackness,* 164.

30. Bruner quotes the late African American emigrant Dr. Robert Lee in "Tourism in Ghana," 291.

31. The term *neoliberal pan-Africanism* is from Jemima Pierre (*Predicament of Blackness,* 150), who also connects the rise of a neoliberal regime and the new heritage tourism economy in Ghana. Bayo Holsey makes the same connection (*Routes of Remembrance,* 231) when she observes that Rawlings's pan-Africanist agenda, "being based on tourism, was firmly ensconced within a capitalist framework" that turned "the remembrance of the slave trade into a commodity that Ghana could sell to diaspora tourists."

32. Muhammad, "President's Initiative at OAU," 1.

33. Ibid.

34. Nyinah, "Lincoln Honors President and Wife," 9. See Holsey (*Routes of Remembrance,* 229) and Pierre (*Predicament of Blackness,* 164) for a similar view that Rawlings positioned himself as the heir of Nkrumah's legacy of pan-African leadership by forging a connection between Ghanaians and members of the African diaspora.

35. Koblah, "President Praised in Harlem." 1.

36. Edusei, "Millennium Summit," 12–19.

37. The author found it hard not to cringe at what seemed to be blatantly misogynistic narratives, but their juxtaposition offers a more complex reading (see Donkor, "Kodzidan Mboguw," 42–43). Whereas the Oweah story blames male suffering on female perfidy, the antelope-thigh story blames female discord on male betrayal. In other words, there is an important etiological difference between the two narratives. Concomitantly, if one views the two stories together—that is, as constituents of a performance repertoire—one sees that as the teller of the antelope-thigh story legitimated the co-identification of co-wives with rivalry, she also produced a counternarrative of man as the father of such discord. Her gesture, like the trickster's double-ness, combined legitimation and subversion in one utterance or act. Viewed together, the two narratives thus assume the dialogic quality of a gendered rhetorical joust.

38. Hynes, "Inconclusive Conclusions," 212.
39. Ebron, *Performing Africa,* 209–11.
40. See Segbefia, "Community Approach."
41. Plair and Heckler, *Goals of FISC,* n.p.
42. Pierre, *Predicament of Blackness,* 3–4, 143, 151.
43. Holsey, *Routes of Remembrance,* 137.
44. For more on "infra-politics," see Scott, *Domination,* 201.

CONCLUSION

1. Chalfin, *Neoliberal Frontiers,* 11.
2. Ibid., 39.
3. Thomson, *Mercenaries, Pirates and Sovereigns,* 224.
4. de Certeau, *Practice of Everyday Life,* 29–42.
5. Chalfin, *Neoliberal Frontiers,* 234.
6. See Harvey, *Brief History of Neoliberalism,* 79–80.
7. Brenner and Theodore, "Cities and the Geographies," 349; Harvey, *Brief History of Neoliberalism,* 39.
8. Chalfin, *Neoliberal Frontiers,* 4, 227.
9. Ferguson, *Global Shadows,* 75–80.
10. Campbell and Loxley, *Structural Adjustment,* 2; Ferguson, *Global Shadows,* 80.
11. Ferguson, *Global Shadows,* 81.
12. The author is not the first to challenge the idea that in Africa, neoliberal rhetoric is the "amoral techno-speak" that Ferguson describes. Brenda Chalfin also maintains that it takes the form of a "deeply contextualized and highly moral discourse in which notions of good and evil, the righteous and the fallen, truth and falsity, are central" (*Neoliberal Frontiers,* 159). The difference is that the author associates the moral underpinnings of neoliberal rhetoric in millennial Ghana specifically with the entrenched status of the postcolonial social compact.
13. Scott, *Domination and the Arts of Resistance,* 14–19.
14. On the definition of radical acts, see Madison, *Acts of Activism,* 18.

BIBLIOGRAPHY

Abdulai, Baba. "Bob Okalla in Concert." *Weekly Spectator* (Ghana), April 27, 1996, p. 6.
———. "Comedy at National Theatre." *Weekly Spectator* (Ghana), December 23, 1996, p. 6.
Abdulai, Ibrahim. *Sectoral Analysis of Foreign Direct Investment in Ghana.* Working paper. Accra: Bank of Ghana, 2004.
Abouharb, M. Rodwan, and David Cingranelli. *Human Rights and Structural Adjustment.* New York: Cambridge University Press, 2007.
Adam, Basiru. "Ghana Regains Her 'Fool' Sense of Humor." *Public Agenda* (Ghana), November 29, 2010, n.p.
Agovi, Kofi. "The Origins of Literary Theatre in Ghana, 1920–1957." *Research Review* 6, no. 1 (1990): 1–23.
Akan Orthography Committee. *The Writing of Akan.* Accra: Bureau of Ghana Languages, 1962.
Akonor, Kwame. *Africa and IMF Conditionalities: The Unevenness of Compliance, 1983–2000.* New York: Routledge, 2006.
Akyea, E. Ofori. "The Atwia Ekumfi Kodzidan: An Experimental African Theatre." *Okyeame* 4, no. 1 (1968): 82–84.
Akyeampong, Emmanuel. *Drink, Power, and Cultural Change: A Social History of Alcohol in Ghana, 1800 to Recent Times.* Portsmouth, NH: Heinemann, 1996.
Alliance for Change. "The Killers of May 11 Are Still at Large." *Ghanaian Chronicle,* September 7–10, 1995, p. 6.
Alomele, Merari. "AAA and Okalla Meet." *Weekly Spectator* (Ghana), September 14, 1996, p. 6.
———. "Bob Okalla at Concert Party." *Weekly Spectator* (Ghana), August 3, 1996, p. 6.
Ankrah, Paa Lewis. "Politics of Thuggery and Money Arrives in Cape Coast." *Ghanaian Chronicle,* May 16–19, 1996, p. 7.
Apter, David E. *The Gold Coast in Transition.* Princeton, NJ: Princeton University Press, 1955.
Arhin, Kwame. "Rank and Class among the Fante and Asante in the Nineteenth Century." *Africa* 53, no. 1 (1983): 2–22.
Arkhurst, Sandy. "Kodzidan." In *The Legacy of Efua Sutherland: Pan-African Cultural Activism,* edited by Anne V. Adams and Esi Sutherland-Addy, 165–74. Banbury, UK: Ayebia Clarke, 2007.

Armah, Ayi Kwei. *The Beautyful Ones Are Not Yet Born*. Oxford: Heinemann, 1969.

Arthur, A. "Sessional Address, 13th December." In *Parliamentary Debates: Official Report,* 286–87. Accra: Ghana National Assembly, 1979.

Asante, K. B. "Nkrumah and State Enterprises." In *The Life and Work of Kwame Nkrumah,* edited by Kwame Arhin, 257–79. Accra: Sedco, 1991.

Ashcroft, Bill, Gareth Griffith, and Helen Tiffin. *Postcolonial Studies: The Key Concepts*. New York: Routledge, 2007.

Ashun, Robert Carlton. *Kotoka and Ghana*. Accra: State Publishing Corporation, 1968.

Asiedu, Alex. "Prospects for an Emerging Tourism Industry in Ghana." *Research Review* 13, no. 1–2 (1997): 11–26.

Asihene, Emmanuel. *Traditional Folk-Tales of Ghana*. Lewiston, NY: Edwin Mellen, 1997.

Austin, Dennis. *Politics in Ghana: 1946–1960*. Oxford: Oxford University Press, 1970.

Ayeh, E. O. *Mmrehua*. Accra: Ghana Publishing, 1978.

Bame, Kwabena N. *Come to Laugh: African Traditional Theatre in Ghana*. New York: Lilian Barber, 1985.

Bangura, Yusuf, and Peter Gibbon. "Adjustment, Authoritarianism and Democracy in Sub-Saharan Africa." In *Authoritarianism, Democracy, and Adjustment,* edited by Peter Gibbon, Yusuf Bangura, and Arve Oftstad, 7–38. Uppsala, Sweden: Nordiska Africainstitutet, 1992.

Barber, Karin, John Collins, and Alain Ricard. *West African Popular Theatre*. Bloomington: Indiana University Press, 1997.

Bargh, Maria. *Resistance: An Indigenous Response to Neoliberalism*. Wellington, New Zealand: Huia, 2007.

Barker, Rodney. *Political Legitimacy and the State*. Oxford: Clarendon, 1990.

Barker, William H. "Nyankopon and Ananse in Gold Coast Folklore." *Folklore* 30, no. 2 (1919): 158–64.

Batta, R. N. *Tourism and the Environment: A Quest for Sustainability*. New Delhi: Indus Publishing, 2002.

Beckman, Bjorn. "Empowerment or Repression? The World Bank and the Politics of African Adjustment." In *Authoritarianism, Democracy, and Adjustment,* edited by Peter Gibbon, Yusuf Bangura, and Arve Oftstad, 83–105. Uppsala, Sweden: Nordiska Africainstitutet, 1992.

Bello, Walden. *Dark Victory: The United States and Global Poverty*. London: Pluto, 1999.

Bhabha, Homi. *The Location of Culture*. New York: Routledge, 1994.

Bienen, Henry, and Jeffrey Herbst. "The Relationship between Political and Economic Reform in Africa." *Comparative Politics* 29, no. 1 (1996): 23–42.

Bittle, William, and Gilbert Geis. *The Longest Way Home: Chief Alfred C. Sam's Back to Africa Movement*. Detroit: Wayne State University Press, 1964.

Blum, William. *Killing Hope: U.S. Military and CIA Interventions since World War II*. London: Zed, 2003.

Boadu, Kwame Asare. "Clash of Women over Evangelist." *The Mirror* (Ghana), June 22, 1996, p. 3.

Bonsu, Adwoa, "Concert Party Fracas." *The Mirror* (Ghana). February 28, 1998, p. 17.

Bosman, Willem. *A New and Accurate Description of the Coast of Guinea, Divided into the Gold, the Slave, and the Ivory Coasts*. Translated from the Dutch. London: James Knapton and Dan Midwinter, 1705.

Botchway, F. Nii Nuertey. "The President, His Vice, and the Constitution of Ghana: Implications of the Rawlings-Arkaah Conflagration." *East African Journal of Peace and Human Rights* 4, no. 2 (1995): 90–101.

Brenner, Neil, and Nik Theodore. "Cities and the Geographies of 'Actually Existing Neoliberalism.'" *Antipode* 34, no. 3 (2002): 349–79.

Brohman, John. "New Directions in Tourism for Third World Development." *Annals of Tourism Research* 23, no. 1 (1996): 48–70.

Bruner, Edward M. "Tourism in Ghana: The Representation of Slavery and the Return of the
Black Diaspora." *American Anthropologist* 98, no. 2 (1996): 290–304.

Buabeng, Ama, and Esi Sutherland-Addy. "Drama in Her Life: The Story of Adeline Ama
Buabeng." In *African Theatre Women*, edited by Jane Plastow, 66–82. Oxford: James
Currey, 2002.

Burke, Timothy. *Lifebuoy Men, Lux Women: Commodification, Consumption, and Cleanliness in
Zimbabwe*. Durham, NC: Duke University Press, 1996.

Burton, Richard. *Afro-Creole: Power, Opposition, and Play in the Caribbean*. Ithaca, NY:
Cornell University Press, 1997.

Butler, Judith. *Gender Trouble: Feminism and the Subversion of Identity*. New York: Routledge,
1999.

Campbell, Bonnie, and John Loxley, eds. *Structural Adjustment in Africa*. New York:
St. Martin's, 1989.

Carroll, Michael P. "The Trickster as Selfish-Buffoon and Culture Hero." *Ethos* 12, no. 2
(1984): 105–31.

Center for Research on Multinational Corporations (SOMO). *Is Foreign Investment Good
for Development?: A Literature Review*. Amsterdam: SOMO, 2008. http://somo.nl
/publications-en/Publication_2478.

Certeau, Michel de. *The Practice of Everyday Life*. Berkeley: University of California Press,
1988.

Chalfin, Brenda. *Neoliberal Frontiers: An Ethnography of Sovereignty in West Africa*. Chicago:
University of Chicago Press, 2013.

Chazan, Naomi. *An Anatomy of Ghanaian Politics: Managing Political Recession 1969–1982*.
Boulder, CO: Westview, 1983.

Chisholm, N. Jamiyla. "Fade to White." *Village Voice*, January 22, 2002. http://www.village
voice.com/2002-01-22/news/fade-to-white.

Cohen, Abner. *The Politics of Elite Culture: Explorations into the Dramaturgy of Power in a
Modern African Society*. Berkeley: University of California Press, 1981.

Cohen, Ronald. "Introduction." In *State Formation and Political Legitimacy*, edited by Ronald
Cohen and Judith Toland, 1–22. New Brunswick, NJ: Transaction, 1988.

Coicaud, Jean-Marc. *Legitimacy and Politics: A Contribution to the Study of Political Right and
Political Responsibility*. New York: Cambridge University Press, 2002.

Colantonio, Andrea, and Robert B. Potter. *Urban Tourism and Development in the Socialist
State*. Burlington, VT: Ashgate, 2006.

Cole, Catherine M. *Ghana's Concert Party Theatre*. Bloomington: Indiana University
Press, 2001.

Collins, John. "Comic Opera in Ghana." *African Arts* 9, no. 2 (1976): 50–57.

Comaroff, Jean, and John L. Comaroff. "Millennial Capitalism: First Thoughts on a Second
Coming." In *Millennial Capitalism and the Culture of Neoliberalism*, edited by Jean Comaroff
and John L. Comaroff, 1–56. Durham, NC: Duke University Press, 2001.

———. "Note on Afro-Modernity and the Neo-World Order: Afterword." In *Producing African
Futures: Ritual and Reproduction in a Neoliberal Age*, edited by Brad Weiss, 329–48. Leiden,
Netherlands: Brill, 2004.

———. *Of Revelation and Revolution: Vol. 1: Christianity, Colonialism, and Consciousness in South Africa*. Chicago: University of Chicago Press, 1991.

Connell, Raewyn. "Understanding Neoliberalism." In *Neoliberalism and Everyday Life*, edited by Susan Braedley and Meg Luxton, 22–36. Montreal: McGill–Queens University Press, 2010.

Conquergood, Dwight. "Beyond the Text: Towards a Performative Cultural Politics." In *Cultural Struggles: Performance, Ethnography, Praxis*, edited by E. Patrick Johnson, 47–63. Ann Arbor: University of Michigan Press, 2013.

———. "Of Caravans and Carnivals: Performance Studies in Motion." In *Cultural Struggles: Performance, Ethnography, Praxis*, edited by E. Patrick Johnson, 26–31. Ann Arbor: University of Michigan Press, 2013.

———. "Performance Studies: Interventions and Radical Research." In *Cultural Struggles: Performance, Ethnography, Praxis*, edited by E. Patrick Johnson, 32–46. Ann Arbor: University of Michigan Press, 2013.

———. "Performing as a Moral Act: Ethical Dimensions of the Ethnography of Performance." In *Cultural Struggles: Performance, Ethnography, Praxis*, edited by E. Patrick Johnson, 65–80. Ann Arbor: University of Michigan Press, 2013.

———. "Performing Cultures: Ethnography, Epistemology and Ethics." In *Cultural Struggles: Performance, Ethnography, Praxis*, edited by E. Patrick Johnson, 15–25. Ann Arbor: University of Michigan Press, 2013.

———. "The Power of Symbols." *One City*. Chicago: Chicago Council on Urban Affairs, 1996.

———. "Rethinking Ethnography: Towards a Critical Cultural Politics." In *Cultural Struggles: Performance, Ethnography, Praxis*, edited by E. Patrick Johnson, 81–103. Ann Arbor: University of Michigan Press, 2013.

Crabbe, Michael. "Bob Okalla on Stage." *The Mirror* (Ghana), April 20, 1996, p. 11.

Dadson, Nanabanyin. "Is Okalla Finished?" *The Mirror* (Ghana), October 28, 1996, p. 11.

Daily Graphic (Ghana). "President Grateful to Supporters, Well Wishers." September 11, 1996, p. 1.

———. "Thugs Threaten O. D. and Okalla." September 23, 1996, p. 1.

Danso, Kwabena. "VAT Has Failed Hopelessly." *Ghanaian Chronicle*, May 11–14, 1995, p. 2.

Davis, Tracy. *Actresses as Working Women: Their Social Identity in Victorian Culture*. New York: Routledge, 1991.

Davis, Tracy, and Thomas Postlewait. "Theatricality: An Introduction." In *Theatricality*, edited by Tracy Davis and Thomas Postlewait, 1–39. New York: Cambridge University Press, 2003.

De Graft, Joe. *Through a Film Darkly*. London: Oxford University Press, 1970.

Derrida, Jacques. *Margins of Philosophy*. Chicago: University of Chicago Press, 1982.

———. *Speech and Performance*. Evanston, IL: Northwestern University Press, 1973.

———. *Writing and Difference*. Chicago: University of Chicago Press, 1978.

Diamond, Elin. "Introduction." In *Performance and Cultural Politics*, edited by Elin Diamond, 1–12. New York: Routledge, 1996.

Diamond, Larry. "Introduction: Political Culture and Democracy." In *Political Culture and Democracy in Developing Countries*, edited by Larry Diamond, 1–36. Boulder, CO: Lynne Rienner, 1993.

Dibua, Jeremiah. "Journey to Nowhere: Neoliberalism and Africa's Development Crisis." *Comparative Studies of South Asia Africa and the Middle East* 18, no. 2 (1998): 119–30.

Dolan, Jill. "Geographies of Learning: Theatre Studies, Performance, and the "Performative." *Theatre Journal* 11, no. 2 (1993): 85–104.

Donkor, David A. "Kodzidan Mboguw: Supplanted Acts, Displaced Narratives, and the Social Logic of a Trickster in the House of Stories." In *The Legacy of Efua Sutherland: Pan-African Cultural Activism,* edited by Anne V. Adams and Esi Sutherland-Addy, 38–46. Banbury, UK: Ayebia Clarke, 2007.

Donkor, Kwabena. *Structural Adjustment and Mass Poverty in Ghana.* Brookfield, MA: Ashgate, 1997.

Doty, William, and William Hynes. "Historical Overview of Theoretical Issues: The Problem of the Trickster." In *Mythical Trickster Figures: Contours, Contexts, and Criticisms,* edited by William Hynes and William Doty, 13–32. Tuscaloosa: University of Alabama Press, 1993.

Drewal, Margaret. "Performance Studies and African Folklore Research." In *African Folklore: An Encyclopedia,* edited by Phillip Peek and Kwesi Yankah, 669–80. New York: Routledge, 2005.

———. "The State of Research on Performance in Africa." *African Studies Review* 34, no. 3 (1991): 1–64.

———. *Yoruba Ritual: Performers, Play, Agency.* Bloomington: Indiana University Press, 1992.

Ebron, Paula. *Performing Africa.* Princeton, NJ: Princeton University Press, 2002.

Economist, The. "Sisters in the Wood: A Survey of the IMF and the World Bank." October 12, 1991, pp. 5–48.

Edelman, Murray. *The Symbolic Uses of Politics.* Urbana: University of Illinois Press, 1985.

Edsman, Bjorn M. *Lawyers in Gold Coast Politics: 1900–1945.* Uppsala, Sweden: Acta Universitatis Upsaliensa, 1979.

Edusei, Eric. "Millennium Summit: The 5th African–African American Summit, Accra, May 1999." *Akwaaba—The Inflight Magazine of Ghana Airways,* May 1999, 13–19.

Ellis, Alfred Burdon. *The Tsi-Speaking Peoples of the Gold Coast of West Africa: Their Religion, Manners, Customs, Laws, Language, Etc.* London: Chapman and Hall, 1887.

Essah, Doris. "Fashioning the Nation: Hairdressing, Professionalism, and the Performance of Gender in Ghana, 1900–2006." PhD diss., University of Michigan, 2008.

Ewusi, Nana. "Stop Bishop Okalla TV Show." *Ghanaian Chronicle,* January 25–28, 1996, p. 2.

Fabienne, Peter. "Political Legitimacy." *Stanford Encyclopedia of Philosophy.* http://plato.stanford.edu/entries/legitimacy.

Feifer, Maxine. *Going Places.* London: Macmillan, 1985.

Ferguson, James. *Global Shadows: Africa in the Neoliberal World Order.* Durham, NC: Duke University Press, 2006.

Field, Kendra, and Ebony Coletu. "The Chief Sam Movement, a Century Later." *Transition* 114 (2014): 108–30.

Fitch, Robert, and Mary Oppenheimer. *Ghana: End of an Illusion.* New York: Monthly Review Press, 1966.

Furtado, Celso. "Post-national Capitalism." *Latin American Research Unit Studies* 2, no. 2 (1978): 1–27.

Fuseini, A. B. A. "NPP Denies Harassing O. D. and Okalla." *Daily Graphic* (Ghana), September 24, 1996, p. 1.

Fuseini, A. B. A., and Joe Okyere. "Mother of All Rallies." *Daily Graphic* (Ghana), September 9, 1996, p. 1.

Gates, Henry Louis Jr. *The Signifying Monkey: A Theory of African-American Literary Criticism.* New York: Oxford University Press, 1988.

Gebauer, Gunter, and Christoph Wulf. *Mimesis: Culture, Art, Society.* Berkeley: University of California Press, 1995.

Genoud, Roger. *Nationalism and Economic Development in Ghana.* New York: Praeger, 1969.

Ghanaian Chronicle. "Hear the Workers Cry, Mr. President." April 24–26, 1995, p. 5.

Ghanaian Times. "Actors, Comedians Update Techniques." November 21, 1995, p. 3.

———. "VAT Takes Off Today." March 1, 1995, p. 1.

Gilley, Bruce. "The Meaning and Measure of State Legitimacy: Results for 72 Countries." *European Journal of Political Research* 45, no. 3 (2006): 499–525.

Gocking, Roger. *The History of Ghana.* Westport, CT: Greenwood, 2005.

Goffman, Erving. *The Presentation of Self in Everyday Life.* Garden City, NY: Doubleday, 1959.

Greenhouse, Carol, ed. *Ethnographies of Neoliberalism.* Philadelphia: University of Pennsylvania Press, 2010.

Guggisberg, Decima More, and Frederick G. Guggisberg. *We Two in West Africa.* New York: Scribner, 1909.

Gyimah-Boadi, Emmanuel. "State Enterprises Divestiture: Recent Ghanaian Experiences." In *Ghana: The Political Economy of Recovery,* edited by Donald Rothchild, 193–208. Boulder, CO: Lynne Rienner, 1991.

Gyimah-Boadi, Emmanuel, and Richard Jeffries. "The Political Economy of Reform." In *Economic Reforms in Ghana: The Miracle and the Mirage,* edited by Ernest Aryeetey, Jane Harrigan, and Machiko Nissanke, 32–50. Trenton, NJ: Africa World Press, 2000.

Gyimah-Boadi, Emmanuel, and Abeeku Essuman Johnson. "The PNDC and Organized Labor." In *Ghana under PNDC Rule,* edited by Gyimah-Boadi, 196–212. Dakar, Senegal: Codesria, 1993.

Hagan, George "Nkrumah's Cultural Policy." In *The Life and Work of Kwame Nkrumah,* edited by Kwame Arhin, 1–26. Accra: Sedco, 1991.

Halm, Ben B. *Theatre and Ideology.* Cranbury, NJ: Associated University Presses, 1995.

Hamera, Judith. *Dancing Communities: Performance, Difference and Connection in the Global City.* New York: Palgrave Macmillan, 2007.

Haraway, Donna J. *Simians, Cyborgs, and Women: The Reinvention of Nature.* New York: Routledge, 1995.

Harvey, David. *A Brief History of Neoliberalism.* Oxford: Oxford University Press, 2005.

Haynes, Jeff. "Ghana: From Personalist to Democratic Rule." In *Democracy and Political Change in Sub-Saharan Africa,* edited by John A. Wiseman, 95–106. New York: Routledge, 1995.

Herbst, Jeffrey. *The Politics of Reform in Ghana: 1981–1991.* Berkeley: University of California Press, 2000.

Hobsbawm, Eric. "Inventing Traditions." In *The Invention of Tradition,* edited by Eric Hobsbawm and Terence Ranger, 1–14. Cambridge: Cambridge University Press, 1992.

Holsey, Bayo. *Routes of Remembrance: Refashioning the Slave Trade in Ghana.* Chicago: University of Chicago Press, 2008.

Hutcheon, Linda. *A Theory of Parody.* New York: Methuen, 1985.

Hutchful, Eboe. "From Revolution to Monetarism in Ghana." In *Structural Adjustment in Africa,* edited by Bonnie K. Campbell and John Loxley, 92–131. New York: St. Martin's, 1989.

———. *Ghana's Adjustment Experience: The Paradox of Reform.* Geneva: United Nations Research Institute for Social Development, 2002.

Hyde, Lewis. *Trickster Makes This World.* New York: North Point, 1999.

Hynes, William. "Inconclusive Conclusions: Tricksters—Metaplayers and Revealers." In *Mythical Trickster Figures: Contours, Contexts, and Criticisms,* edited by William Hynes and William Doty, 202–17. Tuscaloosa: University of Alabama Press, 1993.

———. "Mapping the Characteristics of Mythic Tricksters: A Heuristic Guide." In *Mythical Trickster Figures: Contours, Contexts, and Criticisms,* edited by William Hynes and William Doty, 33–45. Tuscaloosa: University of Alabama Press, 1993.

Hynes, William, and William Doty. "Introducing the Fascinating and Perplexing Trickster Figure." In *Mythical Trickster Figures: Contours, Contexts, and Criticisms,* edited by William Hynes and William Doty, 1–12. Tuscaloosa: University of Alabama Press, 1993.

Jablow, Alta. *An Anthology of West African Folklore.* London: Thames and Hudson, 1962.

Jackson-Opoku, Sandra. *The River Where Blood Is Born.* New York: One World/Ballantine, 1997.

Jeyifo, Biodun. "When Anansesem Begins to Grow: Reading Efua Sutherland Three Decades On." In *The Legacy of Efua Sutherland: Pan-African Cultural Activism,* edited by Anne V. Adams and Esi Sutherland-Addy, 24–37. Banbury, UK: Ayebia Clarke, 2007.

Johnson, E. Patrick, ed. *Dwight Conquergood: Cultural Struggles: Performance, Ethnography, Praxis.* Ann Arbor: University of Michigan Press, 2013.

Jonah, Kwesi. "Nkrumah and the Decolonization of Ghana's Trade Relations." In *The Life and Work of Kwame Nkrumah,* edited by Kwame Arhin, 324–51. Accra: Sedco, 1991.

———. "Political Parties and the Transition to Democracy in Ghana." In *Ghana: Transition to Democracy,* edited by Kwame. A. Ninsin, 84–98. Dakar, Senegal: Codesria, 1998.

Jonas, Joyce. *Ananse in the Great House: Ways of Reading West Indian Fiction.* New York: Greenwood, 1990.

Jones, Geoffrey. *Renewing Unilever: Transformation and Tradition.* New York: Oxford University Press, 2005.

July, Robert W. *An African Voice: The Role of the Humanities in African Independence.* Durham, NC: Duke University Press, 1987.

Jurich, Marilyn. *Scheherazade's Sisters: Trickster Heroines and Their Stories in World Literature.* Westport, CT: Greenwood, 1998.

Kandeh, Jimmy D. *Coups from Below: Armed Subalterns and State Power in West Africa.* New York: Palgrave Macmillan, 2004.

Kassim, Abdallah. "NDC Thugs Attack NPP Chairman." *Ghanaian Chronicle,* May 20–22, 1996, p. 6.

Killick, Tony. *Aid and the Political Economy of Policy Change.* London: Overseas Development Institute, 1998.

———. *Development Economics in Action: A Study of Economic Policies in Ghana.* London: Heinemann, 1978.

Kimble, David. *A Political History of Ghana: The Rise of Gold Coast Nationalism, 1850–1928.* Oxford: Clarendon, 1963.

Koblah, Divine. "President Praised in Harlem." *Daily Graphic* (Ghana), October 23, 1995, pp. 1, 8–9.

Konadu-Agyemang, Kwadwo. "Structural Adjustment Programs and the International Tourism Trade in Ghana, 1983–99: Some Socio-spatial Implications." *Tourism Geographies* 3, no. 2 (2001): 187–206.

Kurtz, Donald. *Political Anthropology: Paradigms and Power.* Boulder, CO: Westview, 2001.

Landay, Lori. *Madcaps, Screwballs, and Con Women: The Female Trickster in American Culture.* Philadelphia: University of Pennsylvania Press, 1998.

Lartey, Joe. "NPP Exposes Bob Okalla." *Statesman* (Ghana), September 26, 1996, p. 1.

Lartey, Osbert. "Bloody Clash after the NPP Rally." *Ghanaian Chronicle,* April 18–21, p. 1.

Lears, T. J. Jackson. "The Concept of Cultural Hegemony: Problems and Possibilities." *American Historical Review* 90, no. 3 (1985): 567–93.

Leistikow, Nicole. "Indian Women Criticize 'Fair and Lovely' Ideal." *Women's eNews,* April 28, 2003. http://womensenews.org/story/the-world/030428/indian-women-criticize-fair -and-lovely-ideal.

Leitner, Helga, Jamie Peck, and Eric S. Sheppard, eds. *Contesting Neoliberalism: Urban Frontiers.* New York: Guilford, 2007.

MacCannell, Dean. "Staged Authenticity: Arrangements of Social Space in Tourist Settings." *American Journal of Sociology* 79, no. 2 (1973): 589–603.

Macdonald, George. *The Gold Coast, Past and Present: A Short Description of the Country and Its People.* New York: Longmans, 1898.

Madison, Soyini. *Acts of Activism: Human Rights as Radical Performance.* Cambridge: Cambridge University Press, 2010.

——. "Co-performative Witnessing." *Cultural Studies* 12, no. 6 (2007): 826–31.

——. *Critical Ethnography: Method, Ethics, and Performance.* Los Angeles: Sage, 2012.

Mensah, Joseph, ed. *Understanding Economic Reforms in Africa: A Tale of Seven Nations.* New York: Palgrave Macmillan, 2006.

Merelman, Richard. "The Dramaturgy of Politics." *Sociological Quarterly* 10, no. 2 (1969): 216–41.

Metraux, Alfred. "Trickster." In *The Standard Dictionary of Folklore, Mythology, and Legend,* edited by Maria Leach, 1123–25. New York: Funk and Wagnalls, 1950.

Miescher, Stephan. "The Life Histories of Boakye Yiadom: Exploring the Subjectivity and 'Voices' of a Teacher-Catechist in Colonial Ghana." In *African Worlds, African Voices: Critical Practices in Oral History,* edited by Luise White, Stephan Miescher, and David Cohen, 162–93. Bloomington: Indiana University Press, 2001.

Mills, Margaret. "The Gender of the Trick: Female Tricksters and Male Narrators." *Asian Folklore Studies* 60, no. 2 (2001): 237–58.

Ministry of Education and Culture. Ghana. *Cultural Policy in Ghana.* Paris: Unesco, 1975.

Mirror, The (Ghana). "Bob Okalla: I'm Not in Politics." September 26, 1996, p. 3.

Mkandawire, Thandika, and Charles Soludo. *Our Continent, Our Future: African Perspectives on Structural Adjustment.* Trenton, NJ: Africa World Press, 1999.

Mosley, Paul. "A Theory of Conditionality." In *Development Finance and Policy Reform: Essays in the Theory and Practice of Conditionality in Less Developed Countries,* edited by Paul Mosley, 129–55. New York: Macmillan, 1992.

Moss, Todd, Vijaya Ramachandran, and Manju Shah. *Is Africa's Skepticism of Foreign Capital Justified?: Evidence from East African Firm Survey Data.* Washington, DC: Center for Global Development, 2004.

Muhammad, A. Akbar. "President's Initiative at OAU Meeting Was Bold." *Daily Graphic* (Ghana). July 9, 1993, p. 1.

Mwakikagile, Godfrey. *Africa after Independence: Realities of Nationhood.* Dar es Salaam, Tanzania: New Africa Press, 2009.

National Theatre of Ghana. *Corporate Plan.* Accra: National Theatre of Ghana, 1998.

——. "Minutes of Key Soap Concert Party Monthly Review Meeting, August 1996." National Theatre of Ghana, Accra, 1996.

——. *National Theatre in Retrospect: An Overview of the First Four Operational Years 1994–1997.* Accra: National Theatre of Ghana, 1997.

Ninsin, Kwame. "Civic Associations and the Transition to Democracy." In *Ghana: Transition to Democracy,* edited by Kwame Ninsin, 4981. Dakar, Senegal: Codesria, 1998.

Nketia, Joseph Hanson. *Funeral Dirges of the Akan People.* Achimota, Ghana: Exeter/J. Townsend, 1955.

Nkrumah, Kwame. *Axioms of Kwame Nkrumah: Freedom Fighters' Edition*. London: Panaf, 1969.
——. *Consciencism*. New York: Monthly Review Press, 1964.
——. *I Speak of Freedom*. New York: Praeger, 1961.
——. *Neocolonialism: The Last Stage of Imperialism*. London: Thomas Nelson, 1965.
Nugent, Paul. *Big Men, Small Boys, and Politics in Ghana*. New York: Pinter, 1991.
Nyinah, Joe Bradford. "Lincoln Honors President and Wife." *Daily Graphic* (Ghana), October 27, 1995, pp. 1, 9.
Okyere, Joe. "President Cuts Sod for ₵100b Sunyani Regional Hospital." *Daily Graphic* (Ghana), September 7, 1996, p. 1.
Omari, Thompson Peter. *Kwame Nkrumah: The Anatomy of an African Dictatorship*. New York: Africana, 1970.
Oquaye, Mike. *Politics in Ghana, 1972–79*. Accra: Tornado, 1980.
——. *Politics in Ghana 1982–1992: Rawlings, Revolution, and Populist Democracy*. Accra: Tornado, 2004.
Organization for Economic Co-operation and Development (OECD). *OECD Benchmark Definition of Foreign Direct Investment*. Paris: OECD, 2008.
Osei, Akwasi P. *Ghana: Recurrence and Change in a Post-independence State*. New York: Peter Lang, 1999.
Owusu, Douglas. "Workers Disrupt May Day." *Ghanaian Times*, May 2, 1995, p. 1.
Oxfam International. *The Emperor's New Clothes: Why Rich Countries Want a WTO Investment Agreement*. Oxfam International Briefing Paper 46. Washington, DC: Oxfam, 2003. http://www.oxfam.org/sites/www.oxfam.org/files/emporer.pdf.
Payne, Ethel L. "Ghana Independence, Africa's Biggest Event." *Chicago Defender*, February 16, 1957, p. 3.
Peck, Jamie, and Adam Tickell. "Conceptualizing Neoliberalism, Thinking Thatcherism." In *Contesting Neoliberalism: Urban Frontiers*, edited by Helga Leitner, Jamie Peck, and Eric Sheppard, 26–50. New York: Guilford, 2007.
Pelton, Robert. *The Trickster in West Africa: A Study of Mythic Irony and Sacred Delight*. Berkeley: University of California Press, 1989.
Pierre, Jemima. *The Predicament of Blackness: Postcolonial Ghana and the Politics of Race*. Chicago: University of Chicago Press, 2013.
Pinkney, Robert. *Ghana under Military Rule, 1966–69*. London: Methuen, 1972.
Pittsburgh Courier. "Celebration Highlights When Gold Coast Becomes New Nation." January 5, 1957, p. A7.
——. "Ghana, Africa, a New Nation Is Born on Historic Gold Coast." January 5, 1957, p. B4.
——. "Ghana—A New African Nation Essay Contest." January 5, 1957, p. A7.
——. "Ghanese Await Day of Independence on March 6 and They Like Americans." January 5, 1957, p. A7.
Plageman, Nate. *Highlife Saturday Night: Popular Music and Social Change in Urban Ghana*. Bloomington: Indiana University Press, 2013.
Plair, Therese, and Mellisa Heckler. *The Goals of FISC*. Program document from the First International Storytelling Conference, 1999.
Plehwe, Dieter, and Bernhard Walpen. "Between Network and Complex Organization." In *Neoliberal Hegemony: A Global Critique*, edited by Dieter Plehwe, Bernhard Walpen, and Gisela Neunhöffer, 27–50. New York: Routledge, 2006.
Plehwe, Dieter, Bernhard Walpen, and Gisela Neunhöffer. "Reconsidering Neoliberal Hegemony." In *Neoliberal Hegemony: A Global Critique*, edited by Dieter Plehwe, Bernhard Walpen, and Gisela Neunhöffer, 1–24. New York: Routledge, 2006.

Poliner, Sharlene. "The Exiled Creature: Ananse Tales and the Search for Afro-Caribbean Identity." *Studies in the Humanities* 2, no. 1 (1984): 13–22.

Rattray, Robert Sutherland. *Akan-Ashanti Folk-Tales*. Oxford: Clarendon, 1930.

———. *Ashanti Proverbs*. Oxford: Clarendon, 1916.

Rawlings, Jerry. "Enhancing the Cultural Life of Our People." *Freedom, Justice, and Accountability: Selected Speeches of Flight Lieutenant. J. J. Rawlings*. Volume 9. Accra: Information Services Department, 1993.

———. "Foreword." In *National Democratic Congress: 1996 Manifesto*, n.p. Accra: National Democratic Congress, 1996.

———. "Let's Go Forward Together." *Daily Graphic* (Ghana), September 12, 1996, p. 6.

Ray, Donald. *Ghana: Politics, Economics, and Society*. Boulder, CO: Lynne Rienner, 1986.

Ray, Shantanu Guha. "India's Unbearable Lightness of Being." *BBC News*, March 23, 2010. http://news.bbc.co.uk/2/hi/south_asia/8546183.stm.

Reder, Deana, and Linda Morra, eds. *Troubling Tricksters: Revisioning Critical Conversations*. Waterloo, Ontario: Wilfrid Laurier University Press, 2010.

Reesman, Jeanne, ed. *Trickster Lives: Culture and Myth in American Fiction*. Athens: University of Georgia Press, 2001.

Richards, Sandra. "Under the Trickster's Sign: Towards a Reading of Ntozanke Shange and Femi Osofisan." In *Critical Theory and Performance*, edited by Janelle Reinelt and Joseph Roach, 65–78. Ann Arbor: University of Michigan Press, 1992.

Roberts, John. *From Trickster to Badman: The Black Folk Hero in Slavery and Freedom*. Philadelphia: University of Pennsylvania Press, 1989.

Rooney, David. *Kwame Nkrumah: Vision and Tragedy*. Accra: Sub-Saharan Publishers, 2007.

Rose, Margaret. *Parody: Ancient, Modern, and Postmodern*. Cambridge: Cambridge University Press, 1996.

Rothchild, Donald, ed. *Ghana: The Political Economy of Recovery*. Boulder, CO: Lynne Rienner, 1991.

Sachs, Jeffrey. "Growth in Africa: It Can Be Done." *The Economist*, June 29, 1996, pp. 19–21.

Safo, Amos. "Kumepreko March Is On Today." *Ghanaian Chronicle*, May 11–14, 1995, p. 12.

Sahn, David, Paul A. Dorosh, and Stephen Younger. *Structural Adjustment Reconsidered: Economic Policy and Poverty in Africa*. Cambridge: Cambridge University Press, 1997.

Sakyi-Addo, Kwaku. "Soap Wars: Unilever vs. Local Soapmakers." *Ghanaian Chronicle*, July 11, 1993, p. 1.

Samwini, Nathan. "VAT: The Mother of All Killer Policies." *Ghanaian Chronicle*, April 24–26, 1995, p. 4.

Schechner, Richard. *Between Theatre and Anthropology*. Philadelphia: University of Pennsylvania Press, 1985.

———. *Performance Studies: An Introduction*. New York: Routledge, 2002.

Scott, James C. *Domination and the Arts of Resistance: Hidden Transcripts*. New Haven, CT: Yale University Press, 1990.

———. *Weapons of the Weak: Everyday Forms of Peasant Resistance*. New Haven, CT: Yale University Press, 1985.

Segbefia, Alexander Y. "Community Approach to Tourism Development in Ghana." In *Tourism in Ghana: A Modern Synthesis*, edited by Oheneba Akyeampong and Alex B. Asiedu, 55–68. Accra: Assemblies of God Literature Center, 2008.

Shillington, Kevin. *Ghana and the Rawlings Factor*. New York: St. Martin's, 1992.

Shipley, Jesse Weaver. "Comedians, Pastors, and the Miraculous Agency of Charisma in Ghana." *Cultural Anthropology* 24, no. 3 (2009): 523–52.

——. *Living the Hiplife: Celebrity and Entrepreneurship in Ghanaian Popular Music.* Durham, NC: Duke University Press, 2013.

Singer, Milton. *Man's Glossy Essence: Explorations in Semiotic Anthropology.* Bloomington: Indiana University Press, 1984.

——, ed. *Traditional India: Structure and Change.* Philadelphia: American Folklore Society, 1959.

——. *When a Great Tradition Modernizes: An Anthropological Approach to Modern Civilization.* New York: Praeger, 1972.

Slater, David. *Geopolitics and the Post-colonial: Rethinking North–South Relations.* Oxford: Blackwell, 2004.

Starobin, Paul. "Politics as Theatre." *National Journal,* October 5, 1996, pp. 2102–7.

Steel, Griet. *Vulnerable Careers: Tourism and Livelihood Dynamics among Street Vendors in Cusco, Peru.* Amsterdam: Rozenberg, 2008.

Stewart, Miranda, and Sunita Jogarajan. "The International Monetary Fund and Tax Reform." *British Tax Review* 2 (2004): 15–17.

Stott, Andrew. *Comedy.* New York: Routledge, 2005.

Sutherland, Efua. *The Marriage of Anansewa* and *Edufa.* Harlow, UK: Longman, 1987.

——. *The Original Bob: The Story of Bob Johnson, Ghana's Ace Comedian.* Accra: Anowuo Educational, 1970.

——. "The Second Phase of the National Theatre Movement in Ghana." In *Fontomfrom: Contemporary Ghanaian Literature, Theatre, and Film,* edited by Kofi Anyidodo and James Gibbs, 45–57. Amsterdam: Rodopi, 2000.

Taussig, Michael. *Mimesis and Alterity: A Particular History of the Senses.* New York: Routledge, 1993.

Taylor, Diana. *The Archive and the Repertoire: Performing Cultural Memories in the Americas.* Durham, NC: Duke University Press, 2003.

Taylor, J. N. K. "Some Unconstitutional Aspects of J. J. Rawlings's Rule in the Fourth Republic." *Ghanaian Chronicle,* July 17–19, 1996, p. 5.

Tekpetey, Kwawisi. "Kweku Ananse: A Psychoanalytic Approach." *Research in African Literatures* 37, no. 2 (2006): 74–82.

Thomson, Janice. *Mercenaries, Pirates, and Sovereigns.* Princeton, NJ: Princeton University Press, 1994.

Tsikata, Kwaku G., Yaw Asante, and E. M. Gyasi. *Determinants of Foreign Direct Investment in Ghana.* London: Overseas Development Institute, 2000.

Tuafo, Kofi Yeboah. *Kwame Nkrumah: The Man Who Took the First Piece of Britain's African Empire.* Accra: Elaine Books, 2012.

Turner, Rachel. *Neo-liberal Ideology: History, Concepts, and Policies.* Edinburgh: Edinburgh University Press, 2008.

Turner, Victor. *The Anthropology of Performance.* New York: Performing Arts Journal Publications, 1988.

——. *Dramas, Fields, and Metaphors: Symbolic Action in Human Society.* Ithaca, NY: Cornell University Press, 1974.

——. *From Ritual to Theatre: The Human Seriousness of Play.* New York: Performing Arts Journal Publications, 1982.

United Nations. *World Economic Survey.* New York: United Nations, 1989.

United Nations Conference on Trade and Development. *Foreign Direct Investment in Africa: Performance and Potential.* Geneva: United Nations, 1999.

——. *World Investment Report: Foreign Direct Investment and the Challenge of Development.* Geneva: United Nations, 1999.

van Dyck, Charles. "An Analytical Study of the Folktales of Selected Peoples of West Africa." PhD diss., Oxford University, 1966.

Vescey, Christopher. "The Exception Who Proves the Rule: Ananse, the Akan Trickster." In *Mythic Trickster Figures: Contours, Contexts, and Criticisms,* edited by William Hynes and William Doty, 106–21. Tuscaloosa: University of Alabama Press, 1993.

Weekly Spectator (Ghana). "Concert Parties Making a Comeback." November 4, 1996, p. 6.

Wellington, Henry Nii-Adziri. "Architecture: Spatial Deployment for Community Experience (Encounter with Efua T. Sutherland)." In *The Legacy of Efua Sutherland: Pan-African Cultural Activism,* edited by Anne V. Adams and Esi Sutherland-Addy, 179–92. Banbury, UK: Ayebia Clarke, 2007.

Willis, Katie, Adrian Smith, and Alison Stenning, eds. *Social Justice and Neoliberalism: Global Perspectives.* New York: Zed, 2008.

Woods, Ngaire. *The Globalizers: The IMF, the World Bank, and their Borrowers.* Ithaca, NY: Cornell University Press, 2006.

World Bank. *Accelerated Development in Sub-Saharan Africa: An Agenda for Action.* Washington, DC: World Bank, 1981.

——. *Ghana: Structural Adjustment for Growth.* Washington, DC: World Bank, 1989.

World Tourism Organization. *News from the World Tourism Organization.* Madrid: World Tourism Organization, 2000.

——. *Report to the Secretary-General on the Activities of the Organization.* Madrid: World Tourism Organization, 1987.

Yankah, Kwesi. "Leave Okalla Alone." *The Mirror* (Ghana), October 5, 1996, p. 5.

——. "Nana Kwame Ampadu and the Sung Tale as Metaphor for Protest Discourse." In *Fontomfrom: Contemporary Ghanaian Literature, Theatre, and Film,* edited by Kofi Anyidodo and James Gibbs, 135–53. Amsterdam: Rodopi, 2000.

——. "The Question of Ananse in Akan Mythology." In *Perspectives on Mythology,* edited by Esi Sutherland-Addy, 134–47. Accra, Ghana: Woeli, 1997.

——. *Speaking for the Chief.* Bloomington: Indiana University Press, 1995.

——. *The Trial of J. J. Rawlings: Echoes of the 31st December Revolution.* Tema: Ghana Publishing, 1987.

Yeboa-Danqua, Jonas. "Storytelling of the Akan and Guan in Ghana." In *Ghanaian Literatures,* edited by Richard K. Priebe, 29–42. Westport, CT: Greenwood, 1988.

Yeebo, Zaya. *Ghana, the Struggle for Popular Power: Rawlings, Savior or Demagogue.* London: New Beacon, 1991.

Yirenkyi, Asiedu "Kobina Sekyi: Founding Father of the Ghanaian Theatre." *The Legacy* 3, no. 3 (1977): 39–47.

Zingaro. "Watch These Things." *Statesman* (Ghana), September 26, 1996, p. 1.

Ziorklui, Emmanuel *Ghana, Nkrumah to Rawlings.* Accra: Emzed, 1993.

INDEX

Page numbers in italics refer to photographs and tables.

DAVID AFRIYIE DONKOR

⸙

is Assistant Professor in Performance and Africana Studies at
Texas A&M University. He is also an actor and a director who has
adapted several folktales, personal narratives, and literary works
for the stage.

www.ingramcontent.com/pod-product-compliance
Lightning Source LLC
Chambersburg PA
CBHW070359270326
41926CB00014B/2622